THE
TRANSITIONAL APPROACH
TO CHANGE

The Harold Bridger Transitional Series

THE HAROLD BRIDGER TRANSITIONAL SERIES

THE
TRANSITIONAL APPROACH
TO CHANGE

Edited by
Gilles Amado & Anthony Ambrose

in collaboration with
Rachel Amato

Foreword by
Harold Bridger

Prologue by
Eric Trist

London & New York
KARNAC BOOKS

First published in 2001 by
H. Karnac (Books) Ltd.
6 Pembroke Buildings, London NW10 6RE
A subsidiary of Other Press LLC, New York

British Library Cataloguing in Publication Data

A C.I.P. for this book is available from the British Library

ISBN 1 85575 226 3

10 9 8 7 6 5 4 3 2 1

Edited, designed, and produced by Communication Crafts

www.karnacbooks.com

Printed and bound in Great Britain by Biddles Ltd, *www.biddles.co.uk*

CONTENTS

ACKNOWLEDGEMENTS

The contents of this book have been produced by authors most of whom are members of the Transitional Dynamics Network (TDN). This network, however, is an evolution from a previous organization, the Institute for Transitional Dynamics (ITD), which was a group of management consultants and social scientists who over many years held annual meetings in Lucerne, Switzerland, known by the name of "Gütsch Meetings" after the name of the hotel overlooking the city. Much of the substance of transitional thinking that emerged during those previous meetings derives not only from the present authors but also from the contributions of others, notably Arthur Zobrist (who organized the meetings in Lucerne), Claude Faucheux, and Sidney Gray who with Harold Bridger were all co-founders of the Institute of Human Relations in 1985 (prior to ITD); also Mahib Abed, Ricardo Edström, Rina Bar Lev Elieli, Chris and Kirk MacNulty, Michael O'Farell, Bridget Ramsay, Steve Rossell, Margaret Legum, and numerous specially invited contributors. Our thanks go to all of these and also to Hanna Krieg, who played an important part in assisting the organization and recording of the meetings

A special mention for Leopold Vansina, a companion in the transitional arena with whom we shared views during the past years and whose editorial help has been generous.

We are particularly grateful to Anne Ambrose, who, with devotion and care, typed the manuscript of the book, also to Alain Keravel for his technical support. A special mention goes to the members of the HEC School of Management in Jouy-en-Josas who hosted numerous editorial meetings for the book and provided help for the preparation of the manuscript.

The completion of the book would not have been possible without the generous support of the Foundation for Adaptation in Changing Environments (FACE). This allowed TDN the full use of its word processor, and it provided a loan to meet a great part of the editorial and typing costs. We acknowledge this support with gratitude.

CONTRIBUTORS

Gilles Amado, Psy Dr, is Professor of Organizational Behaviour in the HEC School of Management, Paris, a consultant, and an action researcher. He is a founding member of the International Society for the Psychoanalytic Study of Organizations, co-editor-in-chief of the *Revue Internationale de Psychosociologie,* and a member of the French Society for Psychoanalytic Group Psychotherapy.

Anthony Ambrose, PhD, is a social scientist whose early career was in research in development psychology. His later work with sociotechnical systems and change processes led him to be a Council member of the Tavistock Institute of Human Relations, Director of the Foundation for Adaptation in changing Environments, and consultant to the WHO and other organizations.

Rachel Amato is a consultant and researcher in the area of organizational analysis and change management, with a special interest in intercultural management and post-merger integration processes. She has carried out consulting missions with a variety of multinationals in France, Scandinavia, and the United Kingdom, in both services and industry as well as in the public sector.

Harold Bridger is a founder member of Tavistock Institute of Human Relations and a member of the British Psycho-Analytical Society. He is currently concerned with organizational review and cross-cultural and career development in many countries. He is a past president of the International Forum for Organisational Health and is a Fellow of the Institute of Management.

Lisl Klein is founder and Director of the Bayswater Institute, currently working in NHS hospitals and in industry. She is an industrial sociologist and has been Social Sciences Adviser to Esso Petroleum Company and consultant to the German government's Humanization of Work Programme. For nineteen years, she was a member of the Tavistock Institute of Human Relations.

Colin Legum is a South African journalist. After early training at the Tavistock Institute of Human Relations, he became the author and editor of over 40 books on Africa, the Middle East, and other Third World countries. He was for many years associate editor of *The Observer* (London) and editor/publisher of *Third World Reports*.

John Sharpe is President of Unilever's Home and Personal Care Businesses in Europe. Since the late 1980s he has been following a "Business Excellence" approach in managing companies in the United Kingdom and across Europe. He is a member of the Governing Board of the European Foundation for Quality Management.

Eric Trist was one of the founders of the Tavistock Institute for Social Research in London and Professor Emeritus of Social System Science at the Wharton School of Business. He collaborated with K. W. Bamforth in research at the Haighmoor mines in South Yorkshire and co-authored the resulting 1951 *Human Relations* article, "Some Social and Psychological Consequences of the Longwall Method of Coal Getting." His later collaboration with Fred Emery resulted in what is known as the sociotechnical systems approach to work design.

FOREWORD

Harold Bridger

The nature of change can take many forms, and all too readily we use the term for many different kinds of movement from one state of being to another.

To appreciate the nature and characteristics of a transitional process of change as distinct from these other forms of adaptation and movement from one phase or situation to another, we need to differentiate between the many terms frequently represented by the prefix "trans-"—for example, translation, transformation, transfer, transporting, transaction, and so on—all of which represent forms of change in one way or another. But in attempting to identify the nature and characteristics of a continuous unrecognized "undercurrent" as well as more obvious identification of step-change, we need to use that more appropriate dynamic, "transitional".

The importance of these distinctions becomes apparent when we make comparisons between such dynamic aspects of change as in human development from conception through birth onwards.

The inevitable but vital distinction between "me/not me" of earliest times now occurs also in our institutional and organizational lives in endeavouring to establish not just "identity" but also a purpose, choice, and actions forward. The parallel with the learning/ unlearning process of transition of early human development becomes increasingly apparent when faced equally with attempting to develop and establish an understanding of ourselves in relation to that widening awareness of "others" who also have power and competences to affect our effectiveness, growth, and futures and thus our fulfilment in that complex uncertainty around us.

The transitional processes of change require (1) time and space and (2) a form of "cover". In early childhood, this "cover" may be the piece of cloth, the teddy bear, or some other "transitional object" (Winnicott, 1951) selected by the infant from the range of objects either offered or found around him/her (the "linus blanket" of the Peanuts cartoons). Thus, the perception of this relationship with that object as that of "comforter" is of a very superficial, minimal kind; it can, of course, perform that function of a comforter, but predominantly it permits of some expression of relationship with an uncertain external world while using fantasy exploration/working-through phases of the transitional process to be developed and carried out.

There is also the time and space required for the unconscious working-through of taking on new elements and letting go old ones to move towards continuing life and work in changing conditions. An example involving international consequences—the Viet-Cong–U.S. relationship at the conclusion of the Vietnam War—may help to illustrate how this dynamic process of transitional change has its parallel in the current and future turbulent open-system world.

Months of uncertainty as to where and how steps towards a form of official peace could be achieved terminated when Paris—a city in the "West" but nevertheless the capital of a country that had been defeated by the Viet Cong in an earlier war, when the French were driven out—was agreed as the location for talks. That is, Paris was a transitional-object "cover" of requisite elements. But this was not sufficient even to permit the open "testing-out" of issues, and certainly not of reaching the working-through phase. The protocol positioning of those taking part in the peace negotiations was questioned by the Viet Cong and other parties. For months, the "shape of the table" became an international press joke. But clearly one might say that "beneath the table", metaphorically, preliminary issues of various kinds were continually being exchanged, attitudes tested, and much "unofficial" material analysed. These would then be related back to central governments until such time as a relevant range and understanding of those actual issues could be openly declared as the ones to be discussed "at the table", with the equal awareness of the possible—if not the definitive—results!

Equivalent transitional experiences can, of course, be recounted in a variety of situations and circumstances of life, whether between "parts of oneself" or between "parties" of so-called unity—for example, the family. In the latter case, an extended detailed study of pets and their position/function in the family (see chapter five) yielded a rich series of examples of a similar nature. The reality object does indeed have to be that "good-enough cover", both with an external *raison d'être* and of a kind "good enough to provide" the time–space opportunity for the working-through of unconscious and learning–unlearning processes.

The "transitional object" in today's and tomorrow's world and the understanding of why and how that may be used will need to become increasingly critical. In particular, the "double feature" in transitional changes is matched by what I call the "double-task" and its relevance today: an equivalent "time–space" requirement to review and work through the tension systems between the purpose of the group or the strategic objectives of the organizations and the interpersonal relationships among those carrying out required activities, and between their roles and accountabilities—that is, the (interdependent) relationships when operating in a turbulent environment.

That review on how one has been carrying out these activities to achieve objectives is demanded even when physical time–space either is not appropriate or is regarded as deflecting time required for the overt purpose!

The recognition of its importance for management is reflected in the answer of a former president of Unilever who, when asked how he influenced the choice of the top-management triumvirate members, replied that he imposed a veto: "They have to be people with whom I can be silly"—that is, with whom he could spend the time on purposes other than the overt ones.

These key issues are usually inadequately dealt with on an intuitive or reflective basis, rather than being confronted by those in relevant positions with the recognition of the need to invest in that space–time requirement.

Thus, whether at institutional level or in specific operational circumstances, the transitional process will need to be undertaken more seriously than it has been heretofore.

The challenge attempted in this book is not just to indicate the special importance of certain specific characteristics of a transitional approach for working in multiple contexts and interdependent networks in an open-system world and in society generally, but to describe and demonstrate—within the limitations of the written word—the value and significance of that transitional process through a range of experiences. Equally, independently of the instances given, readers are offered the kind of description that might also provide them with opportunities for relating its relevance to their own experiences, roles, and current settings.

INTRODUCTION

Unlike many books available on the management of change, this one is not a "how-to-do-it" book giving prescriptions or formulae for what has to be done. Its concern is a more basic one: namely, to describe and illustrate the emergence of new thinking and practice which is gradually altering long-standing conceptions of "change" and of what is required for its effective management.

Over the past two to three decades, as executives, managers, and employees have had to face up to the need for profound changes in the strategy and structure of their organizations if they are to survive, the need for such new thinking has become increasingly acute. It is not just that old ideas of how to bring about fundamental change have proved to be largely ineffective and too simplistic. The turbulence of rapidly changing environments has led to tremendous uncertainty in every aspect of managerial decision-making. Furthermore, the ever-growing interdependence of operating systems, both within and between organizations, has resulted in a degree of complexity within the total field of organizational functioning which has become extremely difficult to unravel. Indeed, with today's imperative of adapting to continuous and often unexpected change in the world, many executives and managers have the greatest difficulty not only in being able to formulate the nature of the problematic confronting them, but in knowing even how to think about fundamental change in the technical and social systems for which they are responsible.

It is within the context of this basic problem of how to think and act about change, especially of how to frame the problems of fundamental change in organizations and in social systems of all kinds within society, that the present book has originated.

The original sources and inspiration for the development of our understanding of transitional processes were Donald Winnicott and Harold Bridger. It was Winnicott, a paediatrician and psychoanalyst, who first identified and explained the process as it occurs in early infancy. It was Bridger, a management consultant and psychoanalyst at the Tavistock Institute (of which he was a co-founder), who first recognized the relevance of Winnicott's insights for understanding what happens when major change and development takes place, not only in adult individuals but in social systems of all kinds.

Bridger has never found it easy to set down his ideas in writing— he has always been much more interested in *doing* action research with his clients and in *talking* about it with his colleagues. What he did do, however, was to form a network of such colleagues who met together, and still do, at regular intervals to examine and discuss in depth transitional thinking and its application to many specific problems of change being encountered by the network members. While some of these colleagues had received their training directly from Bridger, others were already specialists of change—organizational consultants and clinicians inspired by Winnicott or by approaches to change having some similarity to that which we now call "transitional". It was in these meetings over a number of years that many of the ideas developed in this book were expressed in detail, clarified, and often developed further.

The transitional approach to the management of change presented here places much emphasis on enabling people to change the way they think about the problems around them, to alter their perspectives, and to discover new possibilities for action which can never occur to them as long as they remain on the secure railtracks of their habitual mind-sets.

The contributors to this first volume, and to the subsequent volumes, each in their own way describe how this has been done in the settings in which they work and the remarkable changes brought about as a result. There is, in fact, nothing really new about the approach they have used. Many of the success stories of social system change that have become familiar to us in recent times can be attributed, at least in part, to the use of a transitional approach to their management by individuals who had no explicit knowledge of it but who, as natural change-agents, had an intuitive understanding of—a spontaneous feel for—doing some of the things that the approach involves. What is new about its description in this book is that it brings together all the different facets of the approach into a coherent whole. It formalizes this whole into a distinctive paradigm of managerial thought and action, one that seems fully consistent with the new directions in social science theory that have emerged over the last decade or two.

Probably the most significant theoretical feature that the book attempts to clarify is the fact that transition is essentially a psychosocial process. The meaning of this concept and its significance for the management of fundamental change have for too long been overlooked both by practising managers and by theorists of social change. The concept of "psychosocial" draws attention to the fact that what we are dealing with in social system transitions is fundamental change at two distinct levels at the same time. Furthermore, the principles by which change takes place at each of these levels are quite different. At one level are the "social" factors: the products and services, the technologies, the organizational structures, the culture, and the rules and procedures that are the stuff of people's everyday life and work, the external realities around them. These operate according to principles that may be technical, economic, sociological, legal, or environmental in nature. At the other level are the "psycho" factors: the beliefs and values, the hopes, anxieties, and defence mechanisms, the ideas and ways of thinking of these same people that both determine how they perceive the external realities and shape their actions towards them. These are phenomena of subjective experience located within the minds of people, and they operate according to the principles of psychology, especially those studied in the fields of social cognition and of psychoanalysis. These two levels—the external and the internal worlds of people—are in continual interaction: what goes on in the minds of people is partly reactive to what happens around them, but it is also very much proactive. People's ideas and ways of thinking influence the way they act upon their surroundings to bring about change in them.

The effect of this two-level psychological perspective, which is basic to the transitional approach to management, is to shift the emphasis in managerial thinking about fundamental change. This shift is *away* from a primary, if not exclusive, concern with the strategic, technological, and organizational issues that, though critical for the survival and viability of any organization, are so difficult to plan, let alone to change, because of both their complexity and the uncertainties of our time. It is *towards* a much greater concern with the ability of an organization to change itself into a new kind of social "organism" or system that is capable of continuous adaptation to its continuously changing and complex environmental medium. Such fundamental change certainly requires transformation of the structures by which it operates, just as the dragonfly acquires entirely new capabilities when it develops wings with which to fly instead of having only legs to walk with. But it also requires change in the very "substance" or qualities out of which its parts are made in order that new structures *can* develop.

It is here that the transitional approach to the management of change comes into its own. For you cannot *make* people change their long-established ways of perceiving, thinking, and framing problems. You cannot alter people's deep-seated habits by directive. Only they can do it themselves when they really want to, when they themselves experience a strong need to do so. Humans are self-organizing beings, and the driving forces for reorganizing their internal worlds have to come from within as well as from without. What you *can* do, however, is to provide conditions that will increase the chances that people will make changes themselves. These are conditions that enable people to see things in a new light, to extend their perspectives, to look at the consequences of their actions, to question the validity and relevance of their existing ideas, beliefs, and attitudes that underlie their actions, and to entertain different ones that are more relevant to their new perspectives.

At first sight, the provision of such conditions may seem to be an impossible prospect because our Western culture, which pervades all of our social systems, places severe constraints on flexibility in the mind-sets of people and on their readiness to innovate. These constraints are of many kinds. For example, there are the bureaucratic regimes where people are in the habit of working only to management directives, often reinforced by deep-seated mind-sets from past parental and school influences of the "shut up and do as you're told" variety; there are the sanctions against deviating from group norms and the need for a sense of security that comes from a stable status quo; there is the sheer pressure of work, which allows no time for reflection about alternative, better, ways of doing things; and there are the consequences of highly specialized work and the training for it which confine people's perspectives to only small parts of the whole operational system and its problems in which they are involved. In view of such constraints, it is little wonder that senior managements have for so long been deeply sceptical about the potential within most workforce members to participate in constructive innovative thinking. But while many managements are only too ready to complain about resistance to change and lack of flexibility in their workforces, they remain largely unable to do anything about it other than by forcing conformity to their wishes and plans through assertion of their power.

The transitional approach to the management of change offers an alternative to that approach. We now know that conditions of the kind mentioned above really do exist. In the terms used in this book, the special feature of these conditions is that they have "transitional potential". They empower people, of their own volition, to engage in new ways of thinking that are qualitatively different from before: it is as if their thinking becomes of an altogether different "substance".

The transitional approach is not a set of management techniques that can be learned as modules and applied in some automatic manner as a way of controlling or manipulating people. Indeed, it is not about controlling people at all. It is the expression of a basic attitude towards people that stems both from the psychosocial perspective outlined above and also from ethical considerations. This attitude regards people not just as the parts of social systems in which they live and work, nor just as human resources to be used for carrying out the work to be done. Instead it takes a more personal view, regarding people as having value in their own right by virtue of their conscious awareness and feelings, their unique identities, their capacities, their hopes and ambitions, and their fears and anxieties. People, like plants, grow and develop and come to fruition, and, at any stage of this process, most have the potential for further development. But personal development, again like that of plants, can only take place if the surrounding conditions facilitate it. Just as a basic function of family life is to facilitate and promote the development of the young, so life in society, and especially in its organizations, should also function to promote the continuing development of adult people both in their understanding and in their capacities to contribute to society. Such development in people is most conspicuous when there are challenges to be overcome, when new problems cannot be solved by the habitual methods and require altogether new ways of thought and action. Underlying the transitional approach is an attitude to fundamental societal and organizational change which regards it as an opportunity *par excellence* for the people involved to advance towards a better understanding of the realities around them and of the parts they can play in the whole, towards a new shared vision of the future, and towards an awareness of how they themselves need to change if they are to participate in the realization of that vision. The transitional approach to the management of such change is designed to stimulate, encourage, and facilitate this process in people, to the benefit of themselves and of the social systems in which they are involved.

This book is the first one in the series. It presents the basic theoretical principles of the transitional approach to change and some illustrations of it. Subsequent volumes will deal more concretely with the transitional approach in action, within organizations, within society, and within all sorts of developmental situations.

PROLOGUE

Eric Trist

Eric Trist kindly agreed to write a foreword for this book, but regrettably he died before being able to do so. We therefore reproduce here by kind permission of his wife, Beulah Trist, a paper on transition which he presented at a symposium in 1987 as a discussant for a paper by Harold Bridger (1987b) on the dynamics of transition.

I came to think of transitions as constituting a core problem as a result of work that Fred Emery and I began some 25 years ago on what we called "the causal texture of organizational environments" (Emery & Trist, 1965). Because of the increasing complexity and interdependence of factors in the macro-social environment, which raised the level of uncertainty, we said then that the wider contextual environment was undergoing a phase change from a disturbed-reactive field to a turbulent field. Under these conditions, Kurt Lewin's (1947) celebrated model of change as entailing the unfreezing of a system in a steady state, guiding its passage through a period of turmoil and then refreezing it at a higher system level, was becoming increasingly invalid. The world was moving towards being on a continuous-change gradient. We had gone beyond the stable state (Schön, 1971). In terms used by my former UCLA colleague, Peter Vaill (1982), we are now in permanent white water. It can be said, therefore, that we are always in transition, though just to say this leaves out the large question of the speed of various transitional processes which can vary enormously. This formulation in terms of varying speeds yields a more useful perspective than creating a dichotomy of steady states versus transitions.

I have had several experiences of relations among people in well-conducted organizations deteriorating with great rapidity when the organization became perturbed by an unrecognized change in its larger contextual environment. Particularly worrying has been the increase in the level of aggression. No love was now lost: the internal world of these organizations became a darker and more savage place. Socially amplified regression brings exceedingly primitive defences into play, whether in the form of hostile projection or of alienated withdrawal. Once the imperfect but legitimated structures begin to give way and those concerned can create no effective alternatives, there seems to be no stopping the descent towards a catastrophe of the Thom (1975) kind. Recovery can then begin only very slowly, usually in a different setting.

In facing the problems that arise from being in permanent white water, Harold Bridger has shown that the work of Donald Winnicott (1971) is of the greatest relevance. In addition to internal psychic reality and external social reality, both of which have their own rules, Winnicott introduced a third area, which he called the world of transitional phenomena. This extended from teddy bears and all forms of playing to culture of all kinds. This was the domain in which the inside and the outside became joined together and in which one could make things happen at an appropriate level of reality/irreality in Lewin's (1935) terms or of illusion in Winnicott's terms. This is the area of invention, of serious make-believe, of what my colleague Howard Perlmutter (1965) has called social architecture—the imaginative building of new institutions imbued with emergent values whose relevance then has to be tested out under conditions of full reality. Not that Winnicott spelt all this out. In *Playing and Reality* (1971) he gives no more than a first sketch of the social extension of his original idea of transitional objects in the infant situation. It has been left to such people as Harold Bridger to take up their organizational and societal implications in the adult world.

When looking through Winnicott's 1971 book recently, it seemed to me that I had heard a number of the main points in another language—that of Kurt Lewin (1935), whom I have already mentioned. After all, it was Lewin who introduced the notions of boundaries and the permeability of border regions, of creating psychosocial spaces, zones of free movement, and so on. If anyone believed in the value of making things up, it was Lewin.

Not long before he died in 1947, Lewin had become interested in object-relations theory and was planning to spend a sabbatical year at the Tavistock Institute. Of several prominent analysts in the British Society at that time, Winnicott has always seemed to me the one to whom Lewin would have been most attracted. One can never know what would have happened had these two begun to meet. I suspect, however, that developments would have been inaugurated that we are only now getting off the ground.

In some notes and tapes Harold Bridger made two years ago, he mentioned three processes that would have to be effectively managed—a Winnicott term—if transitions were to be successfully made. These were "tuning in", "working-through", and "designing".

Tuning in, as I see it, involves the ability to get in touch with new situations or, more generally, new contexts, to get a feel for their texture. This presupposes environmental scanning. In turbulent environments, it becomes ever more necessary for us to be able to do this. Tuning in involves pattern recognition—the capacity to distinguish between signals and noise. One has to sense all this and so begin to make sense of it—to make an appreciation of it, as Vickers (1965) would say, in emotional as well as cognitive terms. One cannot do this—especially when constrained by time—unless one can to a considerable extent internalize the new material, which is apt to be ambiguous and value-laden, and allow it to come in contact with what is already in oneself. This takes us already into the transitional area. If one's defences are too rigid, one is not going to allow this to happen, so that the novel is likely to be screened out. According to Ashby's (1960) law of requisite variety, if internal variety does not equal the external variety encountered by a system, the penalty is failure to survive.

As regards working-through, one is not going to have much to work on if one has not let very much in. But beyond this, working-through entails the painful process of tolerating all the emotional upheaval that is consequent on coming to realize that one's old famil-

iar world is not going to see one through, that one's security base and
the very foundation of one's identity are being challenged. A new
appreciation of identity, and the serious consequences of disturbing
it, has been offered by Holland (1985). In sociotechnical change
projects, it often happens that when the magnitude of the impending
change is realized, both managers and union people refuse any further working through of the issues. They draw back. They prefer to
hold on to what they have, even if pretty bad, rather than letting go
and moving on to something possibly better but carrying high risk
(Tannenbaum & Hanna, 1985).

So long as the changes taking place in organizations and the wider
society are not of a major order, the individual is not required to work
through their effects on him/herself at the deepest levels of his or her
personality. But when these changes are major—indeed constitute, as
Bridger has said, the beginnings of a paradigm shift, which involves a
discontinuity with the present and the creation amidst uncertainty of
new forms of organizational life—then working-through has to take
place at deep levels of persecutory and depressive anxiety (Klein,
1948). This is the current situation and we are only in the early stages
of it. The organizational and societal paradigm shifts required cannot
take place unless personal paradigm shifts occur in large numbers of
individuals. How to achieve this in time to avoid a number of disas-
ters is an unsolved problem.

One will fall into a trap if one thinks that the new forms and
values—the new culture—will somehow emerge automatically from
what is already there. Winnicott's most pertinent contribution for our
purposes is to have suggested a way out of this trap, which is Harold
Bridger's point of departure: the new values, forms, cultures, and so
on have to be created by those actually concerned, as they proactively
weave together new patterns that, while based on what is already
there (both inside and outside), far transcend existing boundaries.
New spaces have to be found or brought into existence. In the child,
Winnicott has said that this process involves playing; in the adult,
Bridger has now said that it involves what he has called "design".

Unless people are well enough tuned in to the new, and sufficiently worked through regarding its consequences for them, they
will not be free, as persons or stakeholders, to enter into the designing
process. Moreover, under contemporary conditions—and especially
as we look forward into the future—it would seem to be ever more
necessary that processes of organizational and social design should

take place at a highly conscious level. Otherwise, unintended consequences will not be avoided. One can look back in history to inquire
how far major societal change points have been the result of conscious
design. When Howard Perlmutter and I took a look at this some time
back, we could not find a societal paradigm that was designed in full
consciousness, with the agents taking responsibility for what they
were doing, earlier than the American Constitution. To undertake
fully conscious social design at all is a recent step in human history.
We have little experience of it and are only too easily pulled back by
unconscious factors.

The link between making the new and tuning in and working-
through is made by Bridger in his theory of the "double task", for an
organization is not only a "purpose-oriented" but a "learning and
self-reviewing" entity. It will not successfully adapt to a changing and
uncertain future if it observes only its own purposes. It must also take
stock of itself in relation to its environment and learn from this so that
it can reassess its opportunities and constraints and pay attention to
the feelings of, and conflicts among, its members. This second task is
not legitimate in the prevailing bureaucratic culture, and to take out
serious time for getting on with it is not allowed except in rare cases
at the leading edge. I agree entirely with Bridger that if organizations
are going to succeed in the processes of active adaptation necessary
for survival in a turbulent environment, this second task must be built
into their culture and everyday operating procedures.

In a group assembled for the second task any member, including
a consultant if one should be present, may make any comment he or
she feels will help forward the work of the group in making a better
appreciation of its situation. Comments made in these circumstances,
however, are apt to be different from those made in groups whose
object is their own self-study. These latter groups focus on the personal growth of their members, as in group therapy, or on the characteristics of the group, inter-group, or large group, as in group
dynamics. By contrast, the former are focused on the improvement of
the organization in its environment, and of the members through
contributing to this improvement.

Something very crucial was learned about this distinction in the
first large-scale industrial project undertaken by the Tavistock and
led by Elliott Jaques (1951), who found that he had to give up extra-
curricular groups and work directly with groups in their normal
operational settings. This is not to condemn human-relations labora-

tories in their U.S. or U.K. forms but simply to state that they perform a different function. Jaques called the kind of work he did in the Glacier Metal Company "social analysis", to distinguish it from psychoanalysis. I think that Harold Bridger has developed this approach in ways that were not discernible at that time. If there is a "psychoanalysis of organizations", it is likely to consist of various forms of social analysis, grounded on all the understanding that psychoanalysis of the individual has provided but different from it certainly in procedures and to some extent in concepts.

New forms of participant design to handle transitions have begun to appear at the community level in the network-like fields that comprise inter-organizational domains. In a turbulent environment, the higher level of interdependence makes it difficult for single organizations to go it alone. They have to collaborate. The value reversal from competition is easier to achieve under pressures of crisis. In four communities with which I have consulted for periods of several years, local stakeholders have fashioned what I like to call "independent innovating organizations". Established organizations have failed; the gap is filled by a new body created by the interest groups concerned, even though they have previously been in conflict. As these organizations succeed, they become what I have called "referent organizations" (Trist, 1983), which also have the property of being "continuant" (Trist, 1987). These organizations have no formal authority over their constituents but nevertheless acquire the power to undertake an overall change mission on behalf of the community. They establish enabling conditions for substantive changes both to be initiated and to be sustained. They have, therefore, to display stability as persisting good objects—to be continuants that can contain (Bion, 1970) the change-making anxieties and the volatilities these produce.

These organizations are examples of fully conscious social design brought about by leadership networks among those directly concerned. The communities had developed a strong negative identity. Until this negative identity could be changed into a positive identity, no progress could be made. Such a positive identity could only be established when the leadership network had worked through the problems of the negative identity. This involved them in refusing any longer to accept the negative image ascribed to them by outside groups and, at the same time, withdrawing the projections of their own badness onto such outside groups. This took a considerable time and then had to be diffused among a sufficient number of people to gain a "mandate" for taking social action.

My own role in such projects has been simply to supply an addition to the pool of resources, internal and external, already available. This sense of being one among a number of resources, a co-learner and co-contributor, rather than an expert, made me change the name of the type of work involved from "action research" to "action learning"—a term used by Revans (1973) in a context of management education. In many meetings and conversations during these projects, which lasted over several years, I found myself speaking from my own depths to the depths of many others. For everyone was using all of him/herself at all levels in the tasks of tuning in, working-through, and designing. A leading-edge example of work of this kind is well described by Weisbord (1987).

It is also becoming evident that technocratic bureaucracies that infantalize the individual do not work beyond a certain level of complexity and that forms of self-regulating organization perform at levels far above their bureaucratic predecessors. When given the opportunity to participate and be creative, the vast majority of people avail themselves of it. This finding is congruent with basic psychoanalytic postulates.

What is certain is that a major paradigm shift in values, beliefs, and social norms has to take place in order to design a desirable and viable human future. The application and further development of a knowledge base that stems ultimately, however indirectly, from psychoanalysis is a necessary condition for this to come about at the requisite level of consciousness. We know that the resistances to change of this order are major. We do not know how far they will become manageable.

THE
TRANSITIONAL APPROACH
TO CHANGE

CHAPTER ONE

An introduction
to transitional thinking

Anthony Ambrose

Transitions, particularly those occurring in organizations, are notoriously difficult to manage: the best-made plans easily go awry, whether due to unanticipated side-effects, to the unexpected intrusion of new influences, or to lack of cooperation by the workforce. Not only are transitions fraught with uncertainty about the outcome, in many cases they are continuous and open-ended.

It is because of the problems of managing organizational and societal transitions that a network of management consultants and social scientists has been giving special attention to the analysis and guidance of transition as a particular kind of change. Transition has been looked at in a number of different but related fields: in society as a whole (Perlmutter & Trist, 1986), in organizational and community change (Bridger, 1980a, 1980b, 1981), and in developmental change within the human life-cycle (Winnicott, 1951, 1963). As a result of such a wide-ranging perspective, it has become apparent that transition is not just a particular kind of change: it is also a particular kind of process that works itself out in the same basic manner whatever the human context in which it occurs, be it societal, organizational, or personal. It will be referred to here as "transition process", and a main

1

aim in this chapter is to unravel the nature of this process and to describe its properties and how they operate.

Management literature in the last two or three decades has burgeoned with ideas about and solutions to the problems of managing organizational change. (All organizations—whether commercial companies, institutions, charitable organizations, and so forth—are social systems. What differentiates them is their purpose, the nature of their task. Therefore, one can say that all are confronted with managerial problems.) Some of these ideas emphasize the importance of inculcating certain developments throughout the workforce, such as the capacity for innovation, flexibility, and excellence in job performance. Others direct attention to the effectiveness of certain processes that managers should promote, such as the flattening of management hierarchies, getting greater autonomy in work groups, retraining, inspired leadership, organizational learning, and changes in organizational culture. Yet others point to the value of certain conceptual frameworks for approaching the problems of organizational restructuring such as systems thinking, sociotechnical thinking, holographic thinking, and futures thinking. These ideas, themes, and conceptualizations have all made major contributions to the repertoire of knowledge relevant to the management of change.

Nevertheless, there is a growing feeling that there is something missing in all this. It has to do with the fact that, although there is so much rhetoric for change, the problems in making it happen effectively seem so great and so complex. The position adopted in this chapter, and indeed in the whole book, however, is that this feeling is due to the fact that the phenomenon of transition itself is being insufficiently understood and therefore not taken into account appropriately. Consequently, there is little or no appreciation of the fact that transitional change processes in organizations and social groups differ in important respects from other kinds of change mechanisms commonly discussed in the literature. Getting to grips with transitional change therefore first entails gaining an understanding of how the transition process itself operates—a process in its own right, which it is possible to study, and which, if not allowed for, can be an unrecognized source of many of the difficulties with which managements today are having to grapple.

Transition is a process in which a previously established structure or set of structures that composed the system is modified or even relinquished, new forms of structure may emerge, and the mutual alignment of structures within the whole is altered. In the physical and biological spheres, such transitions just happen as a result of the physical and chemical properties of different types of matter which, combined into different types of dynamic system, interact with one another in ways that are partially determined by forces acting upon them from their environmental context.

In the human sphere, however, where our concern may be with transition in human activity systems such as organizations or social groups, although the process is basically similar to that in non-human fields it becomes vastly more complex because of the intervention of human awareness, motivation and purpose, thought and choice, and unconscious phenomena. It is not just that we are concerned with alterations in structures that are of a quite different type—namely, technological and social-organizational structures—but that transition in these does not just happen automatically as it does in physical fields. It will only happen as a result of the voluntary choice of the people who are involved in the system, or of a set of characteristics that facilitate such a process. Even then, it may not happen effectively if their choices and decisions are not based on a real understanding due to the process. For it is people who modify or relinquish structures, it is people who create new ones and realign the whole. Transition process in this field, therefore, heavily implicates what goes on in the minds of the people involved as they try to bring about, or to resist, alterations in organizational or group purpose, structure, and functioning. It is a process that involves human perception, cognition, and feeling as much as it also involves organizational and social interactional variables.

Since transitional thinking is based on an understanding of the process of organizational transition, its introduction in this chapter is necessarily preceded by an analysis of this process. In order to highlight as simply as possible the main features of both, the chapter proceeds in a number of steps. It starts by considering the process of transition as it occurs in organizations, showing it to be a two-level process involving both an objective sociotechnical system in which individuals participate and also the subjective, experiential, cognitive-affective, and unconscious systems of the individuals concerned. The chapter goes on to describe the basis of transitional thinking. This, founded upon studies of ongoing transition process, is a way of thinking about and approaching the most difficult of all the problems associated with organizational transition—namely, how to manage it.

Its central concern is with the way the people involved in such transition actually experience it, referred to as "transitional experience". The work of Donald Winnicott and of Harold Bridger, and his colleagues, directs attention to key variables in this experience and to the conditions affecting them which can critically determine whether or not the transition process is able to take place. The chapter culminates in a description of the key features of transitional thinking as they are applied to the management of change in organizations.

Societal and organizational transition as a psychosocial process

Conceptualizing the process of societal or organizational transition is a particularly complex task because, as we have seen, the scope of such transition covers changes that are of very different kinds. On the one hand, they include changes in technology, the environment, and social structure which people perceive and act upon as aspects of the real world that are outside them. On the other, they include changes in paradigms, values, and other internal representations which are felt as existing inside their minds, as parts of their selves.

This contrast can be put another way: the changes in societal and organizational transition involve both changes in social groups and organizations and their concerns, and changes in human beings and their concerns. It has been recognized for a long time that the processes of change in each of these two areas, even though related, are quite different. After all, organizations are phenomena at a system level different from that of the human beings who constitute them, with different system properties (Vickers, 1978): the processes in organizations have to be understood in social and technological terms, whereas the processes in individual human beings have to be understood in psychological terms. Indeed, the concepts used to describe these different types of processes are at different logical levels and only make sense at their own level. It is because of this that study of these different processes has traditionally been divided up into different scientific disciplines, each with its own distinctive concepts, theories, and methods. Social phenomena such as social institutions, social structure and process, and small groups of all kinds have been the domain of sociology, social psychology, and social anthropology.

Concepts at this level include status, roles, relationships, authority, collaboration and competition, group norms, conformity and deviation, social conflict, and culture. Phenomena at the level of the individual—such as motivation, learning, perception, thinking, and individual differences—have been the domain of individual psychology, biological psychology, cognitive psychology, and psychoanalysis. The concepts used at this level include behaviour, thoughts, feelings, needs, anxiety, reward and punishment, cognitive maps and models, memory, and the unconscious.

As progress in these different disciplines has also revealed their limitations, a new image of the human has gradually emerged, and such artificial divisions no longer seem relevant. Correspondingly, the long-standing dualistic view of the individual versus society is gradually giving way to an integrated view that each is part of the other. The influence of culture on the individual is ubiquitous: it is not just because of their genes or their conditioning that individuals are what and who they are; it is also because of the internal representations of their social worlds which they have constructed from the cultural realities they have experienced. Similarly, organizations and other organs of society are what they are because they are composed of individuals—that is, individuals in social relations who strive to achieve together what none could do alone. The strategies, rules, and operations of an organization, and the undertaking of change within it, only happen as a result of what goes on in the minds of those individuals, in their social and technological context, as members of the organization.

It follows, therefore, that in order to understand and deal with the real-life problems of society and organizations, we have to adopt a multidisciplinary perspective that focuses as much on psychological processes within individuals as on social processes that operate beyond the level of the individual. This means, in particular, that in order to understand the process of transition we have to conceptualize it as a process that is both psychological and social at the same time. As Trist (1990) pointed out, social systems are "more than a mere admixture of psychological and social factors, each studied separately by different disciplines". He proposed that we regard them as "psychosocial systems, a frame of reference that would focus research on processes that are essentially psychosocial in nature" (p. 540). He defined psychosocial processes as being "resultant compounds in which the psychological component attains social existence while the social component attains psychological existence" (p. 541). In achieving such attainments he attributed a central, pivotal, role to the function of culture which "as a psycho-social process, is to permit the psycho-physical human organism to operate socially and the institutional structure to operate psychologically" (p. 541).

Social and organizational transition are therefore now to be regarded as a psychosocial process that takes place in psychosocial systems. What this means, in effect, is that each of the two aspects of the process interact, giving rise to changes in the other. On the one hand, the fundamental technological, social, and organizational changes that are explicit and observable in the system are causally determined by the actions of people resulting from what goes on in their minds or psychological systems: their perceptions, their interpretations of meanings, their values and beliefs, their motivations and feelings, their habitual ways of thinking, their readiness to innovate, and the way they come to decisions. On the other hand, the content of these psychological processes is in turn determined not just by the psychological make-up and past learning of the people, but also by the explicit situation in which they find themselves—that is, by the technological, social, and organizational realities around them which call for action. In other words, there is a continual interaction between the external objective features of their surroundings and their "internal" subjective experience, and it is precisely this interaction that constitutes the psychosocial framework of transition process. It is therefore not possible to understand, let alone influence, this process without taking account of the subjective conscious and unconscious experience of the people involved.

Transitional thinking, as understood and presented in this book, is based on this frame of reference. Although much of the recent thinking in management science about organizational change has paid lip-service to it, it has nevertheless tended to concentrate on organizational, social, and cultural factors regarded as "outside" the individual. Transitional thinking seeks to redress this imbalance by drawing attention to the importance of psychological factors "inside" the individuals who, in collaboration with others, are engaged in trying to bring about fundamental change in the external factors. It does this by taking into account the way in which the individual actors actually experience the many challenges and problems that confront them in the course of organizational transition and particularly how such experiences affect thinking to generate new possibilities for constructive action. It is also concerned with the conditions in the social context, such as organizational culture and its norms and working practices, which can influence these aspects of experience by making them more likely to promote or to retard actions that will facilitate transition.

From Winnicott to Harold Bridger

What is so significant about transitional phenomena is that, besides being a revealing entry point for consideration of the subjective experience of organizational and group transition, it focuses attention on certain features of this experience that are uniquely part of the transition process and are of critical importance in determining the nature and causes of the action taken for change. Some of the subjective accompaniments of involvement in organizational transition are the sense of loss at having to relinquish current as well as long-held and valued ideas and cognitive maps, the sense of insecurity at being in an unstable situation that is far from equilibrium, the tension associated with conflicting demands and possibilities, and intense uncertainty about the future. The aspects now to be described draw attention to what is probably the deepest area of people's transitional experience and the most difficult to cope with: change in the sense of personal identity, of who one really is, as one's long-held ideas, values, beliefs, and practices are relinquished and new ones gradually take their place. Often felt as a threat to one's habitual sense of self, such change is commonly accompanied by illusory thinking which can interfere with attempts to come to terms realistically with the problems of organizational transition. It is because of difficulties in this domain that so much rhetoric for change remains as rhetoric and fails to translate into constructive action.

The work of Winnicott

Winnicott (1951) studied personal transition at a stage in the human life-span when the process could be seen in its simplest and most transparent form—namely, in early infancy. The transition was from a phase during the weeks after birth when the infant is psychologically in a state of near union or fusion with its mother to a phase a few months later when it is increasingly able to discriminate itself and its mother as different beings and eventually to have a relationship with her as a separate person. Observing infants during this period in situations where they interacted with their mothers or played quietly on their own, Winnicott was able to unravel critical variables that affected the progress of the transition.

Initially, the infant has the greatest difficulty in experiencing any distinction between the self and the mother, between "me" and "not me". There is a near fusion or merging with the environment. The infant experiences the illusion that the caring parts of its mother— such as the breast, the holding arms, the voice—are parts of itself. The contents of conscious experience begin to arrive, as if spontaneously created by the infant. They are a succession of pleasing and un-pleasing sensations and feelings, and the infant has difficulty in dif-ferentiating their source as being external or internal. There is just the near oneness of an undifferentiated subjective state in which an objec-tive environment is barely existent. The "good-enough mother" con-tributes to the maintenance of gradual recognition by her "holding", both literally and emotionally. Her caring for the helpless infant en-sures that the infant's pleasing experiences accompany as far as pos-sible the unpleasing ones, thus laying the foundations for a sense of basic security. To the extent that the mother is adapting to her infant's needs, the infant can maintain for a while the illusion that it can create pleasing experiences as and when it wishes. It is for this reason that this phase is sometimes described as one of omnipotence.

Later in the process, growth in the distinction between the self and the mother, the "me" and the "not me", becomes more apparent. The environment becomes an increasingly objective experience; the infant now more readily distinguishes between external reality and its inner reality of wishes, imaginings, and fantasies. Furthermore, the infant develops further capacity to indicate a greater sense of individual desire with people and things around it and an awareness that it is separate from them. It more clearly realizes that the environment is not under its control and can often be frustrating. It is able to recog-nize a greater degree of reality; it is more able to have a relationship with its mother, who is part of this reality that is "not me", and to recognize its increasing autonomy and capacity to make a difference on the world around it. It has begun to find its self as an objective as well as a subjective reality. Such a profound qualitative change from the infant's initial experience is a developmental transition.

In this process, the good-enough mother is still adapted to the needs of her maturing infant, and some degree of illusion persists, but it goes along with a growing recognition that the mother is "not me". There is an overlap between what the mother supplies and what the infant might conceive as being created by its own fantasies. This is an "intermediate area of experience" to which inner reality and outer reality both contribute; the name that Winnicott gave it was "potential space". This potential space stems from the infant's dawning realization that it can actually have an effect on its environment, that "I" can make things happen around "me". This realization is now due to two factors. On the one hand, an area of illusion, though declining, still persists such that what the mother does for her infant during care-taking happens to coincide with what the infant wishes, and the thought is magically transferred into the deed. On the other hand, with its growing perceptual and manipulative abilities, the infant discovers that its own actions bring about interesting changes in the things it touches and handles. Its spontaneous play begins to open up an area of reality on which the infant is capable of voluntarily having an influence, and which then exists along with the area of illusion.

It was largely during this time that Winnicott observed what he called "transitional phenomena"—that is, phenomena that he regarded as characteristic of, and caused by, the infant's experience of transition at that age. Most infants developed a strong attachment to a piece of cloth, the corner of a blanket, or some other soft toy such as a teddy bear: they would play with it incessantly, whether sucking it, loving it, or mutilating it. This object, whatever form it took, Winnicott described as the first "not-me" possession, a piece of the real world that the infant could own and do with it as it wished and whose rights over it were not open to question. He called it a "transitional object" and regarded it as having a critically important role in the transition. In the journey from purely internal experience to confrontation with the outside world, it enabled the infant to pass from magical omnipotent control based on illusion to a form of control more suited to the experience of the real world. In the intermediate area where both kinds of control coexist or alternate, it facilitated the whole process by which the infant gave up a way of experiencing and relating to an increasingly dysfunctional world and discovered a new way that took account of the nature of actual reality and produced desired results in it.

During this process, there are two features that are of the highest significance. One is that the infant engages in action and makes things happen in its environment. Quite spontaneously, it does things that, both as it plays with a transitional object and as it interacts with its mother, it begins to realize have effects, whether pleasing or unpleasing. This is creativity in its earliest form: the transition of inner imaginings and fantasies into effects on the real external world. But freedom to engage in genuinely creative action only becomes possible as the infant gives up and becomes free from the constraints of its earlier conceptions of reality. Moving from an old status quo and moving to a new and better one thus go hand in hand, and the indispensable means for the journey are the infant's own spontaneous actions, whether these be deliberate or accidental. In effect, the transitional object provides the cover, for the "space-time" required for this transitional purpose. (Cover, in the sense intended, suggests hiding, comforting, and enabling other "activities" to be carried out and observed.)

The other feature of the process is the frequent presence of a "good-enough" mother. This means a mother who not only adequately meets her infant's physiological needs but who also provides a framework of security for the development of the infant's conscious self such that it can feel its world to have the necessary degree of benevolence. It is a mother who allows and encourages her infant to interact with her in mutually satisfying ways and who understands its need to play both with parts of her and with objects. For example, she will often engage in holding, smiling at, and vocalizing with her infant and provide simple toys for playing with, such as a teddy bear. She will also provide the space and time necessary for her infant to enjoy this play, during which it is able to explore the relative effects of experience based on illusion and experience based on reality. In other words, she is able to provide for the infant what has become known as a "holding environment"—which is another indispensable condition for the transition described above to take place.

To Winnicott, then, transitional phenomena occur during the transition from being merged with the environment to being separate from it. They serve the purpose of enabling the infant to cope with the difficult coexistent experience of illusion and reality as the basis of its thinking moves from the former to the latter. Yet the capacity for illusory thinking is never completely given up; indeed, it continues to perform a valuable creative function throughout life. Winnicott (1951) summarizes its status, and that of transitional phenomena, in the following manner:

> The transitional objects and transitional phenomena belong to the realm of illusion which is at the basis of initiation of experience. This early stage in development is made possible by the mother's special capacity for making adaptation to the needs of her infant, thus allowing the infant the illusion that what the infant creates really exists.
>
> This intermediate area of experience, unchallenged in respect of its belonging to inner or external (shared) reality, constitutes the greater part of the infant's experience and throughout life is retained in the intense experiencing that belongs to the arts and to religion and to imaginative living, and to creative scientific work. A positive value of illusion can therefore be stated. An infant's transitional object ordinarily becomes gradually decathected, especially as cultural interests develop. [p. 242]

As Grolnick (1990) points out, transitional phenomena are observable in the normal development of most infants in Western society, and they come in many different forms. He concludes as follows:

> To the extent one accepts this Winnicottian developmental line, it seems reasonable to posit that each child will "transitionalise" some part of his or her environment and use it as an adjustor and balancer of the complicated process of separating from, while still feeling a bond with, the mother. [p. 242]

The work of Harold Bridger

The significance of transitional phenomena in child development to help understanding of the psychosocial process of organizational and social transition was first grasped by Harold Bridger in the 1950s. His background up until this time included many influences that led him in this direction.

Harold Bridger, a Founder Member of the Tavistock Institute, undertook training in psychoanalysis at the end of World War II, in 1946, after an unusual range of experiences. As a senior mathematics master he had also held a commission in the Territorial Army, and as war progressed he was a battery commander in the Royal Artillery.

He later transferred to serve as Military Observer at the War Office Selection Boards (WOSB), where he met all the members of the Tavistock Clinic and the other psychodynamics staff—for example, Wilfred Bion, John Rickman, Eric Trist, John Bowlby, John Sutherland, Ronald Hargreaves, Tom Wilson, and others. When Bion was later to return to the WOSB after conducting the first therapeutic-community experiment for those who had "broken down" in battle or in units, Bridger was sent to replace him and developed the therapeutic community on a "hospital-as-a-whole" basis—that is, as an open system—a feature that has now become a characteristic of all forms of organization in our turbulent environment. Together with Wilson and Trist, Bridger towards the end of the war developed a series of "Transitional Communities" for the returning prisoners of war to ensure their productive resettlement. And it was following the setting up of the Tavistock Institute that Ronald Hargreaves, who then became Chief Medical Officer for Unilever, suggested that the company might develop its management development schemes on a basis that utilized what had been learned in the armed forces, but might now be relevant to industry. Consultancy in this and many other facets of business life became a feature of Bridger's work (together with his psychoanalytic practice, as well as allied forms of consultancy in both social as well as industrial life) in the areas of group dynamics and its relationship with the psychodynamics of individual development, of career development, and of management consultancy in organizational development.

That background, in addition to making him familiar with Winnicott's work, inevitably led him always, in organizational and group settings, to be closely in touch with the content and quality of people's experience, be they executives, managers, or workforce members. In dealing with problems of organizational change, for example, he realized that the way people in their group settings act or fail to act is greatly affected by how they perceive, experience, and interpret the meaning of the events, situations, and problems with which they are confronted. Understanding the decisions they came to involved taking into account a host of complex factors—not just the external objective realities of the problems they faced and the group pressures to which they were subject, but also the internal realities of their conscious and unconscious experience as they faced these problems. He frequently found, for example, that the underlying assumptions that guided decision-making were inappropriate and outdated, and that the feelings and motivations that made people cling to them resulted from defence mechanisms used to minimize insecurity and anxiety. Hence, he was interested not only in what people said but also in "the music behind the words": not just in their rhetoric, but also in the thoughts and feelings conveyed by their actions or lack of action. Thus, one of his central interests as a consultant was in trying to understand and to reveal the experiential basis of the discrepancy he so often found between the rhetoric for organizational change on the one hand and action for change on the other.

The second factor to be taken into account is Bridger's multi-disciplinary approach. Like many of his colleagues at the Tavistock Institute, much of his thinking was firmly within the framework provided by systems thinking, sociotechnical thinking, and action learning. Nevertheless, he was always ready, and had the courage, to reach outside theoretical strait-jackets and to take the unpopular route of exploring hitherto unrecognized relations between different fields of thought. For example, he was always aware that psychoanalysis and organizational theory were two entirely different areas of thought developed for different purposes. Indeed, most psychoanalysts have little understanding of how groups and organizations function, and most organizational theorists have little time for psychoanalysis. Nevertheless, as he applied, tested, and refined his ideas over the years he became more and more convinced that there really were important links to be made between the two fields, and that major organizational change could be enlightened, and facilitated in practice, by learning from the psychoanalytic perspective. Moreover, psychic processes and behaviour cannot be understood *per se*: they occur in a specific social context which itself has to be understood.

In parallel to this, he holds the deep conviction that there is no such thing as a group without a task. Here we can see the influence of Bion, which he confirms. This conviction led him to disagree with "purely" psychoanalytic group-relations training sessions, the type that Elliott Jaques (1995) called "free-wheeling" groups. As there is no such thing as a baby without a mother (Winnicott), there is no group without a task, and it is in the context of a task that we can make sense of conscious and unconscious processes operating within the working group. This theoretical orientation gave Bridger a special place within the Tavistock Institute, and it was put into practice in his transitional working conferences, which have taken place every year around the world for several decades.

Coming back to Bridger's findings as a basis for gaining better understanding of the psychosocial process of transitions, this process requires people to engage in three different, though related, types of transitional experience:

- Relinquishing earlier and dysfunctional, but still valued, roles, ideas, and practices.

- Creating, finding, or discovering new, more adaptive and viable, ideas and ways of thinking and acting.

- Coping with the instability of the changing conditions, both outside and within the organizational system, and with the sense of insecurity arising from it.

Bridger found repeatedly that these three essential elements of the transition process could all give rise to serious difficulties. Indeed, he often found himself witnessing, in adults faced with such types of experience, phenomena that were, in their essentials, very similar to what Winnicott had described in infants during transition. Those he observed in executive and managerial positions included the following:

- Illusory instead of realistic thinking, making it difficult to relinquish dysfunctional practices because of the illusion that they were still relevant.

- A kind of merging with the environment—that is, the habitually experienced ways of life and work in the organization with which the self had become identified. This made it difficult to separate the self from the "not me" and for the self to see the environment as an objective reality that can be changed by action upon it.

- A sense of loss of personal identity as long-standing practices were relinquished.

- Clinging to certain seemingly irrelevant procedures or norms as conditions became increasingly unstable in the course of organizational change. Retaining these seemed to provide a sense of security, as if they were transitional objects, before ultimately being given up.

- Management attempts to force through organizational changes by directives, without gaining the understanding and collaboration of the workforce members and without encouraging and taking account of their initiatives. Such attempts commonly evoked serious resistance or ended in failure.

As a result of observations such as these, Bridger (1981) became convinced of the need for a management approach to organizational transition which took account of the experiential difficulties and which would facilitate the process by the provision of conditions that would enable the people and groups involved to become committed to making needed changes. Having succeeded both in organizational consultations and in designing a training experience that demonstrated the value and success of such an approach to change, he invited a selected group of social scientists and consultants working in the same direction to join him in what is now known as the Transitional Dynamics Network (TDN), in order to develop this approach still further.

Key features of the transitional approach to change management

The principal feature of a transitional type of management is the design and provision of conditions that enable the transition process to take place at both the psychological and social levels and facilitate its progress. There are several types of conditions, each relevant to different aspects of the process, which can be outlined as follows.

Open-system perspective

If organizations and communities are to maintain their health in rapidly changing environments, an open-system perspective is essential on the part of those who manage change within them.

Such a perspective recognizes not only the interdependence of the different parts that make up the organization as a whole system, but also the exposure and vulnerability of the whole to environmental forces impinging on it. To a much greater extent than ever before, managements now have to reconcile institutional needs with those outside forces. Coping with the ailments afflicting an organization or a community is different from coping with those affecting the individuals who comprise it. Internal malfunctioning and conflicts, whether of individuals or of groups, can no longer be managed as if in a closed-system. They have now to be seen in the context of the wider environment of the organization, with all its complexity, uncertainty, and unpredictability.

An open-system perspective aims to balance and optimize the interplay of forces at work both within and outside the system. This means not only balancing the internal interdependence of objectives, activities, structure, technologies, people, and other resources; it also means assessing the range of options generated by environmental changes and introducing mechanisms that enable variability and flexibility in the internal situation. The functioning of an organization can only be said to be optimal in the context of the opportunities and limitations of the environment in which it operates.

If managers and those working with them are to develop such a perspective and operate with it, this entails several fundamental changes in their mode of thinking that represent departures from the traditional managerial approach. First, there has to be a broadening of consciousness—their cognitive maps in terms of which they perceive their organization in its environment will need to be expanded. The boundaries of closed-system thinking have to be permeable so that the impact of forces from outside the organization can be appreciated, recognized, and understood as far as possible. Furthermore, there has to be sensitivity to the unpredictable nature of forces and events and a readiness to cope with them and learn from them. Consequently, the management of uncertainty and complexity become central concerns as consciousness expands to an open-system perspective.

Second, the interdependence of all parts within the system of the organization in adjusting to external changes has to be faced squarely. An organization is a system of interacting parts. Each, therefore, requires to be open and flexible enough to identify and work through changes in the other parts. Conflicts inevitably arise in this process, and these have to be managed in the interests of the whole, not just of one part or another. Mutual awareness becomes essential to maintain a shifting balance between maintaining the existing state, structure, and culture of each part on the one hand, and endeavours to be creative and adaptive in fulfilling the purpose, growth, and development of the whole on the other. In this difficult process, the only viable approach to handling the interplay of forces, internal and external, is a collaborative approach. What is required from top-level management nowadays is sanction for collaborative innovative work at and between all levels. Only in this way will viable solutions stand any hope of emerging and of being implemented.

Third, as an open-system perspective increases awareness of needs for adjustment to changing external forces, so it inevitably highlights rigidities within the system. The need to increase flexibility and the range of variability within the system in order to meet external changes becomes paramount. In order to bring about the conditions where innovation and collaborative implementation can thrive, structural changes may well be required towards not just decentralization, but horizontal information-flow. Correspondingly, and more fundamentally, each part of the system and the individuals that compose it will become increasingly holographic in relation to the system as a whole. That is, each will need to possess information and knowledge pertaining to the functioning of the other parts as well as to the external environment. Such an expansion of knowledge and awareness of the organizational system as a whole as it attempts to adapt to outside changes means that it has to become a learning system. Accordingly, individuals will be perceived and treated more and more in terms of their developmental potential as capable of spontaneous learning, rather than just as possessing skills that can be activated by orders from above.

A collaborative management style

Versatility in individuals and in working groups is ultimately dependent on the extent to which they can be autonomous, thinking and acting spontaneously and voluntarily. It involves responsible self-management and initiative from within rather than being directed from without. In an organizational setting where coordination within and between interdependent working groups is mandatory, self-management—to whatever degree it is allowed—is only possible if there is collaborative working and collaborative management. The outcome of this can, of course, never be certain. While the initiative for change in strategy and structure usually comes from the top, it is collaborative working at and between all levels down the line that provides the best chance for the implementation of change and particularly for its modification and even redirection as the need arises. This implies the need for top management, while being accountable for all organizational changes, to share its responsibility for the management of transition as far as possible right down the line. It has to be recognized that such sharing of management responsibility is too risky for some managers to tolerate; also that not all employees want it, preferring to work only from directives. This said, the important issue for transitional change in an organization is that there be a sufficient number of people to form a critical mass that can actively collaborate in the steering and implementing of transition.

Organizational transition is likely to take effect only if executives, and particularly the line management, extend their horizon beyond the boundaries and widen their perspectives to the interdependencies between sub-systems within the boundaries. Bridger (1980a, 1980b) has shown that there are ways of reorganizing so that a largely closed system becomes an open system such that responsibility for boundary management is no longer confined to the senior managers but extends right down the line. Along with such reorganization it is desirable that specialist training for managers be provided concerning the realities of transition process and the complexities of bringing about change in work systems.

Providing a "holding environment"

Transitional management, in addition to its necessary controlling and directing function, seeks to maximize an enabling function by fostering transitional change within organizational members. As a result of designing and arranging conditions under which this can take place, change agents are likely to find all kinds of new ideas emerging regarding strategy, structure, and ways of working. Some of these will be realistic and full of potential, others may be unrealistic and illusory. At the same time, however, change agents will also be confronted with transitional phenomena arising from the inherent instability of being in a transitional state. People, including the change agents, will express their insecurity in a number of ways such as by tunnel vision, by envy and destructiveness, engaging in conflicts with others, and by adopting seemingly irrational courses of behaviour like clinging to dysfunctional outmoded practices. All of these "negatives" have to be managed in such a way that they are "contained" within the organization and allowed to resolve themselves without unduly damaging it. For this to happen, people need to feel that they are allowed sufficient "elbow-room" or space to express whatever ideas and feelings come spontaneously, even if the ideas prove to be mistaken and if the feelings are hostile ones. They need to feel that the organization will not reject them for expressing these and that it can provide sufficient tolerance, space, and time for a process of working-through that may lead to resolution. This also applies to the necessity to find creative solutions, to innovate, for which a safe space is required.

Problem toleration

Perhaps the most difficult aspect of transitional thinking arises as a consequence of adopting an open-system perspective. Managers are faced with the complexities and uncertainties of the system's environment, with assessing their implications for the system, and with tolerating the dissonance between the two, arriving at solutions, and coping with the conflicts and resistance and hostility that become generated within the system. How will they then cope with their own uncertainty, confusion, and anxiety as they attempt to act constructively?

It is evident in many organizations and communities today that those who are attempting to manage change are unable to tolerate these feelings. As T. S. Eliot has said, "Humankind cannot bear much reality". As a result people falter, fail to cope, and seek a false haven. We tend so easily to shut away the more awkward consequences of our social existence today that upset our current ideas. We thus become vulnerable to the "quick fix". We may believe, and may give the appearance, that we are managing change, without in fact doing more than just scratching the surface. This phenomenon is indeed well known in the life of groups of people at work who, in setting out to achieve the tasks of the group, may sooner or later come to operate in the "as-if" mode (Bion)—that is, when the group settles for courses of action that appear relevant but ensure that the difficulties and implications of the more appropriate course are avoided.

To engage in the transition process therefore requires that people, particularly managers, must not only expand their consciousnesses and become aware both of the whole range of realities that are impinging on the system and of the implicit consequences for it. They also have to live with these realities, however disturbing they may be, and to tolerate them, not step aside from them. In other words, they require a capacity for being concerned, for being "bothered", as Bridger would say, that enables them to stay with unpleasant realities until such time as real solutions can be found and be effectively implemented.

To allow the experience to continue means inevitably facing up to inadequacies within the system and to identifying the problems. This may mean recognizing that certain long-held values, objectives, or methods may have become outdated and may have to be given up. It certainly means engaging in innovative thinking and collaborative exploration if new and more appropriate approaches are to be discovered and put into operation. But even if this creative process is allowed to get under way, new problems are likely to emerge in reaction to it.

Creativity can engender destructiveness in one form or another, and shifting the status quo in an organization is likely to lead to rivalry and other negative feelings in some quarters. Any manager embarking on the transition of a social system from an established status quo to a new and more effective form of functioning that will survive and indeed thrive in a new type of environment can succeed only if he or she is able to tolerate and work with problems of these kinds.

Potential space and playing

The way an organization adapts to new demands can be regarded as much a function of the creativity and learning capacities of those in a position to guide and influence its internal changes as it is of the nature of the external demands and of the internal limitations. In the process of seeking new solutions to new problems, the quality of their innovative thinking will be crucial in determining the range of options that can be identified and the choices that are made of new, more appropriate, forms of organizational design, ways of working, planning, and control. "Potential space" is a concept that refers to a process that has to take place if such innovative thinking is to be optimally productive.

This innovative thinking is by no means just a rational process: it is much more akin to the play of a small child as it explores and tries out new possibilities among the toys, objects, and people that make up its expanding world. It is a process of discovering: of new relations and alignments between old and familiar things, of how to integrate new things with the old, of new meanings and new action possibilities that lead to more effective or more satisfying results. For such exploratory play and discovery to be fruitful, it needs to be allowed plenty of scope, in range and in depth, so that a whole variety of new possibilities can be perceived and experimented with. Restrictions on this scope and variety may impede or even negate the process. There are external ones, such as lack of play materials or parental pressures, that impede the quality of play. Even more significant are internal restrictions that prevent the child from playing in a free and variable manner, whether these be the "rail-track" strength of its previous habits or a sense of insecurity that inhibits response to new experiences. Potential space is that space, in the minds of those who play, within which they still feel able to exercise freedom to explore in thought and act. It is a space in which their perceptions, imaginations, even illusions can mingle kaleidoscopically, in which new meanings and action possibilities can be stumbled upon almost accidentally, in which quantum leaps can be made, and in which the ownership of ideas—their own or other people's—is not an issue. Obviously, the greater the opportunity for such space, the greater are the possibilities for the players to modify their internal representations and therefore their perceptions of their world so that they can develop new action capabilities and order their world in new and fruitful directions.

It is precisely this awareness and opportunity that people need to develop if they are to succeed in the creative, innovative aspects of transition process. It is an important basis on which they can realistically cope with the dissonances and disequilibriums that come to concern or bother them as they face up to the needs for change in the system in which they are involved.

A further example is where the use of inner potential space is essential when it comes to actually finding solutions to problems that have been formulated. Not only has the range of possible options to be generated and identified; choices have to be made between them. Only by the full use of this "inner potential space" can the fuller variability of the system be appreciated so that new and effective strategies and ways of working can be chosen and put in hand.

Facilitating transitional learning: the design and double task

Potential space within the mind has all the characteristics of a catalyst. The many different ideas and feelings that go into it interact with each other and, under the influence of the enabling medium, undergo transformation. The elements of some structures become free and able to recombine into new structures. As the restructuring takes place, new ideas, new objectives, and new strategies may emerge. But what comes out, being new and fresh, are only possibilities for change, as yet untried in the real world. The process by which such new possibilities can be applied by people in bringing about needed changes, even transformation, in the real system is a very different one. It is called "transitional learning".

Transitional learning is one approach for implementing new ideas for bringing about change in a system. It is a way of trying out the new ideas, honing or modifying them, so that they become workable in reality, and steering the whole developmental process around the inevitable obstacles while ensuring that it continues to go in the direction that is needed. Where the system needing to change is a highly complex one made up of many interacting parts, such as an organization or a community, each of the parts has to be involved in the transition process. The key to it in an organizational context, therefore, lies in the manager gaining the collaboration and commitment of relevant people in each part who themselves also engage in the trying-out, modification, and steering in their particular areas of responsibility.

Transitional learning has three key characteristics, which Bridger refers as "testing-out", "working-through", and "design". "Working-through" is a concept derived from the field of psychotherapy. Here, it refers to the process whereby an individual who, having gained a new insight into why she or he behaves in a peculiar way in a particular situation, gradually realizes the implications for his or her psychic processes and their link with the external system.

Working-through, however, is not just an intellectual process to be carried out in a conceptual vacuum. In order to be useful for action, it must be linked with a real purpose or task (i.e. through design). This process of linking the ultimate purpose to the working-through of the tension system in those concerned has been called by Bridger the "double-task process". This means that while a group, for example, is completing a task with official procedures, some underlying psychosocial processes are taking place. These have been explained by social psychologists and group psychoanalysts (Bion, Anzieu, Kaës, among others). The double task requires being able to acknowledge those underlying processes in order to gain an increased awareness (and possibly more effectiveness) regarding the total process taking place. The process of increasing one's awareness of the psychosocial side of what is taking place is known as "review".

Designing entails developing a specific strategy or actions likely to facilitate the required change. This is the part that draws upon both creativity from the participants concerned and their willingness to increase others' awareness of the various stakes of the change undertaken. Thus, the first aspect of process design is to get working groups to "suspend business" from time to time and engage in what is referred to as "group review". Interactive discourse in a group of people whose work makes them interdependent provokes and releases all kinds of potentially valuable ideas, which are either critical of existing practices or provide new ways of looking at problems which lead to innovative possibilities. Furthermore, when such groups meet at successive intervals they also facilitate a process of "working-through", such that any change introduced into the functioning of one part of a group or organizational system can be followed through for its consequences and side-effects on other parts of the system.

The second aspect of process design concerns the agenda of review groups. The nature of the work that people do in any organization and the ideas that lie behind it have direct or indirect links to the mission and strategy of the organization, the objectives of its various sub-systems, and the goals to be achieved by the performance of individual tasks, as well as other links to individual psychosocial make-up. If a review group is to succeed in enabling people, individually and as a group, to develop new, more effective, ways of thinking and acting in their work therefore, it is essential that purposes—both those of the organization as a whole and those of the individual—should never be lost sight of. In the past, however, the reason why group discussions such as occurred in T-groups (see chapter two) became controversial was because they raised difficult psychological issues. For transitional social scientists, it is legitimate that interpersonal issues be examined in review groups because they are an aspect of people's interdependence in most work situations. However, a central or underlying theme should also be people's and groups' performance of their tasks and the objectives they set themselves in the context of the work situation.

The concept of the double task has sometimes been likened by Bridger to the double-helix structure of DNA—that is, the interaction of one form of helix with another. The intention was to convey the idea that, as far as possible, every organizational member should be encouraged to regard their task as in fact consisting of two inter-related tasks. Task 1 is their explicit productive task. Task 2 is the task of critically appraising both their performance of it and the objective(s) they are seeking to fulfil by means of it. In other words, the interaction is between the purpose and the tension system. With this type of mind-set, they will become more alert to needed changes, more likely to develop ideas as to what these should be, and more ready to collaborate in group endeavours to bring about change. Faced with transitional change, managements need to support this kind of mind-set as part of their organization's culture. Donald Schön (1983) refers to a similar experience in his reference to "reflection-in-action".

Developmental potential

Attempting to impose change on groups of people within organizations or communities who are either unprepared for it or who show no spontaneous inclination themselves to have change brought about is usually counter-productive. No matter at what level within an organization or community, there are tremendous differences between individuals in the extent to which they are ready for change. Some people prefer the security of an established status quo, with its regularities, its absence of uncertainty, and its seemingly reliable permanence. By contrast, there are other people who are able to take on a wider perspective on their own lives and on the functioning of the organization in which they work or of the community in which they live. They are people who have an awareness of new possibilities within themselves or their environments, and who are responsive to opportunities for developmental changes. They are people who, in one way or another, show initiative, creativity, and capacity for innovation and who, therefore, do not feel tied to maintaining the status quo. Such people, furthermore, tend not to be threatened by external changes that impinge upon them or their organization but, rather, perceive these as chances for development in new directions. These are the people who can be said to show developmental potential. While, in fact, all human beings have such potential, many are either unaware or it or feel unable to do anything about it. It is those who recognize and respond to it, however, whether in themselves or in their organization, who are the driving forces for change.

They are like the green shoots that push up in the garden whatever the weather. When confronted with a challenge, an opportunity, or need for change, these are the people most likely to respond positively, to become involved and participate in finding solutions, and, most of all, to give direction and momentum to the implementation of such changes. Such potential is to be found at any level within an organization. They have also, however, to be ready to engage others, enabling their green shoots to be identified and nurtured. This means that in order to achieve significant changes, the more resistant and reluctant people should also be invited to participate, as important parts of the system to be taken into account.

The role of "transitional objects" or situations in facilitating transformation

Although Winnicott referred to the transitional object in relation to infant development, there are many examples of transitional-object equivalents to be found in adult life associated with other forms of developmental process. Two such examples are the role of the shape of the table in the Vietnam negotiations and the role of pets in human society (see chapter six).

Not only transitional objects but also transitional situations can have the same effect in facilitating or acting as a catalyst in the development or change process. The difficulties and the instability of relinquishing the old and outlived and of discovering new and more viable options can be greatly eased by situations or features, whether designed or spontaneous, that have effects that both reduce anxiety and open up new possibilities. Examples in organizations may be the continued use of a procedure or a piece of structure or culture which may come to assume special significance during a transition and be retained even though it is no longer relevant; or the coffee machine installed at a central point between the offices of different departments, which enables barriers between those departments to be broken down through the informal encounters at coffee breaks. Organizational life is full of opportunities for making unconventional but fruitful approaches to problems by making use of chance or deliberate happenings that are usually unexpected or even frivolous.

Transitional space and containment

However much a manager and those collaborating with him or her may wish, and be ready, to use the transitional approach in bringing about change in their system, they will not be able to do so unless the conditions are right. If conditions are not right, they will first have to be created.

In the normal daily life of many organizations and communities, people usually feel under pressure to get on with the job, to perform, to achieve objectives. The prime criterion for judging a person's or group's contribution to the purpose of the system as a whole is the "first task"—namely, their success in producing whatever they are expected to according to the needs of the system. Consequently, there is usually little room for manoeuvre for those wishing to engage in transitional learning—that is, to review their performance and their objectives and to use their potential space in exploring their developmental potential in the context of an open-system perspective. What is required for this is transitional space–time.

Transitional space is the space available, within the pressures of everyday life, for an individual or a group to engage in transitional learning. It is an external condition for such learning to take place and is to be distinguished from potential space, which is an internal condition for innovative thinking to occur. The two concepts are, however, related. Where the conditions of work organization and working relationships are, for example, very rigid or very authoritarian, it is likely to be difficult for individuals to mobilize their potential space. On the other hand, even under adverse conditions, the more

strength and independence an individual has to use his or her potential space, the more that individual is likely to find ways of changing
the conditions so that his or her own learning, and that of others, can
emerge.

There are four components of transitional space. The first is time:
depending on the duration of the task of a group, one or several
occasions may need to be made and set aside for "suspending business". The second component is place: depending on the nature of the
task, its location may or may not be suitable for engaging in group
review. The third component is sanction: no part of a system is likely
to achieve transitional space of sufficient suitability and frequency
unless it is at least tolerated by the rest of the system.

Last, but by no means least in importance, is group toleration.
Even if the other three components exist, a group will not experience
much transitional space unless all its members create it among themselves. Each individual should be able to feel free enough to express
whatever thoughts and feelings seem relevant for the group's transitional learning and reviewing, however uncharacteristic or "out of
role" they may appear. For this to happen, each individual must feel
that he or she is allowed such expression by others. Toleration by all
members, therefore, of deviations from the norm is a minimum requirement for a group to experience its own transitional space. As
time goes on, furthermore, such toleration may well turn into facilitation, with the recognition that deviation is in fact a prerequisite for the
emergence of the group's potential for variability and therefore for its
own development. Such a situation has been described as one of
"containment". The group is able to contain the variability within it,
even if this at times becomes negative or hostile, without rejecting
deviance. Similarly, the individual members are able to feel contained—that is, located in a space that is encompassed by a boundary
within which there is security, support, and nourishment for spontaneous efforts at development.

Transitional space within a system is that which, because of
the pressures impinging on it, will clearly be subject to expansion
and contraction. If a system succeeds in transforming itself, however,
from a task system to one that is also a learning system, this presupposes that such space will, in the long run, expand to become
a permanent feature of the system, or in other words, part of its
culture.

Preaching to the converted?

On reviewing the key features outlined above, some, or even many, change agents and managers will recognize most or at least part of their own thinking and practice. In fact, we are convinced that there are plenty of people who are working "transitionally" even though they may not be aware of it. One of the purposes of this book is to make explicit the various aspects of this approach and its theoretical foundations. In the course of reading the following chapters, however, it should become apparent that this approach can be successful only if certain conditions are put in place.

CHAPTER TWO

Organizational change theories and practices: a critical review

Gilles Amado & Rachel Amato

The transitional approach to change does not break completely with previous or concurrent approaches to change, although it is in many respects distinct from them. It is for this reason that we will explore these other "parent" approaches here. We will be talking mainly of change in organizations, in institutions, and in groups and less of societal change, although many parallels can be made between the two. In this chapter, we first look at the wider context of the major schools of thought, movements, or "paradigms" of organizational change since the end of World War II. Then, in the following chapters, we go on to describe the transitional approach to change and its distinctive characteristics. By "paradigms" we mean not major revolutions of thought, but simply a series of quasi–ideal-types implying a distinctive way of conceiving of change and addressing the problem of intervention. The notion of "paradigm" is useful here as it captures the way in which these approaches break with other conceptions of the organization and therefore also with the prevalent methods of organizational change at particular points in time.

Of course, it gives a false impression of linearity to trace chronologically the different "paradigms" of the theory and practice of

29

organizational change. This form of presentation has been broadly adopted for reasons of clarity, but it is necessary to bear in mind that the evolution of thinking and practice in this area is continuous and multi-directional: different schools of thought overlap, feed into each other, and are not necessarily mutually exclusive. Furthermore, it is often practically impossible to determine a precise event that marked their start. A "paradigm" of organizational change often results from a combination of simultaneous and dispersed conceptualizations and initiatives that converge approximately at a more or less specific time; it then proceeds to evolve over time as it takes on the different interpretations, contributions, and adaptations of the thinkers and practitioners that work with it. This is, of course, as much true of transitional thinking as it is of the different approaches that have preceded it or existed alongside it. The aim of the introductory chapters in this book, chapters one to three, is to get to the heart of transitional thinking and its roots, to show what are the main elements that the different transitional practices, exemplified in chapters four to eight, have in common with one another. This chapter is a contribution to describing those key elements.

We begin with a brief overview of the approaches to organizational change, which we have divided into two broad periods: postwar from the 1940s to the 1970s, and the 1980s and 1990s.

I

THE FOUNDATIONS:
FROM THE 1940s TO THE 1970s

The period immediately after World War II marked the start of several important influences in the area of organizational change. First, there were two types of training that had a long-lasting theoretical and methodological impact: laboratory training (or sensitivity training or T-group training), developed by Lewin and later based at the National Training Laboratories in the United States; and human relations training, at the Tavistock Institute in London. Other important influences of this period were the sociotechnical approach, developed through Trist's work and later also based at the Tavistock Institute, survey research and feedback, founded on the work of Likert to do with attitudes and perceptions at work; and action research, initially developed by Lewin.

The above roots of organizational change efforts originated mainly in the United States and Britain. Parallel to them, in France, arose a particular form of sociological diagnosis based on the work of Michel Crozier, as well as psychosociology inspired by psychoanalysis and group dynamics, among other influences.

I.1. The seminal work of Kurt Lewin

The work of Kurt Lewin had a significant impact on all sorts of organizational change practices and theories, and his mark can still be seen in this field today.

Lewin, a German psychologist forced to emigrate to the United States to escape the Nazi regime, began his research by looking at topics in the area of individual psychology, such as frustration, learning, and levels of aspiration. Between 1939 and 1947 (the year of his early death), he was concerned mainly with developing a psychology of groups that would be both dynamic and gestaltist—that is, articulated and defined with constant reference to the social context within which groups are formed, integrated, gravitate, and disintegrate (Mailhiot, 1968). It is in this way that he came to be interested in the real and existential dimensions of group phenomena in contexts in which social actions are being restructured or reoriented in order to become more functional, more effective, or more creative.

In 1945, at the request of the Massachusetts Institute of Technology (MIT), which was at the time the most famous American centre for nuclear research, Lewin created the Research Center for Group Dynamics. He conceived of group dynamics as social engineering; however, bitterly regretted that some of his students had been quick to use this approach as a form of science of group manipulation, for Lewin had always been preoccupied with the question of ethics (cf. his 1946 work on psychological minorities). According to Lewin, in order to deal with such issues in a scientific way, the only valid approach is a multidimensional one, involving the various social sciences. It is this conviction that underlay his preference for field research as opposed to laboratory research.

He was influenced both by North-American pragmatism and the Hegelian conception of becoming, which was a constant inspiration throughout his life. He later became a supporter of operationism, a dominant movement towards the end of the 1930s in the United States, which posited that theories and hypotheses in group psychology are only valid if they enable researchers to have an impact on the phenomena being studied. Furthermore, social phenomena cannot be observed from the outside; they can only be understood by researchers involved in their evolution.

It was Lewin who developed the notions of social field and topological psychology (1964), according to which any set of interdependent elements constitutes a dynamic whole. Lewin viewed the social field as a gestalt—that is, as a whole totally bound up with both the sub-groups and the individuals that coexist within it. Social adaptation is a question of bringing the aspirations of that whole to the fore while maintaining functional links with its environment. It is interesting to note that Lewin explored group phenomena in many different contexts (spontaneous groups, teaching groups, work groups, and others) but was always careful to distinguish between socio-groups (task groups) and psycho-groups (training groups) (Lewin, 1944, 1945).

For Lewin, engendering real individual and group development depends on the social climate that prevails within the group, on the creative possibilities available, and on the setting up of structures that are both flexible and functional. In order for social change to take place, the dialectical relationship between three elements of the social situation must be modified:

• its structure;
• the structure of the conscious forces at work within it;
• the events taking place in it.

Two factors are of prime importance to this readjustment: the climate in the group, and a new, more open style of authority.

Lewin's conception of change, together with his scientific approach, are without doubt two major sources of inspiration for the transitional approach discussed throughout this book.

1.2. *Organization development*

One of the most important approaches to organizational change is organization development (OD), which was born around the end of the 1950s in the United States. It is associated by French and Bell (1990, 1994, 1999) with at least three stems: (1) laboratory training of groups, developed initially by Lewin and then continued at the National Training Laboratory, insights from which were later applied to organizations; (2) survey research and feedback methodology; and (3) action research. A further stem, the socio-technical and socio-clinical approaches of the Tavistock Institute, is associated via the links between key actors at that time. The term "organization development" seems to have emerged more or less simultaneously in several places to do with training programmes set up by such people as Robert Blake, Herbert Shepard, Jane Mouton, Douglas McGregor, and Richard Beckhard. A wide variety of concepts and experiences from different contexts and disciplines—clinical and social psychology, psychiatry, family group therapy, systems theory, psychodrama, counselling methodology, action research, industrial relations, and others—contributed to the emergence of organization development. OD has also evolved since its early years by taking on further influences and by diversifying as the OD practitioners and intervention contexts have multiplied.

We need to consider in more detail the three stems that are said, by French and Bell, to have contributed to forming early OD.

Laboratory Training: The T-group.   The Research Center for Group Dynamics, founded in 1945 at MIT under the direction of Lewin, was one of the earliest entities to develop laboratory training, in which participants in reflective small groups learn from the analysis of group processes and the expression of perceptions on individual behaviour. The objective of such reflection is for there to be a change in participants' behaviour upon their return to their usual social context. Above all, it was an experimental approach in which participants were asked to collaborate with facilitators in order to enhance understanding of group functioning. Participants were thus both the object and subject of the research. One of the main features was its anti-positivist side—that is, it sought to move away from exclusively external explanations of reality. Key values in laboratory training were the spirit of inquiry, and democracy, consisting of collaboration and the rational resolution of conflict.

The T-group approach usually consists of a residential break of a week or two, away from any urban centres, during which participants, usually volunteers but sometimes sent by their companies, are essentially cut off from all links with the outside world. An intensive programme is proposed, consisting of group work sessions, alternating with theoretical sessions on group dynamics or exercises on specific aspects of behaviour, and a number of relaxation periods intended to provide the opportunity for informal exchanges. An important characteristic of the T-group is the absence of a predefined agenda or discussion topic. The group generates learning situations focused on the experience of behaviour within the group. Two forms of learning are intended to take place: (1) the enhancement of self-knowledge, and (2) the improvement of people's understanding of group functioning, leading to a greater capacity for managing interpersonal relations and for analysing group situations.

The original proponents of this approach included Marian Radke, Leon Festinger, Ronald Lippitt, and Dorwin Cartwright, who were joined by Kenneth Benne and Leland Bradford in 1946. The National Training Laboratory in Group Development (later to become NTL, and then the NTL Institute for Applied Behavioral Science) was set up in 1947 by Benne, Bradford, and Lippitt and gave rise to contemporary T-group training. Many of the subsequent figures of OD, who tried to apply the insights from laboratory training to complex organizational settings, had been T-group trainers in NTL programs. T-groups became one of the primary tools of OD. From them developed *team building*, which was first practised by McGregor, Tannenbaum, and others.

The T-group type of approach is still alive in its original setting and is also frequently used in modern organizations and institutions, mainly in the United States. In Europe, a psychoanalytic form has been developed, leading to "group analysis". It is important to note that T-groups have replaced the original "task groups" without a proper understanding of the consequences of such a shift (Amado, 1999).

Survey Research and Feedback.   OD was strongly influenced by organizational and industrial psychology. Likert's survey-feedback methodology is one of the most representative examples of such influences. Likert was the director of the Institute for Social Research of the University of Michigan, which, after Lewin's death in 1947, included the Survey Research Center and the Research Center for Group Dynamics, both founded by Lewin in 1946. Likert's method is the result of the combination of these two orientations: organizational analysis through surveys, and group dynamics. The surveys concern employee morale, attitudes at work, and the perception of the organization's management. The data collected is used to introduce changes in the organization by way of feedback to all participants on the results of the questionnaires, starting with the management team and descending the whole formal hierarchy of the organization. The feedback sessions are followed by discussions between management and the rest of the employees on the interpretation of the results, and then the development of an action plan. They are generally facilitated by a consultant. This process is at the centre of most OD interventions, although there may be variations as to the population surveyed or the method of presentation of the results.

Action Research. As was described above, one of the earliest proponents of action research was Lewin. His work on the domestic consumption of meat entrails during the war was one of the first initiatives to be labelled *action research*. Owing to the lack of meat at that time, there was a need to encourage housewives to use meat entrails in their cooking. Comparing the mid-term effects of an advertising campaign on the one hand and discussion groups on the other, Lewin discovered that the participants of the latter were still eating meat entrails six months later. Through this experiment, Lewin pointed out the importance of group discussion for diminishing resistance to change. It is an example of his concern to bridge the gap between social theory and social action, which action research addresses. As he stated: "No action without research, and no research without action."

Chein, Cook, and Harding (1948) identified early on four varieties of action research: diagnostic, participant, empirical, and experimental. In *diagnostic* action research, the researcher analyses a problem situation and recommends appropriate improvement actions derived from his experience or knowledge. *Participant* action research is deemed more effective, as it involves the client in the entire process, which means that they are more likely to carry out the recommended actions. *Empirical* action research means that the researcher keeps a detailed record of his own actions during the intervention and traces their effects. The *experimental* approach is really research on action, involving comparing the effectiveness of different action techniques in a controlled manner with a view to finding the best technique. OD practitioners usually use participant action research and occasionally the experimental variety. OD techniques are even said to be a result of experimental action research (French & Bell, 1999).

Some of the key principles of action research have become a permanent feature of OD, for example:

- Intervention *grounded on data*, usually included in a cyclical or iterative process of data collection, planning, strategic action, and evaluation.

- *Democracy and participation*, usually collaborative work between a facilitator-consultant and multi-level groups of participants from the client organization, with an emphasis on the empowerment of the latter.

- *Action orientation*, based on addressing the real problems faced by the organization and directed towards improving social practice by changing the organization.

The link with the Tavistock Institute

The Tavistock Clinic was set up in 1920 as an outpatient facility to provide psychotherapy based on psychoanalytic theory and learnings from the treatment of psychological disorders related to battle situations in World War I. The Tavistock's work quickly extended to family therapy and took on many of Lewin's ideas, as well as those of its own major figures such as Wilfred Bion and John Rickman. Action research was also very important in assisting families, organizations, and communities.

Certain of the proponents of OD in the United States were strongly influenced by the work of the Tavistock Institute, having spent periods studying, observing, and researching there. A case in point is Robert Blake, whose 16 months spent at the Tavistock led to his taking on some of the ideas of John Bowlby, a specialist of family group therapy, as well as those of Wilfred Bion, Henry Ezriel, Eric Trist, and Elliott Jaques. As Blake remarked:

> Bowlby had the clear notion that treating mental illness of an individual out of context was an . . . ineffective way of aiding a person. . . . As a result, John was unprepared to see patients, particularly children, in isolation from their family settings. He would see the intact family: mother, father, siblings, . . . I am sure you can see from what I have said that if you substitute the word organization for family and substitute the concept of development for therapy, the natural next step in my mind was organization development. [quoted in French & Bell, 1990, p. 30]

Bennis was another prominent OD proponent who spent time at the Tavistock. Major figures from the Tavistock also had frequent contacts with Lewin, Likert, and others in the United States. One result of such links was the joint publication of the journal *Human Relations* by the Tavistock and MIT's Research Center for Group Dynamics (cf. Bridger, Gray, & Trist, 1998).

A further Tavistock influence on OD was the sociotechnical approach, which started with Trist and colleagues' work in the British coal-mining industry (Trist & Bamforth, 1951). It transformed the traditional conception of the relationship between men and machines by insisting on the interdependence between the social system (professional roles, work organization, responsibilities, degree of autonomy, interdependence, subjective perception of roles, etc.) and the technical system (raw materials, machines, physical work conditions, spacio-temporal work organization, organization of tasks, repairs and maintenance, supplies, etc.) of the organization. These are seen as open systems and subject to the influence of their environment (Klein & Eason, 1991). To improve the way an organization functions, it is considered necessary to optimize both aspects simultaneously.

Links to other areas of organization theory and practice

OD can be seen as a variant of applied behavioural science. It of course has strong links with the areas of organizational psychology and organizational behaviour. OD practice has also benefited from the results of studies and interventions showing the effectiveness of various techniques and approaches derived from behavioural science. [Some of the OB concepts and techniques that are brought to the organizational setting by OD practitioners include motivation theory (Sherif, Maslow, McGregor, Herzberg); role theory (Mead); goal-setting in relation to individual behaviour (Locke); social cognitive theory, learning theory, attitude change theories (Bandura, Skinner, McGuire); inter-group behaviour and group dynamics (Sherif, Blake & Mouton, Deutsch, Leavitt, Asch, Cartwright & Zander); laboratory training and group development (Bradford, Benne, & Gibb; Bion, Bennis, Shepard); intervention and consultation theories (Argyris, Blake, & Mouton); theories of planned change (Lippitt, Watson, & Westley; Bennis, Benne, & Chin).]

Collaboration between British and Scandinavian researchers also led to the development of the Quality of Work Life (QWL) movement (Elden, 1979; Elden & Levin, 1991; Emery & Thorsrud, 1969; Thorsrud, 1970) as being closely linked to action research or even a version of action research, although it is concerned more specifically with the democratization of the workplace. Sashkin and Burke (1987) also give an in-depth consideration of the QWL movement and how distinctive it can be considered in relation to OD. The evolving notion of QWL over the 1970s is said to have included worker satisfaction; labour–management cooperation aimed at organization improvement; methods for organization improvement such as teams, autonomous work groups, job enrichment, and sociotechnical change; and a movement focused on improving the social condition. The authors note that the main distinction between QWL and OD is that QWL focuses only on the aim of improving the human condition, whereas OD has a further aim—that is, to improve performance.

The characteristics of OD in brief

OD was for a long time a synonym of planned change, defined by Levy (1986) as the changes introduced deliberately by members of the organization with the aid of outside consultants. Planned change has two important characteristics: (1) there is a deliberate decision to engage in a process of change with a precise objective; (2) a strategy of collaboration and power sharing defines the relationship between client and consultant. An OD intervention involves first defining a strategic plan for improvement, intended to achieve a pre-defined "ideal" organization, and then mobilizing the members of the organization to carry out the plan.

OD is based on a methodological framework made up of three models:

1. The action-research model, action being grounded on the interpretation of data on the organization.

2. The Lewinian model of change in three stages: *unfreezing* (questioning current behaviour or ways of functioning and creating a protective atmosphere to foster openness about difficulties); *moving* (intervening to engender new behaviour or new ways of functioning); and *refreezing* (reinforcing the change carried out and disseminating it throughout the organization).

3. The seven phases of planned change (Lippitt, Watson, & Westley, 1958), in which intermediate phases are added to Lewin's which are oriented towards the management of the client–consultant relationship in such a way that the client appropriates the changes and retains the capacity to solve future problems in the same area.

OD has evolved since its beginnings in the 1960s through the experiences of practitioners during the 1970s and 1980s, and by taking on board something of the organizational change paradigms that developed over that period. In spite of its constant evolution, however, it is possible to define several of the main characteristics of OD as follows:

• It seeks to *replace existing norms* with new ones through a process of re-education.

• It is based on a *systemic* view of organizations, which implies recognition of the interdependence of different phenomena and conceiving of causality as multiple and complex.

• It is based on data collection, seen as the legitimate means by which to demonstrate and *achieve consensus on the need for change*, and to give an orientation to the action to be taken. The data belong to those who produce the data; therefore, an important part of the process is feedback, which enables the change agents to involve the members of the organization in the change process.

• It believes in *learning through action*, and one of the major orientations of the learning is the improvement of organization members' capacity to fix goals and plan the actions of the organization. The procedure includes the comparison of the current organization with an "ideal" organization; the failings of the current organization are the areas in which strategies for improvement can be developed.

- Its activities are centred on *complete work teams*, which means that the pressure of the group to comply with new norms will force individuals to change.

- Its model of intervention is *participative* and favours power sharing. All levels of the organization are involved, for many reasons, including the fact that in this way decisions are more readily accepted and resistance to change is diminished. The underlying belief is that when individuals are given some measure of power, they feel as if they have the possibility to influence events, and therefore their performance and well-being are improved. Furthermore, it means that problems are dealt with by those who are closest to them and/or more expert. The same principles are true of the client–consultant relationship, whereby allowing the client to appropriate the process means that the changes have a better chance of becoming integrated into the organization and therefore of lasting. However, the OD process is essentially managed from the top, in the sense that top management must have knowledge of and commitment to the process and must actively support it. It is usually the entry point into the organization for the OD consultant.

- It has a number of underlying *basic assumptions*. First of all, individuals are seen as having an intrinsic *motivation for self-improvement*, given the right supportive and challenging context. This is closely linked to Carl Rogers's approach to do with personal growth (Faucheux, Amado, & Laurent, 1982). OD interventions seek thus to liberate individual potential for personal development or to modify the organizational constraints that stifle it. The second basic assumption concerns the importance of work teams to individuals, and of the *informal sides of group life*. OD attempts to instil in work-team members some notions of communication, expression of feelings, conflict resolution, problem-solving, leadership, inter-group collaboration, and so forth. Finally, OD sees *managers as linking pins* in the organizational system and uses them in parallel work groups involving the hierarchical levels that are immediately above and below them, in order to disseminate changes.

The perceived limits of OD

The cultural relativity of OD. OD is often accused of having a unique conception of organizations, management, and change processes. This accusation is linked to the debate about the transferability of American management methods to other cultures. Amado, Faucheux, and Laurent (1991) trace the cultural relativity of different approaches to organizational change management to the different cultural contexts in which they originated. They consider that it is for this reason that OD has never really taken root in southern Europe. This would seem to be corroborated by the figures given by French and Bell (1999) concerning the OD Network: of its 1998 membership of 34,000, only 184 were from outside the United States and the majority of those were from Canada.

OD as planned change. The normative nature of OD, including the planning of the change process and the aspiration towards a pre-defined organizational model, has been criticized for being inflexible and unsuited to the variety of organizational forms and contexts. OD used not to allow for a contingent and experimental approach to organizational change: it was a "one best way" approach. However, Glassman and Cummings (1991) note that in recent years OD has evolved so as to take certain contextual factors into consideration and to adapt the implementation of change processes to particular situations.

Survey data as the starting point for OD interventions. In the case of organizations in crisis, it may be helpful to found a change intervention on data perceived as "objective" and "factual", as this may serve to calm conflict and bypass defensive reactions. However, in its extreme form, the rationale behind this type of approach can be seen as functionalist, positivist, and rooted in an ideology of rationality. It would therefore be in contradiction with several areas of organization theory that stem from the interpretative paradigm—for example, clinical social psychology, symbolic constructionism, social representation theory, and so forth. Furthermore, the data collected provide no indication as to the future evolution of the organization and its context and therefore give a false picture of a static organization in a static environment.

Incremental change vs. transformational change. According to Dunphy and Stace (1988), OD is characterized by an ideology of incrementalism. Effective change is seen as a series of small successive and orderly adjustments, and as a process by which employees achieve progressive personal growth. This view of change is in contradiction with the more radical and revolutionary changes taking place in modern organizations through more coercive means.

> It (OD) values evolutionary rather than revolutionary change, order rather than disorder, consensus and collaboration in preference to conflict and power, the use of expert authority and the persuasiveness of data rather than the dictates of positional authority or the emotionality of charismatic leadership. [Dunphy & Stace, 1988, p. 318]

The coercive model is the transformational one. It stands in contrast to the incremental model in that it is reactive rather than proactive. Given the unforeseeable nature of a complex and turbulent environment, it has become necessary at times to respond rapidly and to produce radical transformations. Whether an organization chooses one model or the other is dependent on the fit between the organization and its environment, the time available to complete the change process, and the usual way in which the organization changes (continuous learning throughout the organization, or discontinuous and partial change).

The ideology of participation vs. coercion. There is substantial controversy about the most effective means by which to introduce organizational change. Most theorists favour OD's participative approach for the reasons mentioned above. OD is rooted in the implicit assumption of harmony among different actors' interests, and in the elimination of conflict. In reality, however, participation in OD interventions is controlled by management, as it is kept informal, limited to a consultative role, and can be revoked at will. The OD model of participation contrasts somewhat with the industrial-democracy model, which can be seen as more authentically democratic and focused on the conflict of interests between actors and on the illusory nature of industrial harmony. It creates more permanent participative structures with legitimate powers, which means that they can counter the managerial prerogative in certain circumstances. What is more, employees have real opportunities for participation in the fixing of organizational strategies and objectives, even if this implies changing the established power structure.

A further criticism concerns the universal pretensions of the participative model. Some researchers claim that it does not necessarily produce the best decisions and performance. It can even stifle the emergence of new ideas that challenge the existing organizational paradigm. Furthermore, participation has always been limited to the employees of the organization, whereas it could be beneficial to the organization to have its wider stakeholders participate.

A final point sometimes suggested is that, despite the ethical arguments in favour of participation, in cases where there is a conflict of interests the only realistic solution is coercion.

OD as an apolitical approach.   OD has been criticized for not taking the political aspects of organizations into account, for its naivety regarding the power differential in organizations, and for not considering the effects of politics on change. OD is considered as being in the service of managers, and therefore as incapable of being truly subversive. What is more, the basic assumptions of OD are difficult to reconcile with a view of organizations as battlefields of power.

The implications of the limitation to work units.   OD has traditionally focused on work groups and is not considered appropriate for the introduction of changes in whole organizational systems. One difficulty is that OD relies on close contact between the change agent and the client system, which is difficult to achieve in a whole organization. Another difficulty arises to do with the change process, which is inevitably different when taking place in groups as opposed to whole organizations.

A sophisticated science of manipulation?   Some critics of OD see it as a means by which employees are seduced by humanitarian ideas that make them more ready to orient their actions according to the will of the organization's managers. It is a sort of soft coercion, which poses a problem of ethics.

I.3. *Action research*

As we have seen above, action research has had a significant influence on OD, but it is also a change intervention approach in its own right. Action research is defined by French and Bell (1999) as follows:

> Action research is the process of systematically collecting research data about an on-going system relative to some objective, goal, or need of that system; feeding these data back into the system; taking actions by altering selected variables within the system based both on the data and on hypotheses; and evaluating the results of actions by collecting more data. [p. 130]

Many authors refer to it as a scientific approach to problem-solving, given that it is based on fact-finding. The iterative nature of this fact-finding process is crucial. It is what ensures that the intervention is effectively addressing the real problems of the organization and that it takes on more and more complex problems, as the data collection probes deeper and deeper into the functioning of the organization.

Another distinguishing feature is the collaborative nature of action research. It is this that is said to ensure its efficacy, given that people are believed to support what they have participated in creating. The role of the consultant-facilitator is to help managers identify the problems that need addressing, design their fact-finding procedures, plan actions, and evaluate their results. The process is essentially experimental or heuristic, with the aim of progressively enabling managers to learn more realistic objective-setting and better action-planning.

One of the advantages of action research is said to be its very action orientation. It is this that gives it both its research validity—data are more reliable when coming from people who are having to commit to real action, on a problem that matters to them, as an outcome of the research—and its effectiveness as an organizational change approach. This effectiveness is, of course, moderated by political forces acting to preserve the status quo, the result of which will be an increased difficulty in collecting reliable data.

The early notions of action research have evolved over time, taking on the extensions and innovations of other practitioners, to the extent that at least four different "strains" of action-research-related practices can be identified, under the labels of action learning, action science, participatory action research, and action inquiry. What is more, there is a range of other qualitative research approaches that have characteristics in common with action research—for example, grounded theory and Schein's clinical inquiry (Schein, 1987). This leads a number of authors (e.g. Eden & Huxham, 1996; Peters & Robinson, 1984) to remark that, owing to the proliferation of these different terms, the field of action research is somewhat confusing and it is difficult to establish what are its core characteristics.

Action research is regarded by several practitioners (Argyris, 1980; Kemmis, 1981) as an alternative or challenge to the "positivist" form of social research that had prevailed until its conception. Some give it paradigmatic status as a theory of social science (Argyris, 1980; Elliot, 1978; Kemmis, 1981), whereas others merely consider it a research strategy. According to Peters and Robinson (1984) the former conception includes the importance given to individual value, beliefs and intentions, the potential for emancipation, and the self-critical or learning orientation in relation to social problems seen as linked to the social context. Those who consider action research a methodology emphasize the fact that it deals with real social or practical problems (as opposed to theoretical questions), that it is oriented towards the direct application of knowledge generated during the process, and that it is a collaborative process.

When used as a change-management approach in its own right, and not within an OD context, action research is intended to produce theory, not only useful for the particular situation and organization concerned by the intervention, but also relevant and meaningful to other contexts. Indeed, Lewin referred to two broad categories of action research: the study of general laws, and the diagnosis of particular situations in order to solve immediate problems. Aiming to achieve both in one intervention can be problematic, however, for it means translating the outcomes into more abstract notions, which can lead to jargon and diminish the local impact of the intervention. It is nevertheless possible to generate two forms of research output, one aimed at the client for application to his or her particular situation, and the other aimed at generalization for the benefit of future interventions and other researcher-practitioners.

According to Argyris (1983), Lewin's action research included six main features:

1) It was problem driven, 2) it was client-centred, 3) it challenged the status quo and was simultaneously concerned with 4) produc-

ing empirically disconfirmable propositions that 5) could be systematically interrelated into a theory designed to be 6) useable in everyday life. [p. 115]

Practitioners are reproached by Argyris for either not giving enough attention to redefining the problem presented by the client based on the scientific building and testing of propositions and theories, or producing theories that, however rigorous the research, are disconnected from real life.

As described by Eden and Huxham (1996), an outcome of such generalization is the development of tools, techniques, models, and method. However, one of the principles of action research is that there must be an explicit link between them and the general theories, resulting from the action research, that inform their design. The theory thus developed is said by the authors to be emergent—that is, part of a cycle that sets it in relation to other bodies of theory whereby, in small incremental steps, existing theoretical frameworks are tested in action and the outcomes lead to the development of adjustments to those frameworks, and so on. This stands in contrast to Lewin's argument in favour of hypothesis-testing through action research; there is not confirmation or disconfirmation but, rather, a holding back of a pre-understanding until the data arising from the intervention has been fully interpreted and conceptualized.

Action research interventions are still very much alive, and a new journal on action research, called *Concepts and Transformation*, edited since 1996 in Northern Europe by one of the leaders of the QWL movement, Hans van Beinum, explores epistemological and field intervention issues.

1.4. *The strategic analysis of organizations*

We have chosen to focus on the work of the French sociologist Michel Crozier (mainly from 1963 to 1991) and the type of change intervention it has inspired, given the extent to which this approach broke with the precepts of the American schools of thought which had prevailed until its conception (cf. the Human Relations School). Based at first on his work with public companies and administrations in the 1960s, Crozier developed a conceptual framework for analysing social behaviour in organizations, which later gave rise to a method of intervention with its own specific postulates.

Bernoux (1985) qualifies this approach as belonging to the "interactionist" model, according to which individual behaviour in a social context is seen as resulting from actors acting intentionally to achieve chosen ends by way of strategies. Individuals are considered as having relative freedom of action and as fixing their own objectives within the constraints and resources that constitute their environment. Indeed, both individual action and organizational forms are considered free from the determinism that previous theoreticians had postulated. The organization does not adapt systematically to environmental pressures but results from choices on the part of the actors that make it up, whose decisions are then sanctioned by the environment.

Several concepts are key to Crozier's approach:

- The concept of *actor*, either an individual or a group with common interests, is a fundamental aspect of the strategic analysis of organizations. This perspective focuses both on actor's logics and on the situation of action to explain behaviour, rather than on the personal characteristics of individuals (personal history, psychology, cultural traits, and so on). Action or behaviour is always here and now, it derives from the actor's will to achieve a particular objective, and it is structured in part by the system within which the actor interacts with other actors. Actors are considered autonomous, although interdependent, and they are rational, although their rationality is limited and they will seek satisfactory rather than optimal solutions (cf. Simon, 1957). Strategic analysis views organizations as systems of concrete action in perpetual movement, as their members constantly adjust to changes in the environment, to new internal rules, and to different factors that re-structure the social space within which they work out their responses to the problem of collective action. These factors include the (formal and informal) rules that actors establish to regulate their relationships, as well as the alliances and oppositions that they build up in relation to other actors in the system, both of which represent resources and/or constraints to them in the development of their social game. For in seeking to achieve his objectives, which may be more or less conscious, an actor has certain resources at his disposal (uncertainties, alliances, economic resources, and so on) and is restricted by certain constraints (rules, oppositions, absence of economic resources, and so on). Given those resources and constraints, he develops a rational strategy of action which determines the way he plays the social game, in which he is confronted with the strategies of other actors.

- *Key uncertainties*, or areas of uncertainty, are another important factor structuring actors' social games by reinforcing or diminishing their autonomy and, thereby, their power. Power can be explicit—for example, inherent in the autonomy afforded by hierarchical position—or implicit, and related to the control an actor has over some aspect of organizational life—for example, information that is hard to come by, expertise to do with a crucial area of the organization's activity, relations with the environment (such as a network of useful contacts), and knowledge of the organization's rules. Power thus lies in the margin of freedom available to certain actors in relation to others. Formal rules are of no use in limiting the power of such actors in the organization; rules can even become sources of uncertainty in themselves when used judiciously by the actors subjected to them to counter the constraint imposed by those who wield them. Uncertainties can also be used by those who control them as a resource in negotiations with other actors in the organization. In the face of uncertainties controlled by others, however, actors can resort to various possible solutions to re-establish the balance of power to their own advantage. They are not necessarily totally powerless but can, in turn, choose how best to achieve their own objectives by wielding other sources of uncertainty that are relevant to the actors in question. With regard to the uncertainties that the environment brings to bear on the organization (e.g. changes in technology, legal constraints, strategies adopted by the competition, etc.), strategic analysis does not postulate organizational determinism any more than it does the determinism of individual actors. An organization's management has various choices available to it in developing a response to such uncertainties.

- *Power bases* and *power games* are central to strategic analysis. Crozier is one of very few authors to underline this aspect of organizational life explicitly. In contrast to other approaches according to which harmony and unity prevail in the better-performing organizations, rivalry between members of an organization is viewed by

Crozier as inevitable given the divergent interests of different actors. Power conflicts arise because actors' strategies do not necessarily coincide: they have different objectives and different perspectives on how to deal with the constraints that are brought to bear on the organization and themselves. Power is viewed not as an attribute but as linked to a social relationship in which there is mutual influence of one actor over another, although the influence is necessarily unequal and depends on the situation. The magnitude of an actor's power is related to the stakes involved in a given situation, hence the relevance of the concept of key uncertainty. The more powerful actor has a greater margin of freedom due to the resources at his disposal, as well as a capacity to negotiate his actions.

Crozier's conceptual framework stands in contrast to the postulates of OD in several respects. First, OD's view of the individual is far more optimistic and humanistic. It posits that people are basically good and seek both their own development and, ultimately, the good of the organization. It is founded on values such as respect of the individual as a whole person. Second, OD considers the building blocks of an organization to be groups or teams, whereas Crozier's actors can be either individuals or groups. Third, OD explicitly seeks to reduce conflict and to develop open communication, mutual trust, and confidence between levels and across departments in an organization. For Crozier, harmony and collaboration cannot be decreed. Fourth, OD was very much involved in bringing about changes in organizations by facilitating work on group processes. Crozier's approach, as we shall see below, is not based on long-term "implementation" as such. Neither does it postulate any particular relationship between consultant and client organization.

An organizational change intervention based on Crozier's approach begins with an analysis or "diagnosis" of the organization, according to an analysis grid, intended to: (1) map out the major actors' logics that characterize the functioning of the organization, (2) reveal the key uncertainties from which actors derive their power, and (3) clarify the organizational "disfunctionings". These constitute the "problem" of the organization, which the organization's members often misidentify. Change is intended to follow feedback of the results of the diagnosis, once discussion has enabled the various actors concerned to appropriate the results.

Criticism of the Crozierian approach can be divided broadly into three main themes:

1. *Limited consideration of the influence of culture on individual and collective behaviour*

Crozier refuses the determinism of cultural analysis, which traces a direct causal link between behaviour and cultural traits. He considers culture rather as a learned response to environmental stimuli. Thus, the norms that an individual uses are the result of cultural learning— that is, socialization reinforced by the influence of the environment (Crozier & Friedberg, 1977)—and also, more importantly, as an actor's capacity in the "social game", providing the actor with some of the tools necessary to developing action strategies in the face of those varying stimuli. Although conditioned by the characteristics of the situation, the solutions to the problem of collective action are also "the expression of the relational, that is cultural, capacities of individuals, which they both learn from their family and social settings and acquire, or even create, in the games and structures of collective action in which they participate" (Crozier & Friedberg, 1977, p. 197).*

When talking of the concept of rationality, Crozier does, however, concede its cultural relativity: "Not only is there no universal optimum, but criteria to determine rationality vary enormously from one culture to another . . ." (p. 322). Note especially that some of Crozier's work was also devoted to describing the characteristics of particular national (cultural) models, seen as models of the "social game" in French and American societies. (cf. Crozier, 1963, 1974, 1980).

In later years, Crozier explains his attitude to cultural interpretations of action by describing how he and his colleagues had actually chosen not to embark on cultural-type research, in order to focus on developing their original reasoning and methodology. The two orientations would have been incompatible, not because Crozierian sociological diagnosis goes totally against culturalist interpretations of social systems, but because it is based, rather, on "a prior analysis in terms of power, relationships, and social games" (Colloque de Cerisy, 1994).* However, Crozier argues that his theoretical orientation is actually different from that of cultural analysis, in that it allows for the idea of innovation in relation to learned cultural schemes:

---

*All quotations from Crozier and Friedberg (1977) and from Colloque de Cerisy (1994) translated for this edition.

We came to see individual and group behaviour in an organisation or organised system increasingly as a means to solve problems—the problems of action in a context of constraint and rarity.
In order to solve the problems of collective action humans beings
will have recourse to the cultural schemes they have internalised,
but they will also have to innovate, to learn new things when
those schemes are too inadequate. [p. 241]

The difference between the two orientations used as a research methodology is perceived by Crozier as the split between a form of research whose objective is to

reveal a number of permanent traits by fitting them into a model,
and a more problem-oriented and systemic research approach
which seeks to describe the way people respond to the problem of
collective action in an increasingly complex and changing world.
[p. 242]

2. *Exclusion of interpretations based on individual and group psychology*

In their book *L'acteur et le système* (1977), Crozier and Friedberg flatly
refuse psychological interpretations of behaviour. They consider all
behaviour as rational and consisting of strategies in the face of environmental pressures, although conceding that behavioural strategies
are not necessarily willed or conscious. What they particularly contest
is the determinism inherent in the modelling of individual and group
behaviour according to universal psychological concepts, as well as
the quasi-manipulation that such modelling gives rise to in an intervention situation. Resorting to psychological means of influencing
people's behaviour, among which the authors include charismatic
leadership, is seen rather as using "the various alternative, or parallel,
possibilities for impacting the social game in order to reorient it", and
as giving rise to unanticipated consequences (e.g. passivity in the face
of charismatic leadership). However, the authors do not seem to consider approaches derived from the NTL and Tavistock stems, based
on group dynamics, psychoanalysis, and so forth, which involve
working with the dynamic generated between individuals and in
groups in specific present contexts, and not only referring to the social
pasts of individuals, as Crozier would claim: "they all seek the basis
or foundations of attitude in the social history of individuals" (Crozier & Friedberg, 1977, pp. 465–466).

3. *No real engagement in action*

The revelation of the "hidden" face of the organization's functioning is supposed to be sufficient to produce change in the organization. This stands in contrast to the action research approach, which uses research data to invoke action and is oriented right from the start of the intervention towards joint development of an action strategy involving close collaboration between the consultant and the organization's members.

Crozier explained his position in later years as follows:

> By way of a diagnosis on the state of the system, we reveal the problems and opportunities and suggest a strategy. Unlike the usual approach, we emphasise the diagnosis and the problems it reveals, rather than focusing on finalities and objectives. We refuse to look too quickly to the solutions, which are the apanage of experts, of technocrats and essentially of men of power. [Colloque de Cerisy, 1994, p. 245]

There is also a striking contrast with the OD view of organizational change based on attaining a pre-defined ideal solution or objective, as exemplified in the following statement:

> The only way to truly open up decision-making to a broader set of stakeholders is to concentrate on problems instead of fighting over solutions. . . . Attempting to define things too much, to have clear objectives in advance, inevitably leads to proposing, that is imposing, restrictive measures. A blurred conception of things is indispensable in order for problems to emerge and for a consensus on their existence to develop. . . . If we accept to restrict ourselves to proposing a vague orientation for development and change, it becomes possible to work with the interested parties—those who will be involved in the implementation—on the problems they truly experience, and once a consensus has emerged *they will be able to find the solutions themselves*. [p. 245; emphasis added]

While Crozier's approach respects the self-determination of members of the organization and maintains a certain realism by not positioning the consultant as "master" of reality, in practice it can be questioned, as it relies strongly on the client system's interpretation of the results of the diagnosis. There is little guided working-through of the conclusions to draw out their consequences for action. This sometimes leads to disappointing outcomes, such as the mere "removal" of the people perceived by the interpreters of the analysis (often the company's top managers) as being the main "obstacles" to the smooth functioning of the organization. An action strategy that is true to the findings—and above all to the spirit—of the diagnosis does not necessarily follow.

1.5. Change through centralized leadership

We have chosen to focus on leadership as a "paradigm" of organizational change, because of the significant amount of literature that has been produced, particularly in the 1980s but also much earlier, to attempt to describe what it is that makes leaders, and thereby their organizations, successful (e.g. see Peters & Waterman, 1982). Leaders of some of the world's major companies are seen as having achieved virtually single handed the turnaround of their organizations, owing to some particular form of charisma, whose characteristics the research sets out to analyse in detail. As we shall see below, the "paradigm" of change through leadership stands in stark contrast to the transitional approach, which is why we have given it such attention.

The term "leadership" has taken on a wide variety of meanings in the organizational literature. Katz and Kahn (1966) noted early on that, "leadership is sometimes used as if it were an attribute of personality, sometimes as if it were a characteristic of certain positions, and sometimes as an attribute of behaviour" (p. 334). We shall start from this comment to consider how the concept of leadership is used in the area of organizational change.

Bryman (1997), in his review of the evolving focus of studies on leadership, points to four major perspectives. The first, which predominated until the late 1940s, concerned the *traits* of leaders. This orientation was concerned with the particular personal or innate characteristics of leaders, whether physical characteristics such as height, abilities such as eloquence, or personality traits such as self-confidence. Then followed a focus on leadership *styles*, which persisted until the late 1960s. An important example is the Ohio State University studies on leader behaviour, which identified consideration (concern for employees as people) and initiating structure (clear definition of employee tasks) as key dimensions. Other examples of the style approach are studies on democratic versus autocratic

(Lewin, Lippitt, & White, 1939) and participative versus directive styles of leadership (Vroom & Yetton, 1973); centralizing versus decentralizing decision-making and task versus people orientations have also been analysed (Yukl, 1981). Such studies led to reflection on the training of people whereby it was considered possible for them to acquire the behavioural characteristics of leaders. The contingency approach, which lasted until the early 1980s, set leadership in the context of situational factors, said to influence the effectiveness of different leadership styles. There were many technical problems with studies of this kind, and the contingency approach soon gave way to what is termed "the new leadership approach". The definition of leadership itself is said by the authors to have evolved, after the mid-1980s, from being essentially the process of influencing a group to achieve its goal to being the *management of meaning*.

Various seemingly synonymous terms are used to describe the new leadership: *charismatic* leadership (Conger & Kanungo, 1988; House, 1977; Kotter, 1990), *transformational* leadership (Bass, 1985; Tichy & Devanna, 1986), *visionary* leadership (Sashkin, 1988; Westley & Mintzberg, 1989), and just *leadership* (Bennis & Nanus, 1985; Kotter, 1990). A key publication was Burns' 1978 study of political leadership, in which a dichotomy was established between transactional and transforming leaders whereby transactional leaders establish an implicit contract with their followers based on rewards for compliant behaviour, whereas the transforming (later *transformational*) leader raises the aspirations of his or her followers so that the aspirations of leader and followers become fused. There is something transcendent and heroic about transformational leaders. A link was then made by several authors between transformational leadership and vision (Bass, 1985; Bennis & Nanus, 1985; Tichy & Devanna, 1986). The latter two pairs of researchers suggested a parallel between two dichotomies: transactional/transforming and manager/leader. The manager/leader dichotomy was proposed by Zaleznik (1977) and was also referred to by Kotter (1990). The leader's particular capacity to transform followers through vision then led to the idea of organizational transformation along similar lines.

The concept of charisma, an important ingredient in visionary organizational transformation, is a somewhat elusive phenomenon. Conger and Kanungo (1988) examine the notion of charismatic leadership in some detail. They refer explicitly to the capacity to motivate subordinates and to engender organizational change. What appears to set charismatic leaders apart would be their ability to motivate employees to achieve ambitious goals, with radical transformations of large bureaucratic organizations or the creation of successful entrepreneurial ventures. They emphasize the emotional side of such leadership; they would appear to be unique in there ability to build emotional attachment and enthusiasm among their followers for themselves and their missions. However, they also point out that this carries with it a dark side—that is, charismatic leadership's potential for the generation of psychological dependence, which enables leaders to obtain unconditional support for sometimes rather dubious activities. This aspect is rarely taken into consideration in the mainstream leadership literature.

A further characteristic is the transient nature of charismatic leadership, as discussed in Conger and Kanungo's 1988 review of Max Weber's conception of charismatic authority. Notably, success is seen as a necessary sustaining factor in charismatic leadership, as failure would reveal the charismatic leader to be less than superhuman and therefore he or she would lose his followers. There is an important contrast with the other ideal types of authority described by Weber— the traditional and the rational legal—in which the leader derives legitimacy from traditions or rules rather than from personal qualities. Furthermore, in contrast to traditional authority, which is the guardian of existing institutions, charismatic authority is described by Weber as revolutionary, seeking to overturn the social order where the social system is stagnant or in crisis. Whereas rational revolutions seek to replace tradition with legal systems, charismatic revolutions are a break with traditional and rational norms. The equivalent in organizational change would be, on the one hand, the transition from a family firm to a firm run by a president elected by an executive committee, as opposed, on the other hand, to a radical turnaround or start-up of a successful innovative venture via the personal influence of a charismatic leader who may have rapidly climbed the ranks through his particular relationship skills. Making such parallels, however, brings us to the limit of Weber's relevance for the organizational setting. It is necessary to go beyond Weber to organizational research into the link between charismatic leadership, context, and follower perceptions. Such research established, for example, that charisma is not only a question of personal attributes, but depends on the interplay between the leader's attributes and the needs, beliefs, values, and perceptions of followers (Conger, 1989). While the context is said to have some influence over the emergence of charismatic leaders, it is not as significant as the relational dynamic for most North American authors.

Conger (1989) breaks charismatic leadership down into four stages that are somewhat reminiscent of OD and relate to the idea of organizational transformation:

1. leader's recognition of need and opportunities for change, and formulation of a vision in accordance with those needs;
2. leader communicates vision, which involves presenting the actual situation as unacceptable and generating an understanding of the vision;
3. leader builds trust in the vision;
4. leader helps others to achieve the vision through role-modelling and empowerment.

Other than vision articulation and behavioural role-modelling, the transformational effects of charismatic leaders reside, according to House and Shamir (1993), in the following:

• Charismatic leaders achieve the strong engagement of followers' self-concept: "self-concept theory asserts that some of the most important effects of charismatic leaders are that they increase the intrinsic value of effort and goal accomplishment, as well as followers' level of self-worth and self-efficacy, expectancies of goal or mission accomplishment, faith in a better future, and commitment to the values of the leader's vision and consequently to the goals of the mission set forth by the leader" (p. 90).

• They motivate a shift from a focus on individual interests to a concern with contributing to collective interests.

• They increase individual and collective efficacy by "expressing high-performance expectations of followers, and expressing a high degree of confidence in followers' ability to meet such expectations" (p. 90).

Bass (1985; Bass & Avolio, 1990) developed Burns' (1978) ideas further, describing the components of transformational leadership as charisma (developing vision and engendering pride, respect, and trust), inspiration (motivating through high expectations, modelling behaviour, and using symbols to channel action), individualized consideration (respect and responsibility given to followers), and intellectual stimulation (bringing new ideas and approaches to challenge followers). Bass also considered that transactional leadership, rather than being an opposite form of leadership, was complementary to transformational leadership. He included in transactional leadership the following: contingent rewards (rewarding followers for achieving performance objectives), and management by exception (intervening when task-related activity is not going to plan). Transactional leadership relates to what Nadler and Tushman (1990) refer to as *instrumental leadership*, which they also say is a necessary complement to charismatic leadership as it is concerned with "making sure that individuals in the senior team and throughout the organisation behave in ways needed for change to occur" (p. 85). It is said to focus on "the management of teams, structures, and managerial process to create individual instrumentalities"; in other words, it is the manipulation of some of the more objective aspects of the organizational environment to motivate desired behaviour. They divide this leadership behaviour into three categories: structuring (team building, goal-setting, standard-setting, role definition, and responsibility definition); controlling (setting up measurement, monitoring, and assessment systems and processes focused on both behaviour and results); and rewarding (administering both rewards and sanctions).

Very often, it is difficult for charismatic leaders also to perform the instrumental function; Weber himself referred to the limits of charismatic authority and of the return, once the revolution has taken place, of rational–legal or traditional authority in order to institutionalize the changes. Nadler and Tushman (1990) propose three leverage points for the extension of charismatic leadership to cover this function of institutionalization: the senior team, broader senior management, and the development of leadership throughout the organization. Kets de Vries (1996), who has a psychoanalytic orientation and is one of the most important authors on leadership, refers to a concept similar to instrumental leadership—*architectural leadership*—which means that the leader is an "organizational designer" whose role involves setting up systems and structures that engender high-performance organizations. This can include creating flatter hierarchies and network decision-making; introducing self-managed teams, promoting an IT-controlled but decentralized structure; setting up mechanisms that encourage learning but at the same time make people accountable, creating a climate that fosters innovation and creativity; developing customer-centred organizational processes; fostering speed and engendering a positive attitude towards continuous change; and setting up appropriate and imaginative reward systems. However, the famous leaders he describes also had close senior-manager collaborators to deal with the more "instrumental" of these activities.

Bryman's 1997 critical overview of the new leadership approach points to some of its limits, notably:

1. The approach concentrates heavily on top leaders, the supposed heroes of organizational success. This is seen as a reaction to the preceding focus on groups, which considered leaders in organizations as opposed to leaders of organizations. But this bias means that the majority of leaders are overlooked.

2. Informal leadership processes are little considered.

3. Situational factors are on the whole not taken into account, as transformational leaders are supposed to be able to bring about high performance regardless of the circumstances. In other words, transformational leadership is being correlated with success, which of course is unrealistic. Only recently has there been research to show how contextual factors can inhibit transformational leadership.

4. Similarly, there is a bias towards successful leaders, where an analysis of the experiences of failed transformational leaders could provide valuable learning.

Nevertheless, as Bryman points out, a number of the more recent perspectives on leadership have begun to answer some of the above points. Gilmore (1988) adopts a more strategic view of leadership which does not idealize the leader as much; the leader is seen as having a role in organizational change, but it is both leaders and organizations that are seen as handling the transition. The key is not considered to lie in particular aspects of the leader's personality. Manz and Sims (1991) and Sims and Lorenzi (1992) have developed the idea of *SuperLeadership*, in which a key feature is *"leading others to lead themselves"*—that is, leadership capacity is developed in subordinates, and they are "nurtured" to be self-motivating and to put their own talents to use. There has been a renewed focus on teams as sites of leadership, where leaders are member-facilitators of teams (Katzenbach & Smith, 1993; Kouzes & Posner, 1993). Attention has also become focused on leadership processes and skills that do not necessarily reside in formal leaders—for example, Hosking's (1988, 1991) discussion of leadership as an organizing activity, including such skills as networking. These alternative perspectives view leadership as dispersed in organizations and not necessarily the preserve of formally designated leaders.

According to the new leadership perspective, one of the main tools available to leaders to bring about fundamental change in organizations is culture. Leaders are said to develop a vision that makes a strong contribution to an organization's culture. Culture creation is seen as a key element of leadership in several writings (Bass, 1985; Peters & Waterman, 1982; Schein, 1985). Related literature focuses on the need for cultural change to accompany strategic change or to cope with environmental changes. In these cases, leaders are viewed as having responsibility for cultural reorientations. Some authors even see this as cultural manipulation—that is, a form of management control that operates by the "colonization" of employees' minds (Wilmott, 1993) or by collective illusion (Amado, 1988). However, Martin (1992) adds some nuance to this conception of leadership as cultural manipulation. She sees this perspective as being dominated by a paradigm on organizational culture which she refers to as an *integration* perspective—that is, one in which the cultural components are consistent and reasonably well understood. She distinguishes this from a differentiation perspective and a fragmentation perspective. The differentiation perspective on organizational culture accounts for the lack of cultural consensus, thus allowing for the existence of subcultures and countercultures, and notably for informal leadership as exercised by groups within the organization. The fragmentation perspective diminishes or even eliminates the role of leadership in manipulating organizational culture altogether. Cultures are seen as so diffuse and ambiguous that there are limited possibilities of "managing meaning".

Most of the charismatic leadership and culture-creation approaches have been strongly criticized by European psychosociologists, who take into consideration the "dark" side of influence (Enriquez, 1991) and the complex intricacies at work between uncon-

scious forces, the "political" environment, and all kinds of normaliza-
tion processes (Amado, 1980; Aubert & de Gaulejac, 1981; Enriquez,
1983; Mendel, 1998; Pagès, Bonetti, de Gaulejac, & Descendre, 1979).

I.6. The psychosociological perspective

The psychosociological perspective grew out of World War II in Europe, mainly in the United Kingdom and in France. While close to
many of the OD assumptions and aims, it differs through its reference
to psychoanalytic theory and to the social context of the intervention
process.

I.6. (i) The Tavistock tradition

As Trist and Murray (1990) pointed out in their historical overview of
the Tavistock movement, "experience during World War II had
shown that psychoanalytic object relations theory could unify the
psychological and social fields in a way that no other could" (p. 31).
Melanie Klein's view on the paranoid-schizoid and depressive positions (cf. Riviere, 1952) inspired both Bion and Elliott Jaques in their
applications to the social field. Bion (1959) developed his basic unconscious assumptions (dependency, fight–flight, and pairing) about
group life, while Jaques, through his intervention with the Glacier
Metal Company (Jaques, 1951), built his theory on the use of social
structure as a defence against anxiety. Later, Isabel Menzies Lyth
(1988, 1989) explored the specific anxieties of nurses in the hospital.

Jaques, through his "social analysis" method, aims at a kind of
social therapy with a collaborative approach very much inspired by
the psychoanalytic setting:

- The consultant establishes a relationship with the organization as
  a whole.

- The organization is isolated from its context.

- It is a private relationship, protected by professional secrecy.

- The organization is taken as a unit, an organic entity with its
  history, its structure, its culture, its specific objectives.

- The consultant refuses any individual relationship with the members of the organization and any kind of individual demand for personal help or therapy: internal relationships are defined as public and professional.

- The free association method is used by participants (8–10) in meetings, without any specific agenda, with the help of two consultant-analysts (as in Bion's therapeutic groups)

- Neither the number of sessions nor their content is restricted.

- The members of the organization are the ones allowed to interrupt the process should they decide to do so.

- Reports are distributed to widen the firm–consultant relationship.

- Transference, resistances, and unconscious forces (e.g. social defence against anxiety induced by the contradictions between personality and role requirements) are explored by "working-through".

This type of approach is very close to the one developed by Bion and Bridger in the Northfield therapeutic community in the 1940s (Bridger, 1990). It takes advantage both of the unconscious forces at play within the individuals and of the particular roles, tasks, and organizational context in which they operate.

Various kinds of action research and working conferences have been developed around the world since that early period, using both object relations theory and the open-system approach. They tend to differ from what Jaques called "free wheeling groups" (1995)—that is, training-groups isolated from the social environment, using psychoanalysis without a proper organizational task. Bridger's working conferences have, for about 40 years now, explicitly been designed to address issues of change for managers in all sorts of organizations (see chapter five, this volume).

I. 6. (ii)   *The French psychosociological "school"*

The French psychosociological school first relied largely on OD principles, as noted by Dubost and Levy (in Mendel & Beillerot, 1980). Missions of experts to Bethel in the mid-1950s had enabled the French social psychologists to become familiar with the Lewinian approach, action research, and T-groups. Still under the influence of the cohesive climate engendered by the postwar period of reconstruction, the French social scientists were seduced by the democratic view, Floyd Mann's survey-feedback methods, and Rogers' non-directive approach and growth theory. Nevertheless, an interest in unconscious and collective emotional phenomena was dawning owing to a privileged relationship with the Tavistock Institute (Amado & Guittet, 1991), and many of the French psychosociologists went into analysis in the 1960s. A variety of " revolutionary " influences—the psychoanalytic subversive trend inspired by Lacan and Marxist philosophy, among others—led to a more political approach to social change and intervention (Enriquez, 1972; Faucheux et al., 1982). The principles of the social analysis developed in France have been summarized as follows by Dubost and Levy (1980).

- The engagement of such a process is linked to the suffering of individuals due to social relationships of domination and repression.

- Social analysis is not a process of knowledge transmission. It is above all the confrontation with a situation/problem and knowledge in the making (supported by previous knowledge); but it is also a process of mourning—involving loss of identity, disinvestment of certain objects, and reinvestment of new ones.

- "The initiation of this process originates from group action, often from revolt, which is what engenders a space for thought and research, for un-programmed symbolization, for the transgression of 'orders', of the established authorities, and is thus carried out at the expense of the ideology of the subjects of the analysis—at the expense of their false conscience . . . its significance lies in the movement away from repetition . . ." (p. 102, translated for this edition).

- Despite originating in revolt, this process must produce innovative symbolization, new forms of social action and organization, while at the same time removing action from its central position.

- The change agent must both become involved in the struggles of dominated actors and ensure that the analysis moves beyond the dominant–dominated dialectic and involves all the actors, while preserving their identity.

Thus we can understand that for Dubost (1987), Jaques lacks a consideration of the socio-economic properties of the overall system, of the social determinisms, of the social and ideological contradictions, of the phenomena of domination. The French approach has been called "subversive dialectic" (Amado, 1980).

"Institutional analysis" was born of these "political" considerations. It originated in 1940 in the work of a psychiatrist (Tosquelles, 1966) who was convinced that "it is a question of first taking care of the institution of care" if one wants to help individuals, the relationship between institution and psychotherapeutic behaviour within the institution being dialectically linked. Tosquelles then de-bureaucratizes the psychiatric hospital, stimulates the cooperation of the patients, and establishes micro-institutions (clubs, and such like). We can see some relationship here with the first experiments led by the Tavistock Institute in hospitals (Bridger, 1946; Gray, 1970).

To some extent, the institution is put "in negation", according to the expression of Basaglia (1967), an Italian psychiatrist with a similar orientation, who included in his work the discoveries of anti-psychiatry and took into account Marcuse's theories.

During the 1960s and the 1970s, Lapassade (1967, 1972), Lourau (1970), and their colleagues carried out many institutional analyses and interventions in education and health institutions. Inspired by psychoanalysis (while denouncing the collusion of psychoanalysis with the dominating oppressive power structure) and a radical (somewhat anarchistic) orientation, they put the total institution in analysis in order to unmask the unconscious reality of the organization and the power relationships within it. While a very inspiring approach, it was criticized by Touraine (1981), among others, for attempting to replace social order by "a completely undefined anti-society, a decomposite form of metaphysical aspiration towards transcendence".

The sociopsychoanalytic approach invented by Mendel (1972), and developed further by numerous colleagues (Bitan-Weiszfeld, Mendel, & Roman, 1993; Rueff-Escoubès, 1997), seems much more "realistic". It combines a knowledge of psychoanalysis and social philosophies to produce an innovative methodology. The interventions proceed by dividing the client system into units, based on the technical division of labour, termed homogeneous groups. These groups work separately on daily work problems and then communicate with each other to try to reach solutions acceptable to all parties. Dialogue between groups is exclusively on paper in order to avoid the "pathos", the emotions, and the transference relationships likely to prevent a proper exploration of work requests. Each group is guided (in the initial phases) by a different sociopsychoanalyst who tries to help the group members to get rid of their inhibitions and guilt feelings in the face of figures of authority, and to develop what Mendel calls their "political ego" or, more recently, their "psychosocial personality" (in contrast with their "psycho-family ego", which can only be dealt with in the psychoanalytic cure).

Finally, alongside these "political" types of approach, in the broad sense, there is Kaës' (1979) transitional analysis applied to crisis processes, which is closer to the theme of this book. It is employed in training groups to "seek out the conditions that will make it possible to establish symbols of union in the midst of an experience of breakdown" (p. 61). According to Kaës, transitional thinking concerns "the passage from a state of union with the environment to a state in which the subject relates to it as something external and separate" (p. 61).

More recently, the movement of "work psychodynamics", conducted by Dejours (1993; Dejours, 1996), has grown up. It concerns the psychodynamic analysis of intra- and interpsychic processes mobilized by the work situation and relies on intervention settings close to those proposed by Mendel and his colleagues.

Kaës' transitional analysis is thus a psychoanalytic approach focused on the psychosocial working-through of the experience of breakdown between two states. The process design has three main characteristics:

1. The *frame*
   The frame is the unchanging aspect of the design, "a permanent presence, without which the ego can neither constitute itself nor develop. It is a non-process, that is a series of unvarying elements within whose bounds the process can go on. It is thus that which remains permanent in order for change to take place" (Kaës, 1979, p. 64). It can be seen as the institution that structures the individual's personality. It is silent, never appearing except in cases of crisis. If the frame is not maintained there can be a threat to the individual's safety and identity, and the frame will therefore be attacked by him.

2. The *containing* function
   "The container provides the active support, he is the 'agent' which transforms the imaginary projections of the patient" (p. 69), which

means that he must be capable of tolerating all sorts of projections and making them fruitful.

2. The *potential* or transitional *space*
   According to Kaës, this space must be created by the expression and the practice of a "paternal" law, which is the manifestation of an extra-maternal horizon. Unless it exists, the working-through does not lead to moving beyond the crisis, only to the indefinite repair of the wounds inflicted by separation.

These approaches are still being used in France, particularly through the CIRFIP (Centre International de Recherche, Formation et Intervention Psychosociologiques), to which most of the French psychosociologists of psychoanalytic inspiration and training belong and which has edited the *Revue Internationale de Psychosociologie* since 1994. Barus-Michel, Giust-Desprairie, and Ridel (1996), for example, have explored crisis phenomena from a clinical psychosocial perspective leading to transitional kinds of intervention, while Levy (1997) formalized the role of clinical sciences in understanding organizations. The International Society for the Psychoanalytic Study of Organizations (ISPSO) has also had an important role in promoting these approaches, and its expanding work is strong proof of the renewed importance of the psychoanalytic approach to management and organizational change.

II
RECENT DEVELOPMENTS:
THE 1980s AND 1990s

Other approaches to organizational change emerged particularly from the 1980s onwards, although OD remains as the most prevalent tool and paradigm for organizational change. The other approaches outlined in the previous section also still exist, of course, and continue to evolve as they take on the insights gained from further interventions and a broadening set of practitioners.

Over the last 20 years, OD practitioners have become interested in areas ranging from organizational culture, organizational learning, self-managed teams, total-quality management, visioning and future search, and large system-wide meetings, to the role of OD practition-ers in re-engineering. Some of the techniques of OD have been used in these types of intervention, making it somewhat difficult to distin-guish between them and pure OD change efforts. What is more, OD itself has broadened to embrace new precepts about organizations, as well as developing additional means of addressing oganizational problems. For example, Kilmann (1989) refers to five tracks that are the targets or leverage points of an OD change programme: (1) cul-ture; (2) management skills; (3) team-building; (4) strategy structure; (5) reward system. OD practitioners are said by Sashkin and Burke (1987) to have extended their approach to include process skills and aspects of the organization other than just teams and interpersonal issues. As an indication of the increased attention given to task-pro-cess integration, the sociotechnical systems approach is said to have become more widely used from the early 1980s onwards. Organiza-tional culture has also become a focus of OD, owing to the realization that significant changes can only be brought about if sufficient atten-tion is given to modifying norms and values to support them. Cultural design goes hand in hand with top-level leadership, another more recent focus of OD. The attention to leadership brings OD round full swing back to its participative values, in the concept of empowerment as a means to achieve organizational change. Finally, with more de-centralized organizations and flatter hierarchies, as well as the in-crease in mergers and acquisitions, conflict management is becoming increasingly important in OD interventions. Given all of these evolu-tions, we therefore emphasize again that the approaches presented below are ideal types, or paradigms, although in practice they may involve OD methods or may even be included in OD interventions.

Several "paradigms" from this later period have been selected for more detailed analysis: transition management, organizational trans-formation, organizational culture, organizational learning, chaos theory, and re-engineering. The selection is not intended to be ex-haustive, but to serve the purpose of outlining the main distinctive features of the transitional approach, via a comparison with a number of other approaches that are fairly representative of the organiza-tional change field, and whose value in this exercise lies either in the fact that they have a similar name, such as organizational transition management, and therefore beg to be differentiated, or are founded on precepts that can be readily contrasted with those of the transi-tional approach.

II.1. *Organizational transitions*

A number of researchers coined the term "transition management" (Ackerman, 1982; Beckhard & Harris, 1977; Bridges, 1986; Flamholtz, 1995; Laughlin, 1991; Nadler, 1982) from around the beginning of the 1980s to designate a method for managing complex change—complex, because it involves the whole organization and is associated with rapid and significant internal and external evolutions. Bridges (1986) distinguishes between organizational change and organizational transition:

> Organisational *change* is structural, economic, technological, or demographic, and it can be planned and managed on a more or less rational model. . . . *Transition* on the other hand is a three-part psychological process that extends over a long period of time and cannot be planned or managed by the same rational formulae that work with change. [p. 25]

The concept is based on a sequence of three different states of organizational change: the old state, the state of transition, and the new state. Bridges calls them: the *ending phase*, the *neutral zone phase*, and the *vision* or *new beginning*. Each state requires a particular mode of management.

Transition management is not very different to OD, in that it relies on data collection about the old state to surface the need for change. The new state amounts to an ideal or a vision, developed through the analysis of the old state and of the requirements of the environment. The analysis of the old state is considered necessary to enable the members of the organization to disengage from the former routines and identity and to accept the need for change; in other words, it provides a means by which to manage resistance to change. Inertia is then overcome by communicating a reasoned apology of the new state that is envisioned. What transition management adds to OD is the idea of a state of transition, a sort of neutral zone in which there is confusion and uncertainty but also space for experimentation to create the new state. This transition state requires the setting up of two parallel types of management structure, one for everyday management and the other for transition management—that is, for the development of the new state. The transition team is likely to consist of a transition manager, who has participated in the study stage, and a small team of experts or task forces specializing in different aspects of the transition. Field support or transition coordinators may also be used to provide information to their areas of the company, translate the proposed transition plan for their part of the business, relay information about issues back from the field to the transition team, and manage the resources allocated for their issues and transition tasks. The transition management structure must define and structure new roles, management processes, and tasks. Regular feedback and problem-solving sessions take place between the CEO and transition team.

Nadler (1982) enriches Ackerman's (1982) perspective by looking at transition management in cases where the future state is unstable or uncertain. In such circumstances it becomes even more difficult to manage the transition, as internal political strife intensifies, there is greater anxiety, and the notion of control becomes irrelevant as it is not possible to fix meaningful objectives. The author proposes management techniques to deal with these three areas of difficulty, such as the creation of work groups to develop consensual relations, the setting up of both formal and informal reward systems to acknowledge team (as opposed to individual) performance, the development of a set of principles or a vision of the future which gives some kind of orientation, and the provision of training on how to manage uncertainty, seen as an inevitable part of everyday reality. Furthermore, the management of the transition is broken down into a series of shorter transitions of less magnitude, directed towards a hypothetical future or a series of possible futures. This allows for a more progressive, incremental transition to accommodate a constantly evolving future. Internal communication and feedback from the field are crucial to these short transitions to foster speed of reaction and to correct the orientation before it is too late.

Bridges takes a more psychological perspective on the three phases of transition than does Ackerman. His initial phase, the "ending phase", is characterized by three sets of feeling for those undergoing the transition: disengagement (linked to a perception of loss), dis-identification (in relation to one's former professional identity), and disenchantment. These feelings can be overwhelming and debilitating and need to be consciously managed. Then follows the neutral zone. Although the feelings of the first phase continue to erupt periodically, there is now a new task, that of crossing the neutral zone, an interim period which involves a form of "taking stock" that will eventually lead to creation through the discovery that takes place but which is initially characterized by disorientation and disintegration.

The final phase, which Bridges (1986) calls vision or new beginning, can involve: "developing new competencies, establishing new relationships, becoming comfortable with new policies and procedures, constructing new plans for the future, and learning to think in accordance with new purposes and priorities" (p. 26). Bridges considers this stage of the process the "re-birth", which requires open recognition of the various losses that people have undergone (e.g. loss of turf, of attachments, of meaning, of a career future, of a competence-based identity, of control over events, or even of loss in general) and their replacement by an acceptable alternative through an appropriate means, built around a sufficiently well-defined and well-communicated vision of the future emerging from the neutral zone.

Transition management is likely to achieve more permanent changes than OD, as it manages the uncertainty and the risks inherent in the change process by both allowing for one foot to be kept in the old system while the new system is being built, and acknowledging the difficulties inherent in leaving the old system. Bridges' perspective, particularly, addresses the deeper subjective experience of transition and suggests ways of conceiving of that experience in order better to facilitate it.

II.2. *Organizational transformations*

There are many different interpretations of the notion of transformation in organization theory, so only a selected few will be described. Transformation theory is said to have emerged as a distinctive organizational-change approach during the 1990s. However, it has a number of precursors. Kindler (1979) distinguishes between incremental and transformational change, the former being a step-by-step evolution in the same direction, whereas the latter involves reconceptualization and discontinuity in relation to the initial system. Frame, Nielsen, and Pate (1989) point to the split between OD and transformation theory, by referring to the distinction between the terms *development* and *transformation*. OD interventions are said to be centred on improvements based on learning and on adjusting previous behaviour patterns (i.e. developing the organization), whereas transformation efforts are focused on the desired future state that the transformation is supposed to achieve (i.e. the transformation of the organization).

Similarly, Porras and Silvers (1991) refer to two forms of planned change—organization development (OD) and organizational transformation (OT)—OT being what one could call second-generation OD. Some of the criticisms contained in the above section on OD's early years are answered by second-generation OD. This is really the OD that has taken on the many evolutions of the 1980s and 1990s. Writing at the beginning of the 1990s, the authors consider OT as emerging, ill defined, very experimental, and in a phase of evolution. For Porras and Silvers, the main differences between OD and OT lie in their focus and in their final objective. OD is focused on the work environment (task organization, social factors, technology, physical environment), whereas OT is concerned with the organization's vision (fundamental beliefs and principles, *raison d'être*, mission). OD aims at achieving a better adaptation of the organization to its environment, and OT aims at deeper organizational change, termed paradigmatic. Whereas OD proceeds by developing a vision of the desired future and mobilizing people to achieve it by heightening their dissatisfaction with the present, OT relies on a dual process of *reframing* and *consciousness-raising*.

Levy and Merry's book *Organizational Transformation* (1986) provides an in-depth exploration of the OD perspective on this concept, which they define as follows: "Second-order change is a multi-dimensional, multi-level, qualitative, discontinuous, radical organisational change involving a paradigmatic shift" (p. 5). "Transformations" are distinguished by the proponents of OD from "transitions"—that is, modest, evolutionary, incremental, or fine-tuning change efforts. They are referred to as "frame-bending" (Nadler, 1982) or as fundamental, large-scale changes affecting strategy and culture. In other words, organizational transformations are a more radical break with the former organization than is transition management and stand in total contrast to the incremental approach of OD. According to Kilmann, Covin, and Associates (1988), the main differences between early OD and transformation are as follows:

- Transformation is a response to environmental changes, whereas OD was initially motivated by a will to experiment with new management techniques rather than find a way of surviving in a changing world.
- Transformation is revolutionary rather than evolutionary, as in

OD. In other words, the new state that is envisioned is fundamentally different from the old one.

- Like OD, transformation plays on people's dissatisfaction with the old system but adds to OD the development of a consensual belief in the viability of the new system.

- Transformation involves a qualitative leap in the way people think, perceive, and behave, and not just changes to documents, rules, policies, and so forth.

- Transformation is expected to be system-wide, rather than being limited to one or two entities in the organization.

- OD relies on human-resources-type staff to implement the change process, whereas transformation is driven by line management and preferably involves top management to ensure the necessary resources and commitment.

- Transformation is ongoing and endless, whereas OD ends with the accomplishment of the change programme.

- Transformation involves, ideally, a change management team made up of inside and outside experts as well as line managers. Early OD may not use inside experts, although the consultant–client team idea is prevalent later.

- Transformation is at the forefront of organizational change efforts, which means that it is based on risk-taking and experimentation, as there is little theory available based on the learnings from major transformations. OD has also been reproached for not producing a coherent body of knowledge; however, there is a general OD toolbox.

According to Levy and Merry (1986), organizational transition strategies are oriented towards the achievement of a goal, the change from A to B. Transformation strategies, on the other hand, are oriented towards the process—that is, understanding the different possibilities available and seeking a new vision. They are centred on the emergence of a desired future and not on the achievement of that future. Implementation is supposed to follow naturally from raised consciousness.

Other important authors in this field are Nevis, Lancourt, and Vassallo (1996) who refer to transformation as requiring "a complex series of interlocking, overlapping, and interdependent paradigm shifts", leading to a fundamentally new organizational reality requiring the "resocialization" of organizational members so that they adjust their mental models. It is a constructionist and interactionist perspective, according to which social reality is created in people's consciousness as a result of their interactions. Shared understanding, according to the authors, can be developed through seven methods of behavioural influence: persuasive communication, participation, expectancy (inducing self-fulfilling prophecies), role-modelling, extrinsic rewards, structural rearrangement, and coercion. The combination of these constitutes the strategy for resocialization proposed by the authors as central to achieving transformational change.

Gouillart and Kelly's (1995) book defines transformation as "the orchestrated redesign of the genetic architecture of the corporation, achieved by working simultaneously—although at different speeds—along the four dimensions of Reframing, Restructuring, Revitalisation, and Renewal" (p. 7). These "four Rs" are described as part of a biological metaphor for the organization, which is considered a living organism, needing "holistic medicine" to improve its capacity for survival in a changing environment. A framework is developed around the four Rs by which to work on the various categories of organizational phenomena to improve the organization.

A further conception of transformation is given by Moss Kanter, Stein, and Jick (1992), who see it as the inevitable and necessary change of today's organizations, in the face of environmental changes, to correspond with a new universal model:

> This model describes more flexible organisations, adaptable to change, with relatively few levels of formal hierarchy and loose boundaries among functions and units, sensitive and responsive to the environment; concerned with stakeholders of all sorts—employees, communities, customers, suppliers, and shareholders. These organisations empower people to take action and be entrepreneurial, reward them for contributions and help them gain in skill and "employability". Overall these are global organisations characterised by internal and external relationships, including joint ventures, alliances, consortia, and partnerships. [p. 3]

This model is founded on a number of key postulates:

- Organizations and their component parts function in open systems.

- Consensus is improbable; the choices made by social entities result from negotiations among a multitude of different positions.
- Individual action results in part from the individual's social context.
- The most crucial problem is that of the coordination of specialists.

Change is not seen as having purely negative connotations; it is also associated with opportunities to be seized by the organization, provided that it is sufficiently flexible to do so. Change is seen as a permanent feature of organizational life. The challenge for managers in the 1990s is at once to respond to change, to master change, and to create change where organizations are in a state of fragile equilibrium, given the diversity of activities that have to be coordinated, their blurred boundaries which allow many different influences to bear on the organization, and the variable nature of individuals' relationships to the organization. The authors adopt a prescriptive stance in proposing a model of organizational change that they call the "Big Three Model". It includes three types of movement, to which correspond three types of change and three roles in the change process, as follows:

- Three types of movement
  1. the movement of the whole organization in relation to the movement of its environment (or macro-evolutionary change)
  2. the movement of parts of the organization in relation to each other, depending on the life-cycle of the organization (or micro-evolutionary change)
  3. the power games between individuals or groups in the organization (or political and revolutionary change).
- Three forms of change
  1. change of identity, consisting of a change in the organization's relationship to its environment
  2. change of coordination, related to the internal structuring of the organization's activities
  3. change of control or domination.
- Three roles in the change process
  1. the change strategists (usually top managers)

2. the executors of change (middle managers)
3. the receivers of change (the lower echelons of the organization, those who do not have the power to influence the effects of the change).

Moss Kanter's view of transformation has several aspects in common with prior conceptions of organizational change. For example, the notions of macro- and micro-change are common to other authors, and there are also links with OD in proposing an "ideal" organization, which the change effort should strive to achieve. Although in relation to these authors Kanter et al. are unusual in referring to the political side of organizations, this has been analysed by Crozier. Crozier's strategic analysis would be less deterministic, however, and would emphasize that the lower echelons of the organization are not simply on the receiving end of changes but do have the power to influence them.

II.3. *Organizational culture*

The introduction of the notion of organizational culture into organization theory marks the arrival of a new paradigm: organizations as social constructs and as systems of shared meanings. This conception of organizations implies that they exist only as temporary systems of relationships and transactions between individuals and their environment (Laurent, 1990), made possible by the existence of a common interpretation of experience and a sense of identity. Organizational change thus becomes a question of modifying fundamental values and meanings—that is, it becomes cultural change. Numerous authors, as we have seen above, refer to the importance of leadership for operating such cultural change.

Many definitions of culture originate in the work of anthropologists—for example, Geertz (1973), who sees culture as "the fabrics of meaning out of which human beings interpret their experience and guide their action". Organizational change is thus viewed as a process by which new meanings emerge, giving rise to a reinterpretation of past experience and a reorientation of action, whereby repetitive cycles are interrupted. A key feature of this perspective is that the change concerns shared meanings, and organizational change is thus the institutionalization of new meanings.

There is a whole body of literature focused on the relative efficiency or success of different types of organizational culture (cf. Deal & Kennedy, 1982; Peters & Waterman, 1982), whether they be strong or weak cultures, cultures that perform more or less well in given circumstances, or ideal cultures (customer-oriented, global, innovative, etc.) that must be instilled in order to achieve high performance. Laurent questions this perspective, claiming, for example, that a strong culture can lead to rigidity as much as a weak culture can lead to lack of coordination or direction. What makes for an efficient organization, in his eyes, is its capacity to analyse itself and its environment in order to keep track of its own development. The organization's assumptions concerning its customers, products, activities, employees, mission, and so on translate into behavioural norms. It should be possible for the organization to work on those norms in order to alter people's behaviour in the face of a changing environment.

It is also important to take the intercultural perspective on organizational change into consideration. Various authors (Amado et al., 1991; Hall & Hall, 1990; Hofstede, 1980; d'Iribarne, 1989; Laurent, 1983; Trompenaars, 1993) have shown that national cultures have a significant impact on organizations, and that managers from different cultures hold different assumptions relating to management, authority, structures, organizational relationships, and so forth, which in turn give rise to different practices which reinforce the original assumptions. Strategies that set out to change organizations cannot ignore the specific characteristics of different nationalities and their influence on organizations. The management of multinationals is an interesting example, as it confronts managers with the existence of a multitude of different sets of meanings in one organization. The difficulty is how to engender shared meanings and a common identity while keeping the benefits of diversity.

In addition, certain researchers warn against a universal view of cultural change processes. Wilkins and Dyer (1988), for example, suggest that different cultures (whether national or organizational) change in different ways and that intervention strategies must be developed with the particular characteristics of the culture in mind. They consider the history and past culture of organizations as particularly important in determining their mode and capacity for change. For example, they consider that some organizational cultures are such that cultural transformation would be impossible. This idea is based on the conception of culture as consisting of specific (context-linked) and general (more generic and tacit) frames of reference. Cultural change is said to affect only general frames of reference; changes to specific frames of reference are just minor incremental changes. An organization whose general frames of reference are rigid and strongly invested by its members is less likely to be capable of cultural change.

Both Laurent's (1990) and Meyerson and Martin's (1987) idea of cultures is that they are social constructions and that organizations *are* a form of culture. They are a structured set of values, meanings, and behaviours, and organizational change therefore concerns particularly these aspects. The latter authors also underline the interdependent nature of change strategies and organizational culture: "Leadership at once shapes and is shaped by the organisation of belief and meaning" (p. 624). They propose three "paradigms" of cultural change (very close to the three perspectives on leadership referred to above—integration, differentiation, fragmentation—proposed by Martin) which have different implications for the management of change processes:

1. *Cognitive or attitudinal change* affecting the whole organization, as it involves changing shared meanings. This paradigm is based on a conception of organizational culture as a homogeneous entity, and it focuses on consistent and consensual cultural manifestations. The organization's leaders are the key figures of the culture; they are both the source of cultural content and the masters of revolutionary change.

2. *Change founded on a conception of culture as including differentiation and diversity.* This perspective takes account of the existence of subcultures, of the multiple identifications of individuals (hierarchy, class, ethnic group, gender, etc.), and of the contradictions within a single culture, notably between declared values and real practices. The cultural content is thus not generated by leaders, but comes from multiple sources. It is an open-system perspective, whereby changes are not always intentional but are stimulated by various catalysts. Instead of being revolutionary they are progressive, and they are usually local, although, given the links with the

rest of the system, they may have repercussions elsewhere. (See also Baba, 1995, for an application of the concepts of population ecology to organizational change.)

3. *Change that accepts ambiguity as a permanent feature* of organizational life. In the other paradigms, ambiguity is characteristic of a state of transition only and is seen as an undesirable element to be channelled. In this paradigm, on the contrary, complexity and absence of clarity are legitimate and paradox is embraced. The boundaries between sub-cultures and between the organization and its environment are blurred, as consensus, disagreement, and confusion coexist. Change, in this perspective, is continuous and often unconscious. It takes place through relatively uncontrollable individual adjustments, thus allowing for experimentation and creativity.

Feldman (1986) sees culture as a set of symbols. In examining the link between the symbolic fabric and behaviour in organizations, he comes to criticize the classical conception of the role of symbols in organizations. This conception has led to a dichotomy in the literature between substantive action and symbolic action, whereby the former is associated with decisions based on objective criteria, whereas the latter is associated with the development of the shared meanings necessary to engagement in a common mission. The author questions this distinction, arguing that no action can be dissociated from symbolic representations that serve to analyse and categorize experience. Furthermore, he suggests that symbolic representations are meaningful only in association with other symbols from social activity. Finally, according to Feldman, symbols are not causes of action but a form of predisposition in relation to action. Culture is then the system of symbols used by individuals to make sense of their actions and of those of others. It is what he calls culture as context.

This discussion opposes two conceptions of culture change which we have already encountered in talking of leadership. The first, more classical conception is founded on a view of management as symbolic action—that is, as the manipulation of symbols with the aim of changing mentalities and reorienting behaviour. The other, which Feldman favours, sees cultural change as a process that is itself oriented by the cultural context. According to this conception, in order to be effective a cultural change effort requires a prior analysis of the system of symbolic constructs produced and used by the members of the organization, as it is this system that will define the capacity and possible directions for changing the organization. Finally, it is not through changing the culture that the organization will change, but through changing behaviour.

With regard to intervention strategies linked with the culture paradigm, other than cultural change through leadership there is the set of approaches focused on language (cf. Werr, 1995, for a review), according to which it is necessary to develop common beliefs and cognitions among those concerned by the change in order for a common vision and plans for future work to emerge. Dialogue methods, search seminars, and image tools are used to create a shared present organizational model or local theory and a common vision of the future.

Critics of the more manipulative orientation on culture change (cf. Gilmore, Shea, & Useem, 1997) refer to its side-effects as being, for example, uncertainty over patterns of authority; "polarized images" between visions of the old and the new cultures; mutual blaming between levels of management; false enactments of the new culture leading to disappointment; and an almost ideological promotion of the new culture to the detriment of open discussion of real business constraints, leading to "behavioural inversion".

II.4. Organizational learning

There are many different interpretations of the notion of organizational learning, which is perhaps why no universal model of the phenomenon has been developed. However, one can say very broadly that the organizational-learning paradigm sees organizations as open systems evolving with reference to an environment that both incites change and provides information as to the consequences of actions undertaken. Organizational learning is thus sometimes distinguished from organizational change (Fiol & Lyles, 1985), as learning involves the development of deeper and more extensive perceptions and knowledge linked to an appreciation of causality, whereas organizational change can be considered synonymous with adaptation (stimulus–response) and can take place without learning. Likewise, for Moingeon and Edmondson (1995) organizational change is "learning how" (the improvement and transfer of existing knowledge and routines), whereas organizational learning is "learning why" (the improvement of causal understanding and diagnosis). These two levels of change can also be compared with Argyris and Schön's (1978) single-loop and double-loop learning; singe-loop learning involves error correction without questioning the underlying values that guided the action, whereas double-loop learning involves the examination and correction of guiding values before correcting action accordingly.

Shrivastava (1983) divides the research on organizational learning into four categories:

1. organizational learning as adaptation (Cangelosi & Dill, 1965; Cyert & March, 1963; March & Olsen, 1976);

2. organizational learning as the development of common cognitive maps/theories in use (Argyris & Schön, 1978; Mason & Mitroff, 1981; Mitroff & Emshoff, 1979);

3. organizational learning as acquiring knowledge of causality (Duncan & Weiss, 1978; Dutton & Duncan, 1981);

4. organizational learning as institutionalized experience (Abernathy & Wayne, 1974; Boston Consulting Group, 1968; Yelle, 1979).

Huber (1991) has a more cognitive view of organizational learning which he sees as linked to different modes of information processing: (1) the acquisition of knowledge; (2) the distribution of information; (3) the interpretation of information; (4) organizational memory.

According to Shrivastava, organizational learning is usually considered an organizational and not an individual process, as it is said to be affected by a number of variables of a social, political, or structural nature. Alternatively, as Van der Heijden (1996) puts it, "The learning loop can only work in an institutional sense if people participate together, share ideas about new patterns resulting from reflection on experience, build a common theory, plan and act together. If they do all that they have a common experience without which organisational learning is impossible" (p. 45). Nevertheless, although the process is clearly organization-wide, there is a debate as to whether it is the organization or the individuals that make it up that learn. The key, according to Van der Heijden, is in institutional action, made up of "a coherent set of individual actions which are supported as a set by a self-sustaining critical mass of opinion in the organisation" (p. 45). Otherwise, there are only individual actions, associated with individual and not organizational learning. As with the culture paradigm, shared meaning is crucial.

A link is made in much of the research in this area between experience and learning, as experience is said to contribute to an organization's capacity to select the relevant information and to seek solutions to the organization's problems. Organizational learning is said to lead to a common appreciation of causality (the link between actions and results), which is used in decision-making. It is usually conceived of as a process in which the prevailing world-view (or the "theories in use", referred to by Argyris) is challenged, and in which structural and procedural changes are introduced in order to incorporate a new world-view or new knowledge. Systems of learning can also be institutionalized; they include formal and informal systems of knowledge-sharing, planning, and control. These systems are oriented towards the acquisition, communication, and interpretation of knowledge relevant for decision-making, and they can be linked to the local practices in the organization, seen as a source of learning (see Brown & Duguid, 1991).

There are several methodological orientations to change management within the organizational learning paradigm. Interventions usually attempt to make the organization more aware of changes in its environment and more capable of appropriate responses by developing a capacity for constant watchfulness and for self-examination. Scenario planning is a typical example of an organizational learning tool (cf. Van der Heijden, 1996). As with cultural change, developing a common language, symbolic of shared mental maps, is an important aspect of interventions to improve organizational-learning capacity (Senge, 1990; Van der Heijden, 1996). Van der Heijden refers to this as a *conversational process*, involving people in comparing, challenging, and negotiating "strategic cognitions" leading to a joint understanding. Argyris's perspective on organizational learning, on the other hand, arises from an action science (or action research) background. He states that action scientists consider learning the most importrant objective for researchers, clients, and the social system (1983, 1993). His approach to generating learning in the organization involves overcoming defensive routines designed by individuals, groups, or entire organizations to preserve the status quo in the face of threatening circumstances, but whose effect is to create "self-fulfilling prophecies, self-sealing processes, and escalating error". His approach consists of identifying inconsistencies between "theories in use" and "espoused theories", the sort of inconsistencies that are usually covered up to avoid embarrassment, thereby engendering defensive routines when the pattern of cover-ups gets out of control. His method relies extensively on feedback of observations and interviews made by the consultant, followed by discussion with the interested parties and coaching to improve transparency and thus facilitate double-loop learning.

As with the paradigm of cultural change, the organizational learning paradigm has a tendency towards universalism. Few authors propose looking at each organization as a unique case; instead, typologies such as Argyris' Model I and Model II of organizational learning are deemed to apply to all organizations. In general terms, one could say that this paradigm takes the organization as something of a black box. It is often viewed as a homogeneous entity, rather than a set of diverse individuals or sub-groups. Organizational politics and problems of resistance to change (and certainly the creative potential of these) do not usually enter into the organizational learning literature, which has a generally "positive" conception of organizational relationships, from which it derives its prescriptive or descriptive content. An exception is Argyris' concept of defensive routines based on prevailing value systems. Otherwise, organizational change according to this paradigm seems to follow naturally from the right conditions and preparation. Senge (1990), for example, talks of "motivating people beyond self-interest" and of developing a norm of "openness". This type of postulate does not seem to be challenged by knowledge-based or competence-based management—the organizational learning of the late 1990s.

II.5. Chaos theory

Chaos theory, or the science of complexity as it is sometimes known, introduces yet another paradigm into organizational change theory. It developed initially in the fields of mathematics, computer science, physics, biology, and chemistry (Gleick, 1988; Nicolis & Prigogine,

1989; Prigogine & Stengers, 1984; Waldorp, 1992) and was focused on the evolution of natural systems. It has been increasingly applied to social systems (Anderson, Arrow, & Pines, 1988; Goldstein, 1994; Nonaka, 1988; Peters, 1991; Stacey, 1991, 1992, 1993, 1995, 1996; Wheatley, 1992; Zimmerman, 1992), and represents an alternative way of making sense of life in organizations.

Stacey (1995) contrasts the science of complexity with two established perspectives on organizational renewal. The first is the strategic-choice perspective, which views organizational change as intentional, rational adaptation to environmental changes (usually by restructuring). The second is the ecology perspective, which considers that organizations adapt to environmental change through the adaptation of specific populations within them, based on the principle of competitive selection. What is common to both perspectives is their underlying assumption that all successful organizations tend towards equilibrium—that is, stability, regularity, and predictability. In other words, according to this dominant frame of reference, success is related to "being in control".

Chaos theory views organizations as non-linear feedback systems. Human systems such as organizations are considered a legitimate object for the science of complexity in that, like other systems, they consist of:

> large numbers of agents who interact with each other to produce adaptive survival strategies for themselves and hence for the system, or parts thereof, that they belong to. Their system in turn interacts with others, making up a larger suprasystem in which they are agents that coevolve together. The total system, therefore, has a holographic or fractal aspect in which the parts interact continually to recreate the whole and the whole affects how the parts interact. [Stacey, 1996, pp. 19–21]

The properties of such systems are: (1) bounded instability; (2) spontaneous self-organization and emerging order; to which is related a third property, learning. The first property implies that the play of the forces of stability and instability maintain the organization in a state on the edge of several undetermined possible stable or unstable states. This is known as a state of chaos. The system's long-term future behaviour is unforeseeable and small changes can have huge impacts (cf. the analogy of the butterfly effect), which means that clear-cut links between cause and effect, or actions and results, cannot be traced. Therefore, the results of actions can no longer be the object of intentions. This, of course, challenges one of the basic assumptions of OD and other paradigms founded on intention and determinism.

This is not to say that such systems cannot evolve order out of chaos; what is important here is that chaos, or what Stacey (1996) also calls "mess", is crucial to the process. Mess is what gives the system its creative capacity, or as Stacey puts it, "these are the very conditions required for creativity, an exciting journey into open-ended evolutionary space with no fixed, pre-determined destination" (p. 13). Creativity is described as being inherent to systems operating on the edge of disintegration (another way of putting the notion of bounded instability), a state likened by Stacey to Melanie Klein's "depressive position" and to Winnicott's transitional space (Stacey, 1996, p. 14). Non-linear systems become spontaneously changeable in this state; their behaviour "displays endless unpredictable variety", as no patterns of behaviour are ever exact repeats of previous ones. In the case of organizations, Stacey mentions "true dialogue" as being a source of cross-fertilization leading to creativity, a messy process in which conflict is played out, competition between ideas takes place, and "negative" feelings surface alongside positive ones. In other words, order is not predetermined but emerges from the messy interplay of different forces between which there are tensions. These exist, for example, at the system level between the "legitimate network" and the "shadow network", as well as at the individual agent level "between inspiration and anxiety and its containment, conformity and individualism, leadership and followership, and participant and observer roles" (p. 44). [Stacey defined "legitimate network" as "a legitimate subsystem in which behaviour engages current reality and is driven by a dominant schema that all the agents in the system share, thus leading to conformity" (p. 47), and "shadow network" as "a shadow subsystem in which behaviour is driven, not by current reality, but by recessive schemas, most of which are unique to individual agents, thus leading to diversity" (p. 47).] Small actions generated by agents within the system, through choices emerging from this messy process but made within the constraints of their "decision rules and behavioural scripts" (the forces of stability and equilibrium), can give rise to major outcomes owing to the effects of the self-organizing interactions between other agents and parts of the system and suprasystem.

Non-linear feedback systems are also learning systems. The feedback can be negative or positive. It is negative when the actual outcomes of actions are compared with their intended outcomes, and the information about the deviation is fed back to improve the "discovery–choice–action" loop by removing the deviation—that is, by changing the behavioural pattern. This form of feedback secures stability and is usually the preserve of the legitimate system of an organization. It is akin to Argyris and Schön's (1978) single-loop learning. Positive feedback, on the other hand, is when information is fed back to the "discovery–choice–action" loop that destabilizes it, thus producing change. In this case, both the schemas guiding behaviour and the behaviour itself are changed, as in double-loop learning. The organization's shadow system is often driven by positive feedback. Organizations are said to oscillate between both forms of learning.

II.7. Trends towards the end of the 1990s

The end of the 1990s has seen the emergence of a number of change-management approaches or techniques to which we are reluctant to accord the status of "paradigm" in the sense we have used above. These include re-engineering, the management of new information technologies and their organizational consequences, and competence-based management. Re-engineering, popularized by Hammer and Champy (1993), is an approach focused on the restructuring of basic processes and down-sizing, aimed at improving organizational efficiency. Although relatively new in the managerial literature, this approach has a long past in industrial engineering, where the objective is to improve the relationship between inputs and outputs in manufacturing. Re-engineering takes similar principles and applies them to management systems. It is a rather instrumental technique that is focused on the objective processes involved in carrying out tangible tasks, and it is based on very specific tools and measures.

The preoccupation with new computer-based technologies and their effects on organizations has arisen at about the same time as companies have been engaging in re-engineering processes. Kolodny, Liu, Stymne, and Denis (1996) describe how new technology is considered by some authors (Gerwin & Kolodny, 1992; Weick, 1990) as a facilitator and catalyst for organizational change. It is often seen as a complement to re-engineering, to bring about far-reaching modifications in the way people work, notably in attempting to bring about increased integration with a view to improving efficiency and reducing costs. However, the added uncertainty related to such technologies has meant that roles have had to be redefined and coordination mechanisms adjusted, with varying success, especially after re-engineering has taken out some of the ranks of middle management. One conclusion of Kolodny et al.'s research (1996), however, is that "with the power of 'knowledge-based systems' and the freedom of 'open processes', work organisations will increasingly confront and attempt *to manage the complexity of their situations rather than reduce the complexity*" (p. 1475). There has been limited reflection on how to bring about the evolution in work processes needed to take account of these new possibilities; however, Kolodny et al. identify an emerging paradigm characterized by "a balance between the expanded rationality of technical processes emanating from flexible technology and social systems that recognize open communications and trust-building as foundation stones for creating new relationships" (p. 1479). The Swedish and Japanese models of organization design have been examined for their contribution to this paradigm, as well as evidence from West Germany and North America (cf. Hecksher, 1994).

It is tempting to see these approaches as just another series of techniques for large-scale organizational transformation, rendered inevitable by environmental changes. Perhaps time will tell whether they have been effective, and at what costs.

CHAPTER THREE

Some distinctive characteristics of transitional change

Gilles Amado & Rachel Amato

Change is inherent in our experience of everyday reality and, like the air we breathe, is unnoticed or taken for granted unless circumstances give us cause to take note. This is possible because, under normal conditions, reality for most of us has a certain continuing stability about it: there are frequent periods when things, for a time, seem to be in dynamic equilibrium. In fact, however, there is nothing about reality that is permanently stable in the sense of being static or fixed. We experience it as an ongoing process of interrelated events in which we are involved. We are also continually buffeted by the consequences and implications of actions and events that take place around us without our knowing about them. Change is, therefore, an essential and ongoing feature of reality.

Such a conception of reality leads one to think of change not as a simple mechanical process of a situation moving from one state to another, from A to B, but rather that situation A could have progressed to several alternatives, that the process of changing will have had some effect on the immediate context and, perhaps, on a much wider context, and that B, far from being a stable state, is itself a transitional state. Reality is transitional insofar as "now" is only a temporary resting-place between the past and the future.

All of the approaches to change briefly presented in chapter two have helped in one way or another to think through what we call the transitional approach to change. Some are very close to it, some are included in it (depending on what their aims, methods, and underlying assumptions are), and some are very different. Let us now present what the transitional approach is all about in order to complete the picture.

I
KEY FEATURES

In the light of chapter one of this book, many of the most significant differences between the transitional approach and other approaches already begin to emerge. Just as a reminder, the following are particularly important features of our approach.

- The individual and/or groups involved in the process will undergo both learning and development, mostly leading to better understanding of the complex intricacies between individual, collective, technical, and contextual issues.

- Unconscious processes within individuals and organizations must be taken into account, respected, and worked through—and certainly not used in a manipulative way, otherwise change management is likely to have only short-term effects and to be a manipulative process.

- Although the general direction of the desired outcome can be described at the outset, there is sufficient freedom within the process for all to know that the nature of the final outcome is not predetermined but will be shaped by the interplay of all issues in the process.

- The process provides a context of safety (what might be called "relative safety") that enables people to express any kind of idea or feeling: this is a "containing space" that can accommodate all sorts of feelings, fears, and anxieties.

- The emergent situation will be better adapted to the realities of the whole system and context in which the activity is occurring—that is, the outcome will "resonate" better with the "external reality" than did the preceding situation.

- The emergent situation, shaped by the knowledge and contributions of individuals directly related with the issues, will give more autonomy and responsibility to individuals closer to the system boundaries.

- The emergent situation will contain more variety than previously, and the system should therefore have a greater capacity or resource to respond to future change in its context, as horizons have been broadened leading to better understanding.

Transitional potential will be enhanced by developing a climate in which many views are tolerated and in which it is safe for members to explore beyond the boundaries of current cultural constraints. This potential will be further enhanced by creating time and space within which the process can take place, the objective being to use the time and the space to remove existing cultural constraints in order to permit a more creative exploration of future possibilities to emerge. As described in more detail below, the transitional change agent has a significant role in establishing such a climate.

A way to understand more clearly the main features of the transitional approach is to compare it to other approaches to change management. One of the key dimensions on which transitional thinking can be differentiated from other approaches is the extent to which it embraces *antagonistic or conflicting forces*. The transitional approach acknowledges the existence of such forces within both the individual psyche and organizations and societies, and it works with them in an analytic way rather than against them in a normative way. Another dimension lies in the fact that transitional thinking sees *paradox as part of everyday life*, and, instead of seeking to solve paradoxical situations, it seeks to *balance and optimize* them.

This stands in contrast to most of the other approaches outlined, particularly OD, which are essentially positive and rational, seeing individuals as motivated by a will for self-improvement and high performance, given the right conditions. Likewise, the approaches included in the cultural change paradigm often posit an ideal form of culture enabling organizations to perform better, and the organizational learning paradigm suggests that organizations should, for example, increase openness and clarity of vision to enhance their learning capacity. An exception to this positive perspective is Crozier's sociological diagnosis, in which social actors are not seen as necessarily having any positive or altruistic motivation. Their actions are based on rational strategies and stem from a drive for survival in a social system that provides resources and imposes constraints, rather than from a desire to generate a better functioning organization (unless, of course, it serves their own interests as an actor). Chaos theory is another case in point, in which organizations are likened to living organisms that tend towards equilibrium through spontaneous self-organization emerging from the simultaneous pull between contradictory forces: on the one hand, the need for integration, control, and adaptation to the environment; on the other, the existence of division and decentralization, political games, and defence mechanisms. The idea of a state of instability with a threshold (or a chaotic state), supposedly to allow for change, also has similarities with the notion of potential space in transitional thinking. However, there are major differences between the two approaches: chaos theory postulates self-organization and a return to a state of equilibrium, whereas the transitional approach includes the action of facilitators in the change process (see the final section in this chapter) and proposes how to manage intervention. What is more, chaos theory refers only implicitly to human nature (as part of the contradictory forces at work in organizations), whereas transitional thinking is founded directly on premises to do with human nature.

A further key dimension on which to compare the transitional approach with the others is the relative weight given to a psychological—as opposed to a sociological—interpretation of social situations. Transitional thinking would explore the resonance (cf. Amado, 1993) between psychological and sociological phenomena among others (economic, political, technological, etc.), whereas other approaches tend to adopt one angle to the detriment of the other. A case in point is Crozier's sociological diagnosis, in which the orientation towards explaining social behaviour in terms of rational strategies means that whole areas of behaviour are ignored (how to account for the behaviour resulting from dependence on a leader, for example), and one result of such an orientation is that organizations can be seen as conditioning people to become paranoid. Furthermore, some forms of OD and organizational transformations can be reproached for not focusing enough on the psychological and sociological phenomena behind what is termed *resistance to change* and is usually dismissed as being human nature's destructive or subversive side. Unless enough space is given to exploring such phenomena during the intervention, there is little chance that changes will be both relevant and stable.

The transitional approach can be seen as offering some answers to the criticisms of OD outlined in chapter two. However, it is important to acknowledge the stems common to OD and transitional thinking— that is, T-group training and the approaches of the Tavistock Clinic and the French psychological school, which have given rise to a number of similar values and techniques. We have already mentioned that Lewin was a major source of inspiration to both OD and transitional thinking. To complete the comparison, let us look at the way the settings in T-group training and the transitional approach are designed.

The T-group or laboratory training process includes certain elements that are considered necessary to facilitate learning:

1. Emphasis is placed on the here-and-now.

2. Feedback or review is essential, as it enables participants to evaluate their performance in relation to the achievement of a given objective and to generate representations of the individual and social realities experienced.

3. Learning depends on allowing for the process of *unfreezing* to take place, in which certainties, expectations, routines, and some of the familiar aspects of life are challenged.

4. In order for people to develop the desire to learn and not simply increase their anxiety, it is necessary for unfreezing to be accompanied by a protective environment characterized by the absence of sanctions and the tolerance of failure, where risk-taking and experimentation are encouraged:

    —participants are both actors and observers during the process, a difficult task that involves having a certain detachment while at the same time being engaged in action

    —theoretical sessions during the process aim at building cognitive maps or a framework for the understanding of group functioning, involving the creation of common language for describing group phenomena and the building of a bridge between the laboratory situation and the social system from which participants originate.

Whatever the criticisms that have been levelled at T-group train-ing as a means for change (essentially, that it is a process that takes place outside social reality and its forces), it still remains a reference in terms of setting design: it constitutes an open space where learning takes place by way of exchanges of perceptions and experiences be-tween participants, guided by an analyst who in many respects refuses any form of pre-established normative thinking. It is truly a setting inspired by the principles of action research posited by Lewin. Nevertheless, despite these common roots, it is worth noting that the transitional approach attaches importance to a real group task, and, while participants attempt to understand the "here-and-now", they do not neglect the "there-and-then". It is in this sense that the transi-tional approach is probably more realistic and its effects less disturb-ing than the T-group.

Despite the above links, some major differences between OD and the transitional approach stand out:

- OD is more of a linear, planned approach, in which the end-state is known in advance and described in a vision, and the steps for reaching that end-state are described in a comprehensive change programme, whereas transitional thinking is more experiential and heuristic.

- OD has a positive and rational view of individuals and group dynamics, where transitional thinking takes into account their full complexity—that is, the existence of a "dark" side of the psyche and of the inter-subjective interplay.

- OD is usually managed from the top of the organization. This means that it may result in coercion, as members of the organiza-tion will comply with the OD programme through fear or super-ficial conformity.

- Transitional thinking is somewhat akin to OD in its belief in participation and democracy, except that participation is not taken as an ideal that can sometimes become devoid of anchorage in the task at hand. Naive participation can lead to "group think" (Janis, 1982) and oppressive forms of belonging.

Both chaos theory and transitional thinking challenge the prem-ises of planned change. The transitional approach is more capable than OD of taking on the complexity, the instability, and the uncertainty of an organizational system and its environment. However, the transitional approach is not necessarily in direct confrontation with planned change in that a programme of planned change could result from a transitional intervention. The same is true of action research. These can be seen as tools that can be included in a broader intervention strategy in which model-building and directive approaches are not necessarily excluded. Transitional thinking attempts to take account of the complexity of situations and to engender some meaning from them through group reflection that can lead to action. It shares with action research both collaborative values and an orientation towards action. However, the focus on generating theory is a feature of action research that distinguishes it from most other approaches, including the transitional approach.

Another dimension on which to compare some of the above approaches is their attitude to intervention. Although the transitional approach and the strategic analysis of organizations both consider organizational change as resulting potentially from the proper exploration of social situations, and not as being the preserve of experts employed to impose changes based on a summary external analysis, there is an important difference of perspective to do with intervention. Transitional interventions set up a protected space in which people from the social system in question confront each other directly and engage in a dialogue from which proposed actions emerge. Strategic analysis, on the other hand, relies on the revelation by organizational analysts of a particular social dynamic, the understanding of which is intended to generate the relevant changes. As discussed above, this may have unforeseen and undesirable consequences, particularly when the translation of the analysis into action is left to a select group of top managers. A transitional intervention, although having to take on the difficulties inherent in managing complex group dynamics, does allow for the face-to-face negotiation of an interpretation and its translation into action among the interested parties. As far as the scale of intervention is concerned, unlike OD and transformation, transitional thinking does not specify *a priori* whether it is taking on the whole organizational system or an entity thereof. It has the potential to address all aspects of an organization's functioning, but it does not have a preconceived idea of which predominates or which constitutes a priority. The focus will depend on how the process takes place—that is, on the climate that is generated and on the setting design that emerges. A key aspect of the transitional intervention, as we shall see below, is the attitude of the transitional change agent, who keeps an ethical distance while at the same time maintaining an attitude of empathy, which does not deny the preparedness for being "shot at" (as Bion put it)—that is, for all sorts of negative feelings and countertransference. This position of the transitional approach on the boundaries of the organization may be more effective than other approaches that attack the problem of organizational change head on from the inside, engendering suspicion, frustration, and in many cases burn-out. At least the transitional setting provides a space in which people can express their lack of trust, and it is founded on respect both for what people want to say and what they do not. A well-designed transitional intervention—one that acknowledges anxiety as well as reinforcing the pleasure of effective action—can lead to sounder implementation of changes through increased realism and improved understanding.

Unlike several of the approaches described (leadership, transformation, cultural change), the transitional approach does not take the impetus for change as coming from one particular individual. It thus avoids the potentially perverse side of charismatic leadership—notably the tendency to engender strong dependency (or even sect-like follower behaviour)—as well as its transient nature, whereby inspirational leadership inevitably gives way to more authoritarian, rules-based "management" once the need for institutionalization arises. Transitional change, on the contrary, is founded on democratic or cooperative principles, without idealizing participation as OD tends to do. It sets out to render individuals and groups capable of acting autonomously and in a lucid way, not through the fascination that a seemingly heroic individual inspires in them. Transitional change thus acquires a more permanent quality, one that is closer to the everyday realities experienced by people working in organizations and is less alienating.

Organizational transformation is different to the transitional approach in two main respects: (1) it contains a dimension of obligation; (2) it values change as an ideal in itself. Change is seen as a necessity in the face of a threatening turbulent environment, and people are forced to embrace change as the only means to survive. There is little or no space for dialogue or for mourning the loss of what is past. People are subjected to what amounts to a symbolic aggression, at the same time as being debilitated because they are given limited say or control regarding what happens to them.

As we have seen above, organizational change through culture can take two forms: (1) cultural design or manipulation, often associated with charismatic leadership; (2) cultural understanding with a view to better adjusting the organization's functioning to its multiple cultural realities (whether they be potentially destructive or potentially creative). The transitional approach does not impose a preconceived idea of the new culture that is to emerge from an intervention. Rather than being cultural standardization (instilling the cultural traits necessary for success), it allows for cultural creation through dialogue and negotiation between diverse cultural realities.

The organizational learning paradigm covers a wide variety of concepts and practices, which makes it difficult to generalize when contrasting it with the transitional approach. However, approaches based on this paradigm are often distinct from the transitional approach in that they are driven top-down, and they do not go about exploring individual and collective subjective experience in quite the same way. Argyris and Schön's (1978) approach to change starts with the individual and proceeds by revealing inconsistencies between espoused theories and theories in use, as it is these inconsistencies that lead to defensive routines on an individual and then a collective level. These are said to act as a barrier to self-corrective learning. Intervention is then based on exposing the defensive routines and the inconsistencies behind them at a preconscious level, without considering the "positive" purpose they may serve for the individuals and groups that engage in them. For example, the collective exposure of defensive routines with a view to diminishing them and thus reducing the barriers to organizational learning does not necessarily allow for dealing with the anxieties that led to their development in the first place. Again, it is a normative and somewhat naive perspective that does not take into consideration the irrational, fragile, and destructive sides of human nature (cf. Diamond, 1986, for a psychoanalytic critique of Argyris and Schön's theories). It contains an implicit model of behaviour, founded on the dichotomy between good and bad. Learning in the transitional approach contrasts somewhat with this perspective, as it is based on the notion of review; it is a particular form of learning founded on experimentation (testing out), and upon understanding the interplay of conscious and unconscious forces, both "positive" and "negative".

Psychosociology includes approaches that perhaps come the closest to transitional thinking, particularly as far as their common psy-

choanalytic roots are concerned. In France, however, such
were mainly centred on analysing the dynamics of power in
tions, to the detriment of a full exploration of the creative pot
the dynamic of action, present in social situations (Amado, 19
more recently there seems to be greater openness to this "pos
side of human action. Mendel, who was the first to publish Winn
in France in the 1960s, has produced two recent books (1998, 19
that are a good illustration of this trend.

Transition management also appears to have several elements in
common with transitional thinking, notably the "neutral space" beyond everyday organizational life, in which discovery or exploration
leading to creation of the future can take place. Transition management, in its more psychological form (cf. Bridges), also takes into
consideration psychic phenomena related to change, such as the need
to mourn losses. However, transitional thinking has a much less linear view of change. It is not something to be programmed as such,
and it is not incremental; it is more tumultuous, consisting of continual advances and regressions and of unforeseen happenings,
which it has the capacity to tolerate. It is not seeking to achieve some
pre-defined state of perfection. Furthermore, the transitional approach insists on the protection afforded to those who participate,
and this is inherent in the transitional space. This aspect is not explicitly stated in transition management, although in practice it may of
course be present.

Several attempts have been made in the past to classify approaches
to organizational change (cf. Goodman & Kurke, 1982; Werr, 1995). As
remarked by Werr, the most significant dimension on which to compare them is planned or managed change as opposed to more spontaneous adaptation driven by changes in the environment. Approaches
can then also be differentiated, according to Werr, on whether they
focus on establishing the object of change—that is, the diagnosis (the
what)—or whether they are more concerned with how to go about
implementing change (the *how*). However, the above selection of
"paradigms" of organizational change can in fact be seen as including
both the *what* and the *how*, as they each represent a particular set of
views or basic assumptions on changing an organization, a particular
way of looking at the "elephant" (Smircich, 1983). Subsequent sec-
tions in this chapter describe the transitional approach to organizational change in more detail by focusing on some of the parameters
that distinguish it.

TABLE 3.1.   First- and Second-Order Change

First-order change	Second-order change
Change in one or a few dimensions, components, or aspects	Multidimensional, multi-component change and aspects
Change in one or a few levels (individual and group level)	Multi-level change (individuals, groups, and the whole organisation)
Change in one or two behavioural aspects (attitudes, values)	Changes in all the behavioural aspects (attitudes, norms, values, perceptions, beliefs, world view, and behaviours)
Quantitative change	Qualitative change
Change in content	Change in context
Continuity, improvements, and development in the same direction	Discontinuity, taking a new direction
Incremental changes	Revolutionary jumps
Reversible changes	Irreversible change
Logical and rational change	Seemingly irrational change based on different logic
Change that does not alter the world view, the paradigm	Change that results in a new world view, new paradigm
Change within the old state of being (thinking and acting)	Change that results in a new state of being

From A. Levy & U. Merry, *Organizational Transformation.* Copyright © 1986 by Praeger Publishers. Reproduced with permission of Greenwood Publishing Group, Inc., Westport, CT.

It is useful at this stage to refer to the work of Levy (1986), who distinguishes between first- and second-order change by summarizing the definitions given by researchers from several fields of organization theory in one conceptual model (see Table 3.1). This axis for conceiving of organizational change is useful for distinguishing between the "paradigms" we are describing. OD at its earlier stages can be considered as falling into the first-order change category, whereas the approaches of the 1980s and 1990s are, rather, from the field of second-order change. Other important axes for distinguishing the transitional approach are its underlying conception of individuals and organizations, its view of uncertainty, and its criteria for judging success.

II
DESIGNED VERSUS SPONTANEOUS TRANSITIONAL CHANGE

Day-to-day life shows that we must distinguish between designed change and spontaneous change. Most types of change take either form, except for chaos which is necessarily spontaneous.

II.1. Designed transitional processes

Designed transitional processes are those where people consciously design a process of change in a transitional way. Examples of such processes from a political context and an organizational context are given in this chapter. First, however, let us look at how a process of this kind commences.

The onset of designed transitional processes results, in general, in the existence of one or more of three classes of condition:

• The awareness of a discrepancy between aspiration and the actual state. Such manifestations can be the result of a perception of the inadequacy of a system in its environment or of a purely internal problematic issue, such as difficulties in relations between subsystems.

• An internal necessity that drives forward a development, which is then worked through and consciously implemented.

• A willingness to understand more deeply the roots of an imbalance, and a desire to ameliorate it in an open, deliberate manner, whatever the cost.

Basically, transitional processes seem to be born from the tensions internal to a system coupled with a genuine desire to find the meanings and causes of these tensions as well as ways to rectify them.

A political designed transitional process

A good example of a designed transitional process is the attempt to solve by negotiation the conflict in New Caledonia, an island in the

Pacific Ocean to the east of Australia, which has been a French colony since 1853. The hostility between the two main communities of this French territory—the Caldoches on one side, and the Canaks on the other—led to extreme violence and major risks for the country. While the Caldoches wanted to remain French, the Canaks fought for independence. Various attempts had been made to overcome this polarization. The first major initiative was undertaken by Edgar Pisani, a former government minister, who was sent by the French Socialist government between 1984 and 1986 to try to solve the problem. He failed because he was perceived as being too favourable to independence and could not succeed. His successor, Bernard Pons, a minister sent by the Conservative government between 1986 and 1988, used violence to obtain the liberation of hostages kept in a grotto by Canak rebels; however, he came to be seen as being too biased in favour of the Caldoches.

A new government (mainly socialist, with an openness towards moderate centre politicians), headed by Michel Rocard, immediately created a "Mission of Dialogue". This was a small team of people able to have a deep understanding of the position of individual subgroups in a multi-religious and multicultural society, and each member of the team would dialogue with his or her counterpart in the field in New Caledonia. The purpose of these "missionaries" was then to explore the perceptions, meanings, and proposals of each party in an empathetic way without trying to influence them.

Michel Rocard, who himself did not have any definite idea of what the solution might be, gathered all the data collected with the help of both the Overseas Territory minister and each member of the "Mission of Dialogue". He proposed a conference in Paris with the two representatives of the main communities: Jacques Lafleur for the Caldoches and Jean-Marie Djibaou for the Canaks. Surprisingly, agreement was quickly found between these two "enemies" (after a 10-hour meeting). Among the various factors that contributed to their success, the transitional approach consciously designed by the prime minister undoubtedly played an important part. A film documentary was produced several years later in an attempt to give an account of the various episodes of the process. It has been used since for training negotiators.

The murder of Djibaou by extremists several months later put into question the efficiency of such an approach. Probably the speed with which the conflict was resolved did not allow for sufficient working-through by all of the communities involved in the conflict, especially the extremist ones. Any leader taking part in a transitional process of this kind should take the time to inform his or her "followers" and train them in a transitional approach to managing change. Otherwise, violent reactions come to the surface and can destroy the whole process. Fortunately, the dramatic events of the neo-Caledonian conflict did not decrease the willingness of both sides to go on with the process and, in time, to solve the political issues. A parallel can be made with the Rabin–Arafat peace negotiations in the 1990s.

Organizational designed transitional processes

Within large organizations in the private sector, we can observe two procedures that can be used either just as control systems or, in addition, as transitional processes for the development of people and of the organization: the welcoming of new members and the performance-appraisal interview.

When new members are recruited, they are often guided by the organization, sometimes with the help of a mentor, to get to know several departments and functions, to listen to speeches, and to watch videos about the so-called "reality" of the firm. The implicit message in such a process is: "Learn who we are so that you can adapt to us." An outsider is thus required to internalize the codes, values, and principles of the organization, and the faster the better. This is a classical and widespread example of a social control system.

The transitional approach to such a socialization process would be different. The organization considering itself as an open system would welcome the newcomer as a chance to increase learning and creativity both for the organization and for the new member. The latter, in such a case, would be considered as a kind of consultant using her or his own naivety and sensitivity not only to learn something about the system but also to react, to question, even to propose new ways of functioning. Such an approach requires an atmosphere of dialogue, of cooperation from the insiders, and of openness to change that would be likely to lead to a permanent renewal of the organization. Apart from the basic attitude to such a process, a key assumption is that the reality of the organization is its informal functioning and that outsiders can get deep insights into that "reality", deeper in some areas than those of people already part of the system.

Many firms and managers nowadays have understood this kind of process. For example, some ask newcomers to produce what they call a *rapport d'étonnement* [report of surprise]. The recording of these first impressions is an acknowledgement of the usefulness of surprise to reveal unperceived assets and potential disfunctionings.

The performance-appraisal interview is another feature of the dialectics between adaptation and creativity. It is generally linked to a management by objectives philosophy, if not to a purely bureaucratic process. The idea is to compare the results of work done by a subordinate during a year with the objectives fixed or negotiated by a superior at the beginning of that year. Here again, the process can be a pure control system or a transitional creative process. In the first pattern, the process remains hierarchical, adaptive. The superior's judgement leads to marks and sanctions (positive or negative), with little learning from the experience. By contrast, an open appraisal interview can be the pretext for a collaborative review. In such a situation, several aspects of the work situation will be deeply explored—for example, the context of the objectives, and the strengths and weaknesses not only of the subordinate but of the help given (or not) by the superior and colleagues. The result can be the definition of new objectives, the creation of new procedures; the exploration of new ways of communication, new projects, new areas of learning and training; and an increased awareness concerning organizational, personal, and interpersonal issues. More recently, the limits of purely hierarchical appraisal have come to light. What is known as 360° appraisal, which includes a broad set of partners in the work situation, is implemented in many firms. Again, it can be used either as a social control system or as a transitional process.

As is apparent from these two organizational practices, the transitional approach includes an open and collaborative space where review and working-through lead to creative processes and outputs.

II.2. *Spontaneous (natural) transitional processes*

Spontaneous transitional processes are those that appear without any conscious willingness to design them. As we have seen earlier, many processes are potentially transitional and can produce maturing effects quite naturally.

Spontaneous transitional interactions

If psychotherapy is a designed (voluntary) transitional process, real-life situations provide opportunities whereby personal growth, or a creative personal process, is initiated or stimulated. Observation of such situations leads us to consider that the start of a spontaneous transitional process at a personal level comes most often from an encounter with another person who constitutes:

• a containing function—that is, a "good-enough" mother image, someone able to listen, to suspend judgement, to encourage, to free from inhibitions;

• a reference function—that is, a model to which the person aspires to resemble, an ego ideal;

• a mirroring function, or an alter ego—that is, a person who resembles us, in whom we can find ourselves;

• or a combination of any or all of the functions described above.

These different kinds of persons (or functions) perform a role of ego support in the development of a transitional process. They can be insightful friends, colleagues, or managers. They could be called "shadow gardeners" because they help people to grow without knowing or even wanting to; at the same time, those who grow in that way do not always recognize what kind of interaction helped them to do so. That is why it might be useful to be able to identify those "shadow gardeners" and to give them the recognition they deserve. This would be of key importance for any organization that contains numerous unrecognized internal "shadow consultants".

Spontaneous transitional designs

If we turn now to the notion of spontaneous transitional designs, we can verify several that lead to growth and creativity. One example will shed light on such processes.

The organization committee of a national symposium on a scientific subject was surprised by the great number of applicants, which was totally unexpected and created logistical problems. Because the largest conference-room was too small for 500 participants, they de-

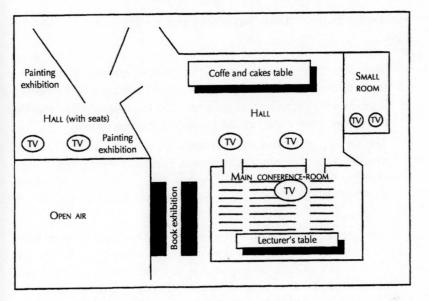

FIGURE 3.1. The conference arrangements

cided to use one room behind, plus a hall close to a painting exhibition displayed next to it. These three places surrounded the permanent coffee-room (with a large permanent buffet); this had a TV set, as did the buffet hall, making it possible from outside the conference-room to listen to and watch the various scientific presentations (see Figure 3.1).

The organization committee was anxious about those participants who could not be accommodated in the main conference-room and would not therefore see the lecturers in the flesh. Although designated group leaders, with microphones, were available in the outside rooms to allow questions to be put to the lecturers from there, it was only in the main conference-room that any questions were raised and discussions took place.

The anxiety of the managers was totally relieved when they got their first feedback (during the conference) about the material organization of the symposium. They were even surprised by the exceptional praise offered by the participants. Analysing more carefully what the participants said and what they themselves observed, the managers discovered the transitional and positive impact of the design.

- The participants who went to the main conference-room were those who were keenest to listen to a specific lecturer and possibly interact with him or her. Therefore, when they were less interested in a presentation, they could move to the other rooms.

- The variety of places where people could listen to the lecturer allowed a continuous movement of people, meeting informally either in the corridor during a tea break or in the painting exhibition. Existing personal links were reinforced and new ones established.

- The architectural design of the symposium not only allowed freedom but also managed to take care of guilt feelings. To leave a room in the middle of a speech is not that easy, so the TV sets performed the function of "guilt-reducers". Indeed, delegates could be in any room without leaving either the subject or the lecturers, who because of the TV sets were everywhere present with the participants. These were able to have superficial, polite relationships with some colleagues, and deeper ones with others.

In their feedback to the managers, delegates reported on the conviviality of this symposium and on the real possibility to exchange ideas, to work through some difficult issues, to meet new people, and to plan creative actions. This spontaneous transitional design in fact helped fulfil in the best way possible the four main functions of symposia:

- transmission of knowledge;
- encounters with other specialists;
- personal working through;
- creative impulse for many participants.

This type of design reminds us of the sociotechnical designs originally developed by British and Northern European specialists (e.g. Cherns, 1976). One can remember how the architecture of the plants and the whole organization in Volvo was designed in such a way that semi-autonomous groups of production workers could function collaboratively from the beginning to the end of the making of a car. But the designing in this case was deliberate. In many cases (as in our example above), transitional processes are unplanned. We can ask if, in that case, managers are likely to regret it? The answer will be "yes" if they want to have more mastery over any organizational change. It will be "no" if they accept that total mastery is impossible, even dangerous, and somehow in contradiction with a real transitional approach. They have to be ready to cope with uncertainty and unexpected events, and to increase their awareness of the creative signs and the "live shoots" likely to emerge anywhere.

II.3. A mixed process:
the Iran–U.S. football game

To conclude this section, we would like to give an account of a recent transitional process that includes both the spontaneous and the designed dimensions. Many societal changes are helped by spontaneous transitional processes. This is a normal feature if we accept that events are not entirely predictable. People are not always aware either of such transitional processes or of their developmental potential. If they were, they might use them for a variety of purposes. This is what happened during the 1998 football World Cup in France.

The key to this illustration is the conflict between Iran and the United States. Some may recall an earlier example of sports diplomacy introduced into the lexicon by the United States and China through the game of ping-pong two decades ago. Like the indoor game, this new example may also, as an Indian journal noted, "have long-term consequences for the world. ... For the thawing relations between Iran and the U.S. fit a global pattern and have the potential to strengthen the forces of peace as much as cause harmful fall-outs" (*The Hindu*, 25 June 1998).

Let us just make a short historical flashback. Diplomatic relationships with Iran were closed by the United States on 7 April 1980, during the hostage crisis (53 American hostages were kept prisoner for 444 days in the U.S. Embassy in Tehran by Islamic fundamentalists). Since that period, a dual containment strategy (against both Iran and Iraq) had been set up by Reagan and followed by Bush.

For geo-strategic motives, Bill Clinton wanted to renew normal relationships with Iran. In 1997, Mohammed Khatami, a moderate cleric, was elected president of Iran in a landslide victory over conservative opponents on a mandate for political and social reforms. Since his election, open clashes between pro-Khatami moderates and conservatives who still control key levers of power, have become a familiar feature of the Iranian political landscape. Khatami received an unexpected boost through the surprising qualification of the Iranian football team for the World Cup after a match against Australia in the autumn of 1997.

Iran had not qualified since 1978 (one year before the hostage crisis). "Hysterical" reactions of happiness were evident in the streets of Tehran after the qualification, especially from thousands of young women who gathered in front of the Azadi stadium, some of them taking off their veils. After short negotiations, and under the control of the police, they were allowed for the first time to enter the stadium to celebrate the event. A first and deep breach had been made in the power of the conservative system. As noted by a French journalist (*Libération*, No. 5315), contrary to the history of the relationship between football and politics, which shows the use of football for fascist purposes (Mussolini's Italy, Argentina under military rule in 1978), the autumn event of 1997 in Iran demonstrates the subversive strength of football. A second similar event occurred when Iran was drawn to play against the United States in December 1997. There was a spontaneous outburst of popular feeling in Tehran in support of a more normal relationship with the rest of the world. Women were prominent in the celebrations, rejecting instructions from conservative Islamic leaders not to attend. One should remember that, when he was elected, Khatami received overwhelming support from women and young people (55% of Iranians are less than 20 years old), who represent a large majority of the Iranian population. As the French journal *Libération* noted: "On November 29th, the Iranian society expressed its aspiration to change as it has never done since the Islamic revolution of 1979" (22 June 1998).

After this, both Khatami and Clinton gave multiple signs of mutual recognition. Politicians used various forms of reasoning in assessing which score in the Iran–U.S. football encounter would be most likely to facilitate reconciliation. As football—in Iran, replacing boxing as the national sport (in spite of the strong reluctance of Islamic leaders)—had become one of the symbols of the political regime's modernity, Iranian and American diplomacy made every effort to make use of the unexpected encounter in the match between the two teams in Paris on 21 June. Madeleine Albright, during her seminal speech at the Asia Society in New York, explained that she wanted to develop a "road map leading to normal relations" with the Islamic Republic of Iran (*Times of India*, 21 June 1998). One journalist wrote that through her speech she "transported policy wonks and Middle East analysts in a magic carpet to a fantasy land inhabited by Aladdins and Sinbads" (*Times of India*, 19 June 1998).

Referring to Islam, which she categorized as "the fastest growing religion in the United States", Mrs Albright pointed out that " We respect deeply its moral teachings and its role as a source of inspiration and instruction for hundreds of millions of people around the world". She then alluded to President Khatami's injunction to all Iranians to get better acquainted with Western civilization, and she added, "I would say, in response, that the same can be said with respect to Eastern civilisation and Islamic civilisation". Her speech, according to *The Independent* (*Libération*, 22 June 1998), was the U.S. administration's first considered response to a television interview given by President Khatami on CNN more than four months before, in which he had called for an end to the hostility with the U.S. and proposed, as a start, more non-diplomatic exchanges.

Paris was, by chance, the right transitional place for symbolic reasons, as one journalist noted: "There could hardly have been a more apt international setting for signalling the thawing relations than France which is hosting the global football show. It was after all from French soil that the father of the Islamic revolution, Ayatollah Khomeini, waged his long and successful war against the Shah of Iran and his patron, The United States" (*The Hindu*, 25 June 1998).

President Clinton himself videotaped a message to the Iranian people that was televised during the game at half-time (Father's Day in America) in which he hoped the match "can be another step toward ending the estrangement between our nations".

One could also say that the International Federation of Football (FIFA) gave some potential help to the process in making 21 June the fair-play day of the World Cup, precisely the day of the Iran–U.S. encounter. Observers of the match indeed noticed several symbolic gestures: before starting the game, the Iranian captain gave flowers to his American counterpart, who in turn gave him U.S. Soccer Federation pennants, and their hand-shaking was "surely the longest of the World Cup" (*Libération*, 22 June 1998). Instead of keeping apart, as is customary, the two teams mixed for the photograph and stood arm in arm.

Iran's 2-1 victory had interesting outputs. According to Reuters News Service, no one in the crowd of thousands even mentioned the losers. "A return to normality", "The first time in twenty years we all have something to celebrate", "We now have a new image" were some of the frequent comments from Iranians in the street. Jubilant Iranians, both boys and girls—normally kept from mingling together—poured onto the streets of Tehran to cheer their first victory in the World Cup finals, stopping traffic and waving flags, chanting "*Iran, Iran, Iran*", many with radios blaring popular music. The World Cup Iranian football coach, Jalab Talebi, said that the United States also deserved to win: "Technically, they were over us and dominated most of the game. They deserved to win too but, at the end of the game, only one team can win and it was our chance to be the winning team."

At the same time, the Iranian politicians kept a "low profile", using the victory to bolster U.S.–Iran reconciliation. President Khatami said: "What counts is the endeavour, hard work, diligence, solidarity, skill and intellect displayed by our young people. . . . It was a victory for the national unity of all Iranians whatever their political opinions. We must learn to tolerate one another regardless of any differences in taste and to undertake discussion on the basis of the rules of the game, that is, laws and regulations." The President spoke of the need to recognize the people's right of sovereignty over their own destiny, adding: "If we accept this principle and adopt a broadminded approach, we will perform better at tasks involving collective work; exactly in the same way as a football team, where you can see one team acting on the basis of rivalry towards the other team, not of enmity. We must implement this at the level of society."

Since that period, negotiations have developed and the political experts predict that normal relationships between Iran and the United States are likely to resume.

This story, as an illustration of transitional processes, demonstrates the importance of unpredicted events, symbols and transitional objects (the football game in this case), playing, and potential space for growth.

III
A CONTINGENT PERSPECTIVE
ON CHANGE MANAGEMENT

III.1. Transitional, regressive, and transitive change

Transitional processes are specific processes leading to a more advanced degree of development and change. To simplify, they can be distinguished from regressive ones and transitive ones. To be realistic, we would like to show how these kinds of change can be legitimate depending on the internal or external constraints of the situation. It is, therefore, important to understand their characteristics.

Regressive change

Regressive change is the opposite of transitional change. Whereas transitional processes aim at further integration and mature development, regressive processes leave the system in a higher state of dependency, with diminished feelings of responsibility; with lower levels of confidence in experimenting, exploring, and taking risks; and sometimes with a climate of fear, anxiety, and uncertainty for individuals, which stifles initiative and reduces commitment. Regressive processes increase entropy in the system.

It might be argued that once a system has moved into a situation that is basically regressive, it does not take long for a vicious spiral to commence that rapidly reduces the effectiveness of the system by diminishing the contribution of individuals in the system and generates suspicion and hostile, destructive forces. Such a view must be qualified, however. The structure and viability of many systems is based on regression—that is, on the dependency of the people within them. Such systems can be called "totalitarian". They all institutionalize, or have people unconsciously internalize, a system of values, norms, and rules that have to be followed precisely. Their functioning can be compared to that of closed systems, such as bureaucracies, sects, and some organizations with a high degree of imposed common ideology and culture. If such a system is to be efficient, it is important to realize that the price to pay is the relinquishing of individual autonomy, responsibility, and creativity and the oppression of subcultures (Amado, 1988).

Regressive changes are generally undertaken in situations where specific constraints exist (see below), or by those in controlling positions who have a strongly authoritarian personality.

Transitive change

Unlike transitional change, transitive change is a process that involves no development or contribution to learning by individuals in the community but simply a change of state in a particular feature from A to B. This change of state from A to B may well have a significant impact on other people or on other systems. The key point here is that the people involved in moving from A to B either take no account of any of the potentialities that are possible in all changes, or are obliged to manage a situation in this mechanical and directive way because of other considerations (see below).

The contrast between transitional change and transitive change can be depicted in the following way:

Transitive	*Transitional*
conditional	creative
mechanistic	experience-based
operational	reflective
automatic	working through
sequential	simultaneous
reactive	responsive
immediate	delayed

Driving a car is transitive to the extent that it involves operating the machinery with learned skills. It is transitional when it involves working one's way through unfamiliar territory, processing contradictory or ambiguous information, deliberating, exploring options, making choices. Driving a car in unfamiliar territory is a transitional process which incorporates transitive operations. Many transitive behaviours, which are based on learned skills, are often embedded in more transitional kinds of conduct that require a reflective deliberating process.

If we turn now to organizational change processes, we understand that transitive change is close to the notion and experience of planned change where management would like the organization or a department to move from an A-state to a B-state. It will be useful here to differentiate more carefully between two modes of transitive change: the open transitive mode and the manipulative transitive mode.

- *The open transitive mode.* In this mode, the initiators of the change process explain as clearly as possible where they start from, where they want to go, and how they propose to get there with the people involved. This mode is "open" because the influence is clearly exposed and perceived. This mode is mostly used by managers who are not afraid of clarity, who feel that they can expose their strategy and their projects to colleagues and subordinates and answer difficult questions about them.

- *The manipulative transitive mode.* By contrast, the manipulative transitive mode is one in which the initiators of the change process try to lead people from A to B without them becoming aware of the process by which they are to get there. The underlying anxiety of such change managers (which could be justified) is that clarity might prevent the occurrence of the change and create more problems than positive results.

III.2.   The relevance of each kind of change design

Through the examination of each of these types of change—transitional, regressive, transitive—one could easily place a positive value on transitional change and a negative one on regressive change, and build something like a hierarchy of modes of change from the lowest value to the highest, as in Figure 3.2.

However, one has to be careful to avoid dichotomous or black-and-white thinking and be prepared to adopt a more situational approach. Such an approach would show the value of each mode according to the specific context in which it takes place.

A *regressive mode* of change can be considered as legitimate when certain characteristics exist in a particular situation:

- high emergency and risk,
- necessity for a strict and collective discipline;
- heavy time constraints.

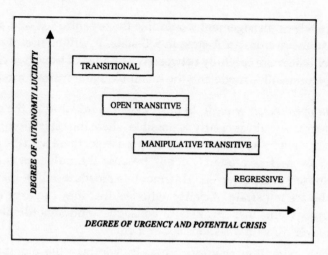

FIGURE 3.2. Types of change design

For example, during a war and at a critical moment of it, some quick decisions must be taken and implemented whose rationale cannot be explained to the soldiers because it might create more confusion, disagreements, or internal conflicts. This might also be true for any life-or-death situation in the operating theatre. In a way, the "non-thinking" at certain moments under such conditions can be a requirement for "success" or survival.

A *manipulative transitive mode* can be considered legitimate as a phase of a change process when the following exist:

- time constraints;
- defensive mechanisms and strong resistances towards positive change and learning.

The teaching–learning situation is the best illustration of such a positive use of a transitive manipulative mode. Any trainer or teacher can choose to put the trainees and students in a "learning" situation where they do not know what or how they are going to learn. A directive and manipulative mode, genuinely imagined and elaborated, can help to promote positive change. The only question is its depth and the awareness about the process of change itself. Provided that the "students" can understand soon afterwards the relevance of such an approach, they will learn. On the contrary, however, if the pedagogical "manipulations" are neither understood nor explained, at some point in time students might get lost or at least very suspicious about the hidden style of the trainer, and this could well increase their reluctance to "play the game" of learning adopted by the trainer.

An *open transitive mode* is, probably, most relevant when both

- time constraints exist,
- the change agent has available, more than anyone else, the best information and data to go from A to B.

In such a situation, one might say that to use a transitional approach would be more manipulative than the use of an open transitive one. Managers who have to collect a lot of data from various sources before reaching a point of view are used to this mode. They use influence in a way that is understood.

What, then, is the status of transitional change in relation to all of these other modes?

III.3. *Processing change with a transitional orientation*

As the above description shows, time is one of the key factors that allows for (or does not allow for) the possibility for a transitional process of change. This view leads us to understand why, if we consider the process over its complete duration, there is not necessarily a contradiction between these three modes of change and the transitional mode. Indeed, regressive and transitive processes can be worked out with a transitional orientation. Such an orientation means that, once regressive or transitive steps have been proposed or taken for specific reasons, there will be moments and spaces for examining with the people involved the rationale of the outcome and the process that took place. In other words, a manager who wants to work transitionally might use regressive or transitive steps but will necessarily at some time, and as frequently as possible, open up the situation for a real working-through as far as possible. Otherwise, he or she can be seen as a manipulator.

These different forms of change management are very much dependent on the role and stance adopted by the change agent. After all, can everyone work transitionally? Are there not some specific characteristics of the behaviour, the attitudes, and even the personality of the so-called transitional change agent? We will attempt to outline these in the section below.

IV
THE TRANSITIONAL CHANGE AGENT/LEADER

The "transitional" change agent is distinguishable from her or his counterparts in other schools of thought more by behaviour than by techniques or "toolbox". In the face of events, projects, and crises she or he reveals particular personality traits, psychic characteristics, and attitudes.

First, the transitional change agent has a strong sense of curiosity, is someone who seeks to understand, who is moved by what Melanie Klein refers to as the epistemophilic drive. Instead of adopting a position of contra-phobic retreat in the face of action or the unknown, she or he tends to have an investigative attitude. This attitude goes hand in hand with a capacity to accept the ambivalence of human emotion, to acknowledge negative feelings, violence, hatred, the death impulse present in all of us alongside Eros. Just as Winnicott talked of seventeen good reasons for a mother to hate her young child, it is easy to imagine the number of times change agents must feel negative emotions in the face of complex and anxiety-provoking situations. It is important to be able to tolerate those negative feelings in oneself for two reasons: first, it is a necessary condition in order to be capable of imagining and recognizing them in others (rather than denying them), and therefore to be able also to accept them as being part of the normal set of phenomena; second, it is a means by which to avoid the illusion of the perfect being, in total control, motivated only by good intentions, setting a false example to those with whom she or he interacts and thereby depriving them of a dynamic and creative frustration. The notion of "good enough" dear to Winnicott—and often misinterpreted—contains this dimension of imperfection which people need to recognize.

A link can be made with the "depressive position" described by Melanie Klein, a phase of development linked to the understanding of complexity. Similarly, the transitional change agent does not artificially separate good from bad. Unlike many adepts of organizational development, she or he does not have a vision of the individual as essentially positive, forced to deal with an unfavourable social context. The inside and the outside are in fact seen as having a close and dialectic relationship. However, this acceptance of the negative side of things which enables people to access the whole individual as well as the full complexity of human interactions does not prevent positive work from being carried out. On the contrary, just as Harold Bridger refers to himself as "a pessimist working optimistically", the transitional agent works essentially towards development. In order to do this, he does not rely on moral discourse or on models. In fact, he refuses them, seeing them as naive, alienating, and reproducing the former scheme of things. Instead, he focuses on the discovery or the invention of confrontational situations designed to enable people to get beyond difficult situations. This approach requires a truly independent spirit, one which is capable of working towards objectives despite the apparent constraints of a difficult context. It is the type of spirit that Winnicott showed when he refused to join the followers of Anna Freud or Melanie Klein and created a third group (King & Steiner, 1992), and when he invented the unconventional technique of the squiggle to facilitate child therapy, while retaining a psychoanalytic approach.

The transitional change agent, because she or he recognizes ambivalence, complexity, and paradox, attempts to create transitional spaces or learning environments that are necessarily imperfect but sufficiently well thought out so that the people concerned are able to interact in terms of the real problems and/or move beyond those problems, sometimes through a form of symbolic playing linked to the real issues.

It goes without saying that the transitional person, while able to cope with loneliness, enjoys doing things with others; she or he has a profound sense of cooperation. Although her or his inventions are often made alone, due to her or his partially external position (both in and out, on the boundary of the situation), they are also generated by others in whom creative forces are unleashed. In order to achieve this, two further qualities are necessary to be a transitional change agent.

The person must have a containing function—that is, the capacity to maintain a work setting, with its rules of the game and its limits, as well as to tolerate more or less furtive movements of destruction within the designed groupings, and to bear and understand the projections of which she or he may become the object, to accept resistance. Furthermore, and most importantly, the person must have the sense of "ontological safety" that Laing (1970) spoke of. It is a quality acquired early by those who were brought up in a protective educational environment that was nevertheless sufficiently frustrating, a quality that develops throughout life in those who are able to face up to difficult and painful experiences and to draw positive lessons from them. In fact, it is this ontological safety that leads to the independence of spirit referred to earlier—the experimental daring, the capacity for loneliness, the pleasure of discoveries made together, the sharing of inexpressible feelings.

Nevertheless, if the above qualities are typical of the transitional person, they are not quite sufficient for the transitional change agent, whether manager, consultant, union leader, politician. These must also have a good knowledge of the context within which they are operating in order to be able to detect the objective social determinants of behaviour and understand the unconscious social defence mechanisms as well as the routes likely to lead to change in organized social systems. It is the combination of the person's transitional qualities and knowledge of the context that will ensure the success of the actions she or he undertakes.

These qualities should not be considered the exclusive reserve of leaders or some form of elite. While there is a great body of literature to this effect, which tends to insist on the quasi-innate positive qualities of leaders, clinical analysis and observation also point to the pathological traits and behaviour of many of them. The very situation in which people have to exercise responsibility (usually meaning they also have a high position in the hierarchy) makes leaders fragile: the uncertainty, the risks inherent in decision-making, the fact that they become cut off from the field both isolate them and weigh on their inner experience. The transitional approach is a means by which to reduce some of the stress inherent in leadership.

But transitional qualities are much more widespread than we think in people. It is important to detect the presence of such people and to observe the role they play in the organizations in which they are employed. It is our hypothesis that they play a central, although usually invisible, role in solving tensions and conflicts as well as in the development of maturity.

The potential nature of such qualities means also that they can be learned. It is not only in-depth personal reflection on the experiences of everyday life and work that add a transitional dimension; in addition, the many working conferences founded on the model developed by Harold Bridger and other transitional experts show how reflection in groups, using the double-task technique, can greatly facilitate and expedite transitional learning. The participants talk of their resulting capacity to act differently in their professional context following these conferences, particularly as a critical mass of people from their organizations have also been through the same experience.

CHAPTER FOUR

Review as a necessary ingredient in transitional change

Gilles Amado & John Sharpe

The process of review is the attempt by any kind of human system to attain an awareness of itself with regard to how it is functioning, at both manifest and latent levels, in order to achieve the tasks and purposes for which it exists. The purpose of review is to make sense of the system's inner life and to optimize its ongoing capability in a conscious way while remaining in tune and in touch with the wider system of which it is part. The vehicle for such a process is mainly the expression of and reflection on feelings, thoughts, cognitive maps, and perceptions about how any tasks are being undertaken by the people involved. Such an expression is mainly verbal, but drawings or any other metaphoric tools can also be used to reach such an objective. The motivation for review is based on a desire for better understanding, which is almost invariably linked to a desire to improve the way and the degree in which the system achieves its goals.

The process of review has also been called "Task 2" by Harold Bridger—that is, the task to be carried out alongside the "primary task", or Task 1. The primary task can vary greatly in its nature: it consists of the immediate job in hand being tackled by a person or a group. It can therefore be operational in nature or concerned with planning or with analysis. The answer to the question, "What are we doing at this point in time?", will be a definition of Task 1. Every Task 1 has space around it which enables the people engaged in Task 1 to put the question: "How are we going about it?" or "Are we approaching this in the best possible way?" This is Task 2—that is, the search for feedback to permit a system to attain a greater awareness and understanding of its own functioning, which enables it to develop and change the way it is working in order better to achieve its goals.

The process of review lies at the root of all learning, be it at an individual, group, or organizational level. The motivations, or drivers, that make an organization want to develop a capacity for review are many and varied. Two classic reasons would be, first, a culture of excellence, such as striving for world-class performance; second, at the other extreme would be a survival crisis that demands fundamental sustainable change in the way an organization works. Whatever the motivation, an organization that commits itself to the review process is committing itself to increasingly open boundaries and an increasing capacity to adapt to changes in the external environment.

Why is it necessary?

Without review, any system can be said to be blind in one way or another. In achieving any particular task, an organization has to bear in mind many different factors that affect that task and how it impacts on the other tasks of the organization and on the individuals in it. If a task is implemented in a blinkered way, with a narrow focus designed simply to achieve the goals exactly as given, it is quite possible for this to create more negatives than positives in the system. This can be for many different reasons: for example, the original goals might have been wrongly defined or there may have been changes in the operational environment which must be taken into account. In order for any task to be completed without developing "blind spots", the review process is necessary to keep checking that the goals and the way the task is being approached are still valid.

It is in this sense that Zobrist (1987) wrote about the role of review as a "maintenance role". It helps to secure the integration of the system within the context of its environment, the health of the system, the restoration of its energy, the careful use of its resources and potential, and the sound functioning of all processes involved.

The review process is also the basic mechanism by which creativity and innovation are built into the work process. An organizational culture that invites individuals involved in the work process to check continually the relevance of the task and how it is being addressed is also inviting the continual creative involvement of all individuals in seeking and implementing new and better solutions than would be available in a more rigid and normalized work approach.

To give a better understanding of the nature of the review process and the levels at which it can operate, we now look at four examples—one in sport, two in business, and one in politics.

Sports example

If we consider a football team playing 40 matches a year, can we imagine what the situation would be like if its members did not have some space to review how they were playing and what was going on between them?

Without a review process the players would not be able to understand:

—the reasons why they win and the reasons why they lose;

—the strengths and weaknesses of their strategy and tactics;

—the motivations of their coach in the way he or she selects certain players, or not;

—the ways available to the players to improve their game.

In a team game, where the individual performances that contribute to the "results" are very visible (through the media) and where to be selected or not is also very visible, another set of issues is always very close to the surface. These are the various feelings, some positive and some negative, that are generated in team members:

—anxiety about one's own performance,

—feelings of inadequacy or "humiliation" when one is not selected for a match;

—resentment towards other team members who did not cooperate with one in the best way;

—superiority or " omnipotent" feelings about performance;

—resentment, in front of the coach, about decisions or tactics or selection.

These sorts of issues, interpersonal tensions, and conflicts can easily develop in a team. In turn, they can lead to a sense of isolation by individual players or by the coach who is responsible for exercising a weekly choice about who should be on the team. Only by being as open as possible and reviewing all issues concerning team performance and team relationships can the climate in a team be sustained in a healthy mode such that all people can understand well enough what is happening.

The situation of a team and the kinds of questions raised by individual performances, team performance, selection, and non-selection are high-profile examples of many of the issues met with in other types of organization. Within corporate organizations, for example, the visibility of the issues may not be so clear, but the basic relationships between performance, selection, success, fame, recognition, and reward are all fundamentally the same.

Business example 1

This example of the need for review concerns the case of Company X. The problem for this company was located in the "operational planning meeting", which was responsible for managing the sales operations of the company. Because sales of promotional packs accounted for over 50% of the company's sales, the process of planning the promotions was of great importance to the company. The business was run in a "no-nonsense" way with a rather status-conscious management climate. Different departments had well-defined briefs as to what they should achieve, and they were assessed on results.

The operational planning meeting involved many departments: marketing, sales, planning, production, and commercial. Over a period of twelve months, the meeting had become more and more unsatisfactory, with many disagreements occurring between departments. The mood of the meeting had become one of frustration and anger.

The company objective of having a smooth, well-planned promotional sales programme was not being met, and various problems kept reappearing in the programme. The sales department rarely managed to sell the stock of goods produced. This resulted in residual packs having to go back to manufacturing to be repacked. Stock levels were rising, and the manufacturing department was regularly being dragged down from very high output to very low output. A point was reached where it was clear to everyone that the system was going dramatically wrong and that the whole process had to be examined. The key decision was then made that everyone in the system should "take a step back" and examine what was going on. This was the start of the review process, provoked by the operational crisis.

In the first review meeting, all departments were asked to state what they were trying to achieve. The marketing department stated that they wanted high targets so that they could sell as much as possible on each promotion, since any one brand had only two promotions per year. They also believed that the sales department would work harder if they were given stretching and challenging targets.

The sales department always argued for low targets, because a large part of their remuneration system was based on exceeding their sales targets. They felt that the targets themselves had little effect on how much they would sell and that lower targets would not hurt the company but would help the department. They argued that lower prices and more discounts were the way to increase sales.

The planning department's main objective was to keep stock levels down to a minimum; therefore, they wanted accurate targets. This would allow them to schedule the minimum production to maintain minimum stock levels. Planning people were frustrated by the big difference between the high sales estimates from the marketing department and the low sales estimates from the sales department.

The manufacturing department's main goal was to keep manufacturing costs low. This required long, smooth production runs, avoiding any peaks and troughs in production. But this is not what happened, because the planning meeting always resulted in last-minute decisions and many changes in the production plan, leading to peaks and troughs. Despite high peaks and low troughs, the output was still not being sold.

The commercial department's role was to ensure that all company operations were profitable. Each promotion was evaluated on its profitability. The way to make promotions profitable was to achieve high sales at high prices. The commercial department ignored sales-department ideas that high prices would mean lower sales.

It was quite clear from this review of departmental goals that many of the goals of the different departments were directly in conflict with each other and that these differences both fuelled the failure of the meeting to do its job and increased the animosity felt between departments. It was clear to all that the company had to continue to mount promotions; otherwise, they would go out of business. However, it was also clear both that the criteria for promotions needed to be redefined in terms of the overall company interest, and that this process would not allow all departments to achieve their own limited goals.

The final solution that emerged from the discussion was as follows. Each promotion individually did not have to make a short-term profit; sales over the whole year would be used to evaluate profitability. The commercial department would focus on the relative cost/benefit of different promotional types rather than the profit of individual promotions. Marketing agreed to let sales make a realistic estimate of what could be sold, and the basis for sales remuneration was moved to six-monthly sales targets rather than for each promotion. In this process, marketing conceded power and influence to sales, and sales moved to a more realistic, but more difficult, reward system.

These decisions removed the largest in-built conflict mechanism, and it was soon clear that the sales targets being set were more realistic and were being achieved. This allowed the planner to plan more accurately, and the peaking and troughing of manufacturing was eased significantly. That is not to say that everything became perfect. But the excesses were taken out of the system, and the people involved agreed to suspend their own limited operational criteria in favour of more broadly based criteria related to the needs of the whole system.

In this review process, the individuals involved had to move from their original viewpoint of what they individually were trying to achieve to one that optimized the performance of the whole system. Such a move in viewpoint involves recognizing important aspects that were mentioned earlier. Many other issues, such as power and status, are also involved in the rebalancing of such a complex system. The review process makes it possible to work on and acknowledge the changed relationships involved in order that changes to the macro-system do not simply create new problems that then emerge in some other place in the operations of the organization.

Business example 2

The second example illustrates what can happen when a regular review process does not take place. Crossbe Company is a brokerage company whose growth has been significant and rapid over a one-and-a-half-year period. Starting with three people, it is now composed of eighteen specialists operating on the MATIF financial market. These specialists were recruited each time there was a shortage in the work force rather than according to strategic objectives. They devote their time to immediate requirements, calling clients and trying to make business with them. The atmosphere is very tense both because of the "stress" of the market itself and because of the relatively uncertain job definitions caused by the rapid growth of the company. Therefore, people work hard but separately most of the time, without any kind of coordination procedure except an informal one during coffee breaks and very occasional meetings. The last review session took place a year ago.

It was in such a context that the members of the company received an internal note (Figure 4.1) one morning from the "so-called" boss. The reactions to the accusations contained in the note were immediate, violent, and ironic. People felt that:

—it was unfair and wrong,
—they were working like mad;
—they got good results thanks to themselves;
—there was no kind of internal coordination;
—their boss was not a boss;
—the management was a paradoxical one ("each of you have your own clients but do not have a clientelist attitude").

The internal note had, then, the dramatic effect of creating a collective accusation by all members of the firm against their boss. This reflected long-standing thoughts about him, which, though discussed in the corridors, had not been communicated to him. It appeared clear

---

INTERNAL NOTE

I am profoundly disgusted by the constant degradation of the service we offer to our clients. Our June's success must have helped us lose the sense of reality. <u>Some examples</u> – Today, nearly none of Kathy's clients has been spontaneously called. – One needs to ask again systematically every morning the same questions: "Have you been calling Mr X . . .?". – I have the impression that, collectively, we make less and less effort to remain informed about national and international economic news. – I notice that the spontaneous disappearance of our morning meeting has been commented upon by nobody, and therefore considered as normal. – Nobody seems to get organized (telephone, arrangement of papers, telephone numbers, daily call program, visits, lunches . . .). – No real initiative is taken about the organization of the work. The enormous number of meetings already held remains hopelessly unfruitful. – A kind of "clientelist" mentality seems to develop. This remark can be linked with my first one. May I remind you that the main objective of our department is to call <u>systematically</u> all our clients at <u>regular times</u> and to tell them what the other agents are unable to tell them. Self-evident truth: the more we get clients and the more they are satisfied with us the more they will bring us new clients. <u>Conclusion</u> We must all succeed together in reaching a <u>steam-roller</u> discipline which "nicely harries" the client even if he is not active on the market. Experience proves that if one doesn't call a client during a week, one does not call him any more. More initiative, more professionalism and our performance and atmosphere will get better and you finally will discover me less grumpy.

FIGURE 4.1

to all members, when they discussed the issues properly for the first time together, that their boss had no idea of how to build a team, to motivate people, to delegate and control work, or to appreciate performances, and finally that he should not be in his position of authority.

There can be little doubt that review sessions, had they been held regularly, would have helped the team to avoid such an unfortunate explosion and would have increased the awareness by each person of the requirements of the business.

Sociopolitical example

At a "macro" societal level, some form of review process is essential in order to prevent societies from slipping into a totalitarian or anarchic state. Various characteristics are built into free societies which permit a public review process to take place. Democracies provide a political review process which is expressed through the secret ballot in a multi-party context. The whole process of political elections at national, regional, and local levels provides a mechanism whereby feedback is given regarding the policies and priorities desired by the people. The concept of freedom of speech is anchored firmly in the concept of review, and the process is also expressed in the freedom of the press and in the independence of the courts. The constitution of many countries is built on "checks and balances" that are designed to prevent any one faction from gaining unfettered control over the whole country. These are mechanisms that are designed to ensure that a collective review process is able to continue in the long-term interests of the country and of all the people in it.

It is all too easy today to identify those countries that have lost this quality of openness and the ability to reflect and review. All forms of totalitarianism, fundamentalism, and absolute dogma deny individuals, groups, and societies the space and freedom to reflect on the reality of their situation and the implications of the changing environments in which they live. This block on any form of open review in turn blocks learning, adaptation, and development within the society. This carries with it the consequence that dysfunctional activities become increasingly prevalent. More and more measures are needed to control review, and over time they become more and more extreme. The control mechanisms must be sustained because to start to question any one part of the system would initiate a process that would finally question the very basis of the system itself.

The only societal system that can remain healthy in the long term is one that gives the highest value to frequent review of its goals, values, and activities in respect of their appropriateness in the ever-changing environment in which it operates and of which it is an integral part.

* * *

All the above cases show the necessity of a review process that maintains awareness and self-consciousness in any kind of social system, whatever its size, and they show the heavy price to pay for its absence. We shall now examine the modalities and specificities of this process.

When should review take place?

The process of review is characterized in this chapter as being a distinct and identifiable activity. It does not refer to the unconscious or semi-conscious reflection on experience which all individuals do as part of everyday life. It is a purposeful review (Task 2), related to a primary task (Task 1), and its objective is to increase the quality of the output or solution to the primary task. It does this by taking account of all those aspects of the whole system that affect the work being done to achieve the primary task.

The fact that "review" is an identifiable task in its own right makes it possible for an individual or group to know whether a review has been done and to be aware of the time at which it was done. It is difficult to define precisely the best time to undertake a review session, because it depends on the context of the task. Nevertheless, we can stress an important requirement: the review session should be regular, and ideally it should be institutionalized into the normal working practice of the group. If we ask "Why should that be so?", the above examples give a first answer. If the review sessions are not regular, they may be perceived and used as crisis regulators only. In other words, someone or several people will ask for a review only when things go wrong. We are not saying that they should not be used to help solve crises: crisis resolution is, indeed, one of their potential strengths. But if they are used solely for that purpose, two negative consequences may follow:

- the crisis difficulties will have developed over an extended period of time and therefore may have become crystallized and hard to sort out;

- the participants are likely to enter the review sessions with anxiety feelings and may therefore give priority to protecting themselves against these instead of contributing with full creativity to solving the problems.

By contrast, if the review sessions are institutionalized:

- people will get accustomed to thinking about their jobs or functions, whatever the pressures are;

- people will gain understanding of the interdependencies between their jobs and those of others;

- people will feel more open to tackle personal as well as interpersonal issues;

- people will have the possibility not only to express anxiety but also to share satisfactions and examine the reasons why things go well;

- regular opportunities to acknowledge positive feelings and outcomes will make it easier to tackle more negative ones.

In many ways, the institutionalization of review sessions gives an open space where self-reflection can take place. That is why managers should avoid building too pressured or complete an agenda for these meetings, especially when there are no topics requiring immediate attention. These are moments for discussion of such questions as: "How do we each feel in the context of our job?" "Have any questions arisen in your mind over the last few weeks?", "Can we discuss our collective way of working?" The raising and consideration of such questions can helpfully reduce the possibility of people keeping problems hidden within themselves.

Many readers of this chapter may be surprised by our insistence on the institutionalization of regular sessions without their necessarily having precise task objectives. Don't we have enough meetings all the time whose efficiency is very low and which create more problems than they solve? We would answer such a legitimate question in the following manner. Yes, review sessions need and cost time, but one of the main reasons for the failure of many formal meetings, apart from the frequent lack of expertise in their leadership, is the absence of space for the expression of the real concerns of people—that is, absence of the review process itself.

Since the absence of review is still a common feature in the functioning of many organizations, it is important to consider why this should be so. The reason lies in the fact that, for some people, the idea of review carries an element of risk.

Risk and review

There is a certain apprehension in some organizational members when it is first suggested that there should be a "review" of a some activity, task, or process. The reason for this is often that the organizational culture is known to turn such a review process into one in which more blaming is done than learning. For the review process to work, the dominant cultural assumption has to be that learning is valued and that blaming is counterproductive.

In organizations where the switch from blaming to learning needs to take place, the real switch that is necessary is in the basic assumptions operating in the organization about people and their work. Organizations that believe that management's role is to tell people what to do and to control their activities, and use fear and censure rather than encouragement and reward, should not bother to try to introduce a review process before making a serious decision to move away from that culture. If they did try to use review without changing the culture, it would simply be seen as another way to allocate blame. On the other hand, for organizations whose basic assumptions about people are positive (e.g. they are intelligent, they wish to identify with the organization they work for, they wish to make a contribution and to develop themselves through their work), the review process becomes an essential and valued way of building a "learning organization". Of course, there are many intermediate positions between these two extremes, but the direction in which organizations should try to move is clear. Whatever the position today, progress can be started in the desired direction as long as the genuine will to change is present in the management.

Another lingering bad memory that could dissuade an organization from starting to implement review sessions is that of "sensitivity groups", which in the past were undertaken by organizations as a form of training. The experiences of some people who went on such events was negative and painful in a personal sense. However, we now understand much better why this was the case and how to avoid it.

There is a very simple rule that should be used in all work-related review sessions: "To undertake a review [Task 2] mainly when there is a clear Task 1 to be reviewed." If it is the case that task performance is being hindered by interpersonal relationships affecting the work climate, experience shows that in dealing with these by review it is important to consider them essentially within the context of the objectives and roles involved in Task 1. When dealing with deeper underlying problems, managers should try to solve them not by review but by face-to-face interaction or by asking for an outside consultant able to deal with both the psychodynamic and the organizational aspects of the reality.

Different levels of task review

An organization, be it small or large, can be regarded as a whole system. The organization will exist within a larger system of which it is part. It, in turn, will usually consist of a number of sub-systems that work together to fulfil its goals. Within each sub-system will exist individual activities that are the tasks that the sub-systems perform in order to make their contribution to the whole system. The primary task (Task 1) can be defined at any level within this hierarchy of nested systems. In an organization, the highest-level task, one of the tasks of the top management, is concerned with defining "mission, goals, and strategy". Similarly, deep within the organization in a sub-sub-system another activity such as the hygienic cleaning of a production line will also be a Task-1 activity. Because every task exists at some level in a nested series of systems, it will be taking place both as part of a larger system and may itself have sub-systems. The majority of tasks involve several people working on the task as a group. The group will have various characteristics, such as cost, reliability, resource demand, and speed. Any group working on a Task-1 activity should be regularly undertaking Task-2 review as a way of ensuring that the outcome of the task is optimal in the light of the whole system's goals and needs.

All tasks have a purpose, which should be contributing to the overall goals of the whole system in which the task takes place. The purpose of the task is some form of output, be that in the form of a product or a service. Many products and services have specifications that may be explicit or implicit; where specifications exist, the objective of the task is to create the products or services to the levels defined, or expected, by the customers of the task.

Because the Task-2 review of Task 1 should encompass all aspects of Task 1, Task-2 review should therefore include five different levels of consideration, as follows:

- *Whole system*: reviewing the appropriateness of the task with regard to the needs of the whole system of which it is a part. This can include an examination of whether the assumptions given at the outset of the task are still valid—for example, has there been a change in the external environment? It could also include an assessment of whether the task affects another part of the organization in a way that had not been foreseen at the outset of the task.

- *Work group*: reviewing how well the group is working together in order to accomplish Task 1. This can include whether the group has the right skills and competences available to do the task, and whether the roles of the people in the group are understood by everyone, whether communications within the group and between the group and the wider organization are being handled well enough.

- *Process design*: reviewing the process design and making necessary changes (mid-course corrections) where these are seen as appropriate, ensuring that creative and innovative approaches are being used so that better solutions are likely, keeping in touch with the external environment to see whether improved approaches are becoming available.

- *Quality of output*: reviewing the output of the group to check whether it is within the declared specifications or looks "good enough" against the group's experience, checking also that there have not been changes in the organization, or in its external environment, which might warrant a change in the targeted specifications.

- *Personal relationship with task*: considering whether each individual, in a group context or not, brings a unique relationship to the task, the group, the whole system, the output, and the customers. All of these have some effect on an individual's feelings and therefore on his or her disposition towards them, and it is desirable that the justification of these be checked from time to time. Furthermore, it should be remembered that personal learning and development is one of the potentially positive outputs from all work situations. This, too, will be maximized if the individual tries to give some conscious, dedicated time to reflect on and review the experiences gathered while working on the task.

In situations where project work is done by project teams, these factors will have been reviewed and defined at the outset of the project and will feature in the project brief. However, in the normal run of daily work in many organizations, such factors are not considered every time a new task is introduced but become part of the general assumptions of the organization. Institutionalizing the review process then ensures that all work in the organization will be managed in a better way.

Task-2 review involves considering all factors that will affect the achievement of the primary task. In reality, each factor has to be reviewed in the light of all the other factors. This means that one is constantly flicking from one frame of reference to another in order to get the full picture.

Requirements and limits of the review

Two difficult issues must now be raised in order to avoid being too emphatic about the merits of the review process. First, it needs a "safe" atmosphere; second, the process is limited by the extent of self-analysis that is possible among the participants. We will try now to develop these two points.

A secure atmosphere

No human beings or human systems can constructively look within themselves unless they can feel that they are on secure ground in one form or another. Indeed, the environment in which a review takes place must be reliable and give some protection during a kind of work that can sometimes feel dangerous. This protection will have two main characteristics:

- *"A search-for-sense" atmosphere.* This means that the primary objective of the review is not to make judgements but more to try to understand, and find meanings in, situations that are more or less confused. This is different from the problem-solving atmosphere that we find in the Task 1 of the double-task process. Let us not forget that the capacity for people to gain insights into situations and into themselves and to be able to make sense of them is a key element in the feeling of personal safety. Use of this capacity requires transitional space, or what Winnicott called an intermediate area of experiencing to which both inner reality and external life contribute.

• *A containing function.* Transitional space has a containing function that creates an atmosphere that is secure and enables a search for sense. What has to be contained? Mostly feelings of aggression, even destructiveness, against others, oneself, the task, and so on. Nevertheless, containing does not mean avoiding. Such feelings must be considered as normal and must be recognized and accepted in order to be able to be overcome. The failure of many meetings and of interpersonal relations often comes from the too rapid repression of such normal feelings. It is the ability to cope with these "negative" feelings that allows one to go deeper into the review process. Managers therefore need to be able to accept such feelings and to make the best "use" of them both for the people and for the tasks in their charge. Those who are able to do this are generally accustomed to self-reviews, which help them to avoid projective and other defensive mechanisms. That is why they are commonly recognized as the best helpers in difficult job or interpersonal situations.

Self-analysis

Whatever the quality of the participants, a difficult question remains: is self-analysis really possible? Either individually or collectively, a self-analytic process is inevitably limited both by unconscious factors and by power issues.

The *unconscious obstacles* are inevitable as long as we accept the existence of the unconscious psychic life (Amado, 1979, 1991). Ambivalent feelings, and rationalization and denial defence mechanisms, are likely to be present in any kind of individual or group review dealing with tasks and outputs. Other unconscious mechanisms may also operate but go unrecognized and not be dealt with by people, even if they are mentally prepared to be good and honest reviewers. These include the basic assumptions (fight–flight, dependency, pairing) described by Bion (1959), group illusion and splitting anxieties (Anzieu, 1984), defensive call for leadership (Bejarano, 1972) or ideology (Kaës, 1971), and projective identification and transference processes of all kinds.

To be in and out is a very difficult task. The best access to the unconscious is the method of free association that Freud invented for psychoanalytic treatment. In a work setting of everyday life, the nearest one can get to this is to allow one's own feelings and thoughts to surge into consciousness from the "back of the mind", to be open to them, make space for them. They should be welcomed as a source of further sense-making, as pointers towards latent realities; and diffuse attention should be allowed to spread evenly to all these resurgences before rushing to conclusions, letting them, rather, fall gradually into place and connecting them into a pattern that makes sense.

The *power issues* are the second difficult obstacle to overcome. These are more or less present in any group review within an organizational setting. The free expression of feelings can be seriously inhibited by the presence of various hierarchical levels in the group or by career aspirations and fears. As we mentioned elsewhere (Amado, 1985), the members of an organization very often fear a strategic use of the truth against themselves. Crozier and Friedberg (1977) explain how such an anticipation is legitimate in bureaucratized organizations where people tend to use any kind of "uncertainty area" both to maximize their own power and to protect themselves against impersonal rules. "Information is power" is a key proverb in those organizations. To keep information private would then be a very "rational" way of behaving. When this happens, one can very easily imagine the difficulty of any kind of review process.

Are these two obstacles too difficult to be overcome? A main reason for being optimistic lies in the relation with the task. As we said earlier, the presence of clear objectives and well-defined roles (unlike in "pure" group-dynamics experiences) creates a vital necessity for review. When this necessity is widely appreciated within an organization, it becomes sensible for the management to support it by providing training in the review process for groups and key individuals so that they can both steer it in constructive directions and help to make the experience fruitful for all participants. Such training will also enhance the participants' understanding of people, groups, and organizational dynamics. Nevertheless, the call for an outside consultant may become a necessity from time to time, to avoid people getting too immersed in their own idiosyncrasies and during critical periods when the sense of safety and understanding are low.

Finally, all these aspects of the review process show the increasing complexity of the manager's role. More and more, the manager requires psychological and social skills if she or he wishes to build a creative organization. But the increasing willingness to pay attention to those skills must not lead to overemphasis on the search for meaning. Just as action can be a defence against insight, so review can become a defence against action. The right balance has to be found, and this is the real art of being a manager.

CHAPTER FIVE

The working conference design

Harold Bridger

The background

Origins

The approach to management training and development to be reported in this chapter rests on a different premise from the purely group dynamics foundation of the study groups of the Leicester model or the T-group tradition of the National Training Laboratories (NTL) in the United States. In both of these traditions, groups concerned with the internal task of self-study and review are given no external task. My own experience, however, has convinced me that in organizational settings the internal task is best undertaken in conjunction with an external task. I have therefore called my approach the double-task model.

This chapter is a revised version of Harold Bridger's chapter, "Courses and Working Conferences as Transitional Learning Institutions", in E. Trist & H. Murray, *The Social Engagement of Social Science. A Tavistock Anthology, Vol. I: The Socio-Psychological Perspective*, The University of Pennsylvania Press, Philadelphia, 1990, and is reproduced by permission of the publisher.

In a note on study groups in the review of the first Leicester Conference (Trist & Sofer, 1959), J. D. Sutherland, the then Director of the Tavistock Clinic, who had himself taken a study group, stated:

The special social situation which experience shows most useful for this purpose consists in having a group meet without the "external" task to be done, but with the specific task of examining the kinds of feelings and attitudes that arise spontaneously, these feelings and attitudes being those which each individual brings to any group situation, or which develop within it independently of whatever the external task may be.

In the follow-up of that conference some six months later, it became apparent that most members of the helping, educational, and social professions had found study-group experience relevant and useful, both personally and professionally. By contrast, most of those concerned with organizational and operational affairs had not found it of value in their back-home situations. Indeed, it created a barrier.

The account of the follow-up meeting quotes me as drawing "a further parallel with the training work being done by the Tavistock Institute in industry, where there was no attempt to turn groups into study groups". The method was to develop insight during the course of working through existing problems.

In organizational projects as early as 1947, I had introduced the procedure of "suspending the agenda" in executive meetings when no progress was being made with the task in hand. This allowed the group to review and reflect on the emotional and conflictual elements that were impeding its progress. In the Glacier project, Jaques (1951) gave up using extra-curricular sessions and relied solely on making interpretative comments in the working sessions of executive or union meetings.

My thinking at that time, and indeed since, has been much influenced by my experience, during the war, as a social therapist at Northfield Military Psychiatric Hospital. The activity groups I created influenced material brought into clinical groups in a positive way as regards therapeutic outcome. The two groups became interlocked and were often, with advantage, the same group in different modes. This interconnection expressed the double task in action.

Shortly after Bion started therapy groups in the Tavistock Clinic in 1945, he gave an extended trial of his method of group-centred interpretation in training groups outside the medical area. One of these consisted of industrial managers, others of people from the educational field. These groups did not fare well. It seemed that a number of the participants were patients in disguise. We thought that it was best to remove this disguise and have the patients admit that they were seeking psychiatric treatment and should therefore be in a therapy group.

In 1946 in Nottingham, under the auspices of the Industrial Welfare Society, the Institute held an exploratory residential conference using Bion's methods. The participants were fairly high-ranking managers from a number of industries. The conference generated such stress that a distinguished member perforated an ulcer. He condemned the conference publicly. This episode had a decidedly chastening effect. Even carefully picked people in industry were not ready for anything of the study or T-group type. Our frontal approach had been a mistake. No more groups outside the medical area were attempted for another ten years, though psychodynamic projects continued and flourished in organizational settings. A seeming exception was a discussion group in the field of teacher training which worked on material provided by the members. This led to their undertaking a project: the production of a report on their proceedings to communicate their group experience to their profession (Herbert & Trist, 1953).

In 1956, four senior people with NTL backgrounds were invited by the European Productivity Agency to make trials of NTL procedures in European countries. These trials were, on the whole, successful, and the Tavistock was approached to work out a design suitable for British conditions. This was how the first Leicester conference originated in 1957—as an experimental endeavour to discover a form of experiential learning acceptable in the United Kingdom.

To make clear that this was not a therapeutic endeavour, the Institute created the conference as a joint venture with the Education Department of a university, the link with education being similar to that made by NTL with the National Education Association. Like NTL, again, we had application groups and theory sessions as well as the study groups, which were our own version of T-groups. Moreover, participants came through a sociological channel; they were nominated by organizations, though the decision whether or not to come was personal. To make relations with the Leicester community, we introduced external operational tasks in which participants engaged with local organizations (e.g. industrial firms, the police, hospitals, and local government) in exploring some specific problem or issue that was of current concern to them. The conference was successful in that no one came to harm, the patient-in-disguise phenomenon was stopped, the shadow of Nottingham was removed, and a relationship with society was made.

On behalf of the Institute, I spent the next summer at NTL, in Bethel, Maine, to make a thorough study of their methods. These summer "labs", as they were called, contained a great variety of activities based on experiential learning, which had established itself as an accepted educational innovation. Nevertheless, and despite the overall success of Leicester, I was still disquieted about T-groups and study groups. It seemed to me that the idea of a group of participants with the task of "learning about groups by being a group" meets Bion and Rickman's (1943) conditions for the "study of its own internal tensions" only when the participants are patients prepared to join such a group with the expectation of "getting better". Then the real-life task of the group is for the patients "to get well". It did not seem to me that there was a compelling real task in the non-patient groups that I had experienced. Since this time, movements such as the human-potential movement emerging from the Esalen Institute, particularly from the influence of Abraham Maslow, have produced groups outside the medical area with a strong commitment to self-study, but such groups are therapeutic or quasi-therapeutic in aim.

Bion's original formulation had emphasized the need for the group's situation to be a real-life one—that is, an action situation. I therefore thought that a suitable real-life situation had to be found for non-medical groups whose members, such as managers, carried out organizational roles. Such a situation might be found if one could discover a way of working with participants in which they could bring into the group problems and concerns arising in their organizational settings. This way of working would entail creating circumstances in which they could recognize and pursue what I have called the double task.

An organization theory basis

In his book *Leadership in Administration*, Selznick (1957) distinguishes between concepts of organization and institution:

> The term organisation suggests ... a system of consciously co-ordinated activities. ... It refers to a rational instrument engi-

neered to do a job. . . . It has a formal system of rules and objectives. Tasks, powers, procedures are set out according to some officially approved pattern.

An institution, on the other hand, is more nearly a natural product of social needs and pressures—a responsive, adaptive organism.

This does not mean that any given enterprise must be either one or the other. While an extreme case may closely approach either an "ideal" organisation or an "ideal" institution, most living associations . . . are complex mixtures of both designed and responsive behaviour.

The process of adapting, of projecting and internalizing, of learning and acting, unconsciously as well as consciously, is the institutional characteristic. For convenience and in deference to present-day usage of "organization" in both senses, the term "organization" will, predominantly, be used.

The organization is an open system with regard to its environment and is both "purpose-oriented" and "learning- and self-reviewing." The capability of carrying out this double task at appropriate times, and in the course of normal working when relevant, is becoming an essential feature in interdependent multidisciplinary work forces.

The more rapid change rate has created a situation of far greater complexity, interdependence, and uncertainty than organizations have previously encountered. Emery and Trist (1965, 1973) have called this situation the "turbulent environment". More initiative is now required of managers, more innovative capability, more flexibility and more recognition of the need to cooperate. Greater understanding of group life at all levels is needed in order more effectively to manage transitions of one kind or another, which are occurring with much greater frequency (Bridger, 1987b).

Internal courses:
the opportunity in Philips Electrical

About this time in the early 1960s the Institute divided into two operating groups, one of which undertook the further development of the Leicester model (Rice, 1965), while the other, to which I belonged, was interested in the double-task approach. It is scarcely accidental that the opportunity required to pursue this arose in an industrial setting with a company beset with problems of increased uncertainty, complexity, and interdependence. The company in question was the British affiliate of Philips, the multinational electronics firm, in itself a very large organization. To meet the challenge of the new conditions, senior management took time out for self-review. As the result of a week's off-site conference, they gave priority to Staff Development.

An immediate job was to develop training designs relevant to the new managerial competences (cf. Morgan, 1988). They were called Practice of Management courses (PMCs) and required attention to process as well as to content. If the attendance was to be secured of the bulk of the most relevant managers for the kind of course contemplated, this could be no longer than a week. The aim was to produce a scheme that would permit extensive use.

Each facet of a pilot course was to be concerned with "managing groups at work", which entailed *understanding* the dynamics of such groups—hence the need to appreciate the role of informal systems and other processes affecting groups as operating entities. The *consultative* aspects of management were becoming increasingly significant, whether for more sophisticated and satisfying appraisal methods and career development, or for reaching the most effective outcome with a work force. I came to see the consultative process as a "basic building block" in the development of a group as well as an important element in its own right within any training scheme for organizational effectiveness (Bridger, 1980b).

The study group became a work group, but with a double task:

- The group had to work on selected issues of importance for group members in their organizational settings and in their roles. It was to manage its own selection of topics and to manage itself. It implicitly posed to itself the problem—and the challenge—of being able to face internal differentiation, thereby enabling leadership and other capabilities to be demonstrated according to the pertinent circumstances.

- The group had to identify the processes operating within it at different times, especially the way the group as a whole, with its particular set of values and norms, was influencing events and modes of working.

An "intergroup" experience (Higgin & Bridger, 1964) could be offered in a variety of forms, but in early models it consisted of an interim review of the course about two-thirds of the way through the week. Each work group would review the experience thus far and prepare recommendations for amending the remainder of the proposed programme so as to meet better the original or changed expectations of members. In addition, each group was to select an appropriate group member (or two) to represent it at a meeting with the staff representative and jointly make some proposals.

"Talk-discussions", which gave a conceptual framework to the experience, were placed at points when they were most likely to be relevant.

The placing and interlocking of these aspects, together with transitions for entry and departure, were carefully thought through to ensure that both the real-life situation and the study processes were operating for each component as well as for the whole. The course itself was regarded as a process consisting of three phases: pre-course, the residential week, and post-course.

The procedure described in what follows represents the mature model that evolved after extensive trials when the demand for a large number of courses had been created. It is based on my joint paper with one of the internal consultants (Low & Bridger, 1979).

Pre-course phase

The pre-course phase consists of two operations. In one, nominations are submitted from constituent parts of the company of those managers who wish to attend. Invitations are sent by the Management Development Adviser (MDA), setting out the purpose and indicating prior work to be done. In the other, the MDA appoints the course staff, and meetings between them are subsequently held two or three weeks before the residential phase.

Nomination and method of invitation

Each participant attends voluntarily. He or she is free to withdraw at any stage. Invitations are sent on the basis that each participant

- has within the scope of his or her management function sufficient opportunity to influence change in methods of working;
- has the motivation to undertake fresh approaches to work and to explore problems without preconceptions;
- is resilient enough to absorb conflicting pressures and to react with sensitivity.

The description of the course states its purpose as follows:

"These courses ... are designed to enable managers to gain, through participation in group exercises and discussions, a fresh insight into management and to derive general principles and practice from particular experiences. The content emerges from members' interests. No attempt is made to teach hard and fast techniques but rather to encourage learning by participation in joint work, aided by the presentation of theoretical concepts."

The phrasing indicates the duality of task: that through a discussion of management topics that are both valid and real, insight can be gained not only about the content of such issues, but about the processes of group activity.

The nominees are asked to bring, for discussion by heterogeneous work groups of which they will be members, subjects important to them in their roles as managers. In addition, they are asked to formulate a specific problem from their own managerial experience which can be discussed in detail within the homogeneous common-interest group of which they will also be members.

Staff selection and staff meetings

The responsibility for inviting people to take part as staff members in the PMCs rests with the MDA, assisted in this task by the Tavistock consultant. The increased numbers of courses has obliged the MDA to create a network of staff assistants. The criteria for inclusion are

- a capacity to understand the motivation of people at work in groups;
- sensitivity to individual and group behaviour;
- organizational roles that have credibility in a professional sense;

- support from managers to do consultant work, whether with training or with operational groups;
- experience as a participant in a PMC.

To avoid any feeling that participants are undergoing a selection process for becoming trainee consultants, individuals are encouraged, on later reflection about the course and its impact on them, to appraise themselves. In this way the initiative can be left with the individual to state whether a consultant role of this type is appealing. The invitation, ultimately, still remains within the prerogative of the MDA, following discussions with the individual.

As group work is a crucial element within the total course design, care is taken in the assignment of individual staff consultants to each group. Unnecessary inhibitions to learning are avoided by ensuring that no staff member has too close a personal or work relationship with any member of his or her group. Although an experienced consultant can work singly with a group of some eight or nine participant managers, it has been found advantageous to have two staff members with each group. Sometimes these are people of equal experience, in which case they work as co-trainers, but more frequently one is a trainee.

Staff meetings are held before the course assembles, and they have a dual purpose—in content terms, to determine the framework for the week's programme; in process terms, to become acquainted with one another, to understand different roles, to recognize overtly the relevance of talent within the staff group, and to agree how the work will be shared between staff members.

From the start, the differences are made clear between teaching and administrative roles. Course members will best understand the importance of role clarity in groups if the staff themselves have made a conscious effort to distinguish their own roles.

The residential phase

First plenary session

At the first plenary session the staff allows time for questions, however trivial these may seem, without creating an undue sense that time is an expendable commodity. The session attempts to be administratively brisk and to explain the rationale of the course design and the roles of the staff. Nevertheless, there is bound to exist, to a certain degree, a sense that participants are the victims of manipulative or even devious stratagems. With the best will in the world, and despite protestations to the contrary, the staff may fail to convince them that such is not their intention.

The course is frequently described as unstructured, not because a basic framework is lacking, but because it starts from the learners' questions, rather than from the teachers' answers. Exploration of problems about managing, about group behaviour, begins with discussion between participants, so that their differing or similar experiences may be brought into the open, before any inferences about behaviour in general can be drawn.

Homogeneous common-interest groups

The next stage consists of initial brief exchanges between members with a common interest—that is, in a homogeneous group.

These are trios or quartets, consisting of managers with similar roles or functions who can explore their own problems and communicate with each other in a familiar language. No staff member is present at this stage, which immediately follows the introductory plenary meeting, unless a group requests clarification. The group's task is to formulate an agenda relevant to some common interest that each member can take to his or her search group. They meet again at later stages for different purposes.

Heterogeneous search groups

At the core of the design are heterogeneous search groups of nine managers, which have the task of understanding how content and process are interdependent in achieving group objectives. (The idea of cognitive search was introduced by Wertheimer, 1945, and developed by Fred and Merrelyn Emery, 1978, at the social level for the purposes of search conferences.) The first of the heterogeneous group periods takes place once there has been an opportunity to share, in a further plenary meeting, the variety of managerial problems that participants have begun to discuss with each other. They now find themselves members of a group with mixed, perhaps conflicting, interests.

Thus at this stage the design has already established a replica of institutional life. The members belong to one group where they speak a recognized language; to another, where they must try to understand the language of others whose ideas and backgrounds are unfamiliar; and to a total organization, represented by a plenary meeting where all participants come together to deal with matters affecting their inter-group requirements.

Alternation of consultation and search groups

For the next two days the common-interest groups (renamed consultative groups) and the heterogeneous groups (renamed search groups) function alternatively. The task of the former is now concerned with learning about the giving and taking of advice between colleagues; the role of the second, to undertake free exploration of problems and issues. By reason of this alternation, course members experience, in a temporary system, the conflict of interest that flows from simultaneous membership in distinct groups, and they learn to sustain the two-way stretch to which they are subjected. It will be the function of the staff to observe and interpret in relation to the processes involved in managing groups exactly how these different aspects of the week's course develop. The content by means of which such awareness develops is represented by the members' own agendas, brought from their trios and quartets to the search groups.

Theory session: the nature of groups

Now that each group has had some experience of handling its own discussions, a plenary period is inserted which takes the form of a theory presentation by a staff member about "The Nature of Groups". Experiences in working groups, however frustrating or uncertain their nature, precede any attempt to draw together more general concepts about groups. The structure is a reflection of the wish to proceed from the known to the unknown. It supports learning by discovery. The expectation is (and experience bears this out) that the participants will relate this talk about groups in general to their own developing perceptions about what is taking place in their own groups.

Thus, about one-third of the way through the course, at the very point where members are feeling that they are lost, that the staff process observations are merely intrusive, unhelpful remarks (not germane to the content discussions), and that confusion is a dominant note, an attempt is made through the plenary presentation to enable them to see their experiences against a fresh set of concepts. There are usually feelings of manipulation, however, as if the course staff have been keeping these revelations up their sleeve.

Inter-group exchange

Not only does the course aim to provide opportunities to look at small groups, it is also concerned—because management involves such experiences—with examining what happens when groups try to work to communicate with each other. About mid-way through the week, therefore, the search groups have the opportunity to share their experiences to date, by means of an inter-group exchange. Two members from each group describe and discuss with each other their separate views of what has occurred in their respective groups. This is arranged as a "fish-bowl" exercise, in which representatives of groups are observed by the colleagues who have chosen them. Members have the chance to evaluate what happens when representatives are faced with conflicting feelings—loyalty to one group yet a desire to understand the attitudes of people from another. The criteria for choice of representatives are also reviewed.

Review and field force analysis

Underlying the initial attempts to create this type of course is a belief in the value of "suspending business" for effecting a review of organizational life. Participants have the opportunity to look back at what has been happening, to make proposals about what might happen, and to come to jointly agreed decisions about what will best suit the future needs of the course as a total institution. A method for doing this is field force analysis (Lewin, 1951), by use of which managers produce maps of those forces that assist and those that detract from the course objectives. It is a method that course members can use back home. This review affords an occasion to examine, with staff feedback, just how course members are proceeding with this task of managing their own temporary institution. They look at the forces—internal and external, such as competitive pressures and drives—that make up group life. The rational, logical aspects of decision-making are seen to be tempered by the irrational. It is at this stage, when awareness of process has been acknowledged, however uncertainly put into words, that the members of each consulting and search group can examine their own group's process and expect to find parallels between them and those in groups in their sponsoring organization. The group discussions towards the latter part of the week focus on the group's own processes and dynamics. The consultant has opportunities to engage with group members about process, even to make, where appropriate, brief statements about organization theory. Papers brought to the course are best received if introduced when members can gain knowledge from them relative to points arising from the course experience itself.

Final stages

The final stages of the residential phase prepare members for return to their organizations. So the trios and quartets are reconstituted and meet immediately prior to the brief plenary session with which the course concludes. Members recall their first uncertain, tentative group meetings and attempt to relate the intervening experience to the pressing tasks they will face beyond the confines of the course. As with a vacation, the descriptions to others not present of an experience not shared is likely to prove frustrating. How does one relate again to colleagues who will be incapable of receiving with comprehension and sympathy one's inability to interpret the significance of the week's events?

The ensuing plenary session when participants and staff alike reconvene from their homogeneous groups—for consultants and observers, too, can benefit from a pause to consider jointly the future against the background of the course—is not an occasion for further public review of the groups' process. The need for business now outweighs the need for any suspension of business. On occasions, the staff find themselves giving a lead on content, while participants, reversing the usual roles, seem to be more concerned with process.

A practical task is provided by a brief discussion of the interim plans for a follow-up meeting (say, after six months) with the need to make arrangements, to coordinate dates, to consult diaries—in fact, to think immediately of that external world to which everyone now must return. Course participants, having shared in a learning experience about membership in, and management of, small groups, are about to take on more familiar roles again. And so they leave the course, as they joined it, as accountants, engineers, production managers, personnel officers and marketing managers.

Post-course phase

The objectives in providing an occasion for course members to reconvene six months or so later are:

- to evaluate the course's relevance to the roles and functions that people will have taken up again;
- to reappraise one's own performance at work and the feelings about one's career development in the light of the course;
- to discover the organizational issues raised as a result of attempting to relate "group dynamics" to problems at work.

The members and staff come back to the same conference centre for a period of two and a half days. The temptation for the staff to concentrate on process comments to the exclusion of any involvement in the content to be examined has to be resisted. This brief follow-up looks back while still continuing to look forward—what is the relevance of group dynamics to problems at work? Staff and members alike share their experiences. After resuming through work groups—and thereby meeting the need to enjoy a reunion—the course members focus attention on special areas of interest. Case studies of organizational problems are carried out, frequently by new groupings made up of people who now have a new common interest. Whether individuals wish to discuss with others the self-appraisals carried out as arranged before coming to the follow-up session is left to them to decide.

The points raised relate to questions of organizational complexity back at work. Thus the relevance to this complexity—familiar and perhaps inevitable in any large multifunctional enterprise—of the

Practice of Management is considered. This leads to work between course members, between members and staff, and between members of different and separate courses, in what may generally be described as "organizational development".

The consultant's role and functions

As these courses proceeded, features of the consultant's role emerged that may be regarded as general for all courses and workshops of this kind. I shall now review these.

Staff consulting roles

Staff roles, like course design, are conceived as enabling resources; in addition to the importance of what a staff member does is the way in which it is done. He or she takes different roles at different stages and in different situations: in the early trios and quartets, to clarify; in the search group, to be an adviser who listens and gives feedback; in seminar activities, to reinforce learning; in the small consultative groups, to observe and coordinate. By differentiating between these roles from the start, the consultant can show the relationship between role clarity and organizational effectiveness.

The point of a consultant's intervention in the early stages is often not perceived, as the group does not yet understand process. It finds difficulty in reconciling the consultant's process comments with its own interests in optimizing task objectives.

The consultant does not refuse to answer relevant questions (i.e. those consistent with the role) but, if asked a question about content (e.g. what is your opinion about the influence of trade unions in industry on the authority of management?), may indicate why, at that moment, the group wishes the consultant to take over their task rather than carry it out themselves.

One way in which a group may cope with uncertainty is to establish a familiar structure, which often means appointing a chairperson and perhaps a secretary. There may be opposition, often unvoiced, to these moves. The consultant notes it for future reference when opposition becomes overt—usually in some rationalized form. Intervention is then designed to produce a realization that a particular structure or procedural form is not a general solution to difficulties of operational functioning. The experience can help later to determine when such a structure or procedure should realistically be brought into play. The timing of interventions is crucial—an opportunity for intervening not taken may not recur. Usually, however, the dynamics of the group behaviour are repeated, though in another or disguised form.

In the later stages, the consultant has to exercise self-discipline, through recognizing the group's own growth in learning potential, so as not to intervene in the same way throughout but allow participants to try their hand on process comment whenever they are ready to do so.

The consultant's relationship to the group

In the early stages, a consultant is liable to be the target for hostile feelings, overt or covert, because a group perceives him or her as having failed to help or lead the group. As time progresses, group members begin to distinguish between manipulating others, being manipulated, and feeling that one is being manipulated. The theme of manipulation itself often becomes a means of learning about integrity and about recognizing when one is either obliged or can choose to conform with certain circumstances. Two forces are usually involved—the urge to get on with the job in hand and the effort to provoke the consultant into "coming clean"—and there are often others.

Later in the process, the group is apt to show frustration over failure to achieve goals in content; it may want its own survival as its aim, or be reluctant to "jell" because it would become too "cosy". In various crises such as these, the group's sense of aggravation may be turned on the consultant for failure to help.

The consultant must understand and learn how best to help the group in these circumstances—for instance, by suspending business to examine those factors that are determining the group's actions. Concentrating on roles ensures that the consultant is seen to be concerned only with group development and not with judgements about individual behaviour. Individuals will be learning about, as well as from, each other and may begin to explore individual aspects; the consultant, however, refers to individuals and their behaviour only insofar as it contributes to the group's process task.

One specific phenomenon usually occurs about a third of the way through the course and is associated with the underlying wish of the group as to the level of learning with which it will proceed. Critical is the group's discovery that the way forward lies in giving reflection on its own behaviour as prominent a place as task achievement. Once this shift is recognized, the consultant can assume that the group is joining him or her and beginning to show a capacity to share in the second task of looking at process as well as content. Soon afterwards, the group sometimes refers to the consultant's having become a "member".

A consultant must "earn the right to be trusted"

A consultant may wish to take notes to help remember incidents in the development of the work group. The group is likely to suspect that the notes are for other ulterior purposes, usually because of past association with authority figures displaying judgemental attitudes. No consultant can expect to be trusted as of right, but has to earn trust. Only through consistency of role, and certainly not just through the use of "techniques", will the trust of participants develop. Trust itself will come to be recognized as a process, not a state. Once, however, a "good-enough" shared experience has developed, a slip out of role by the consultant may be forgiven (or may even lead to being seen as human after all), but basic discrepancies can have most damaging effects. A consultant (or manager) may grossly underestimate the penetrating and subtle sense of the "music behind the words" which groups use at all times.

Findings derived from review of course experience

Anyone who feels it desirable to do this type of work places a high value on it. One should, therefore, be wary of believing that an experience of learning from the here-and-now will be valued by everybody. The following factors influence attitude:

- Commitment to the course objectives by an individual participant, coupled with a willingness to explore, produce a positive attitude to learning.

- An individual who feels that he or she has been sent for some vaguely therapeutic purpose will build resistance to what is seen as an intrusive threat.

- An individual whose own manager is half-hearted or highly sceptical will tend to deny the value of the experience, whatever he or she may personally feel about the method of learning.

- Where a staff member displays, however unconsciously, his or her own uncertainty or anxiety about self, career, or competence, this attitude transfers itself to the participants. They will display anxiety and even aggression towards the staff member and the course in general.

- If a sponsoring manager's behaviour belies his or her words, which may in appearance only support open-ended learning, the subordinate is liable to be guarded in his or her own behaviour.

- No application of learning from experience is possible in any organizational setting that exclusively rewards conformist "safe" behaviour.

To take these points into account, membership of the course is controlled by the criteria for inclusion set out by the MDA.

Naturally, it is not possible to guarantee that course members will be paragons of influence, resilience, and sensitivity. What is essential is that people, with a positive rather than a negative approach, be encouraged to test themselves out in the temporary system of the course environment, provided that they receive "back-home" support for their efforts.

Evaluation

In the early courses, participants completed questionnaires on their attitudes and assumptions about management behaviour. Questions based on concepts of motivation, by such writers as McGregor (1960) and Herzberg (1966), were answered prior to, during, and at the conclusion of the course. The purpose was to help participants examine any significant behavioural change deriving from their learning experiences. However, the anxiety of the course staff to prove the relevance of the training was greater than the participants' need to learn. The process of collecting and comparing the data took an undue emphasis, which interfered with the development of course activity and hindered the consultants in their principal task. Questionnaires are still occasionally used—for example, as a means of introducing a theory session. However, no formal evaluation of the courses is conducted by questionnaire. Currently, however, an attempt is being made to assess their value by means of a survey conducted with all previous participants who have assisted in the preparation of the survey material.

Because of the obvious difficulty, given the number of variables that can affect individual and group behaviour in any organization, no attempt to quantify the value of the courses has been made. Significant outcomes, however, are that individuals have been able to evaluate their careers in the light of their course experience. Training managers have been able to respond to the wishes of their organizations to adopt a more open appraisal method. The need to do so arose from conversations about how relevant the learning was to factories, laboratories, and commercial offices. A number of management teams, including the executive boards of two subsidiary companies, have asked for assistance from training staff in order to carry out reviews of their group's effectiveness, in the same way that work groups suspend their business in the courses. One factory, a number of managers of which have attended the course and whose subordinates have similarly attended off-plant training exercises, has, through its director's initiative, set up project groups comprising people of different disciplines and functions to examine specific problems. Other parts of the company have reviewed the relationship between their objectives and their methods of work through residential conferences. As a result, they have effected their own changes.

Now that many seeds have been sown, the future emphasis in PMCs will be on training the trainers. The recognition of the role that a staff member can take creatively as consultant has brought new demands. It is not the intention to overlay the organization as a whole with courses in behavioural skills, but to increase the possibility of learning from real work groups, whether these be at boardroom level or on the shop floor.

External workshops

The courses in Philips became woven into the texture of the organization. The model was taken up by several other comparable companies. Then a demand for external courses arose in which people from different organizations could meet together and have the advantage of even greater diversity of experience, though internal preparation and follow-up could not be equivalently intensive. These workshops I have come to call Tavistock Working Conferences (TWCs). Efforts are made to ensure that the firms sending participants are supportive of experiential learning and that the interest of the participant is authentic. Preferably, two people come from any one organization.

For a number of years, TWCs have been held at least annually, first in conjunction with Bath University, then at the conference centre of the Foundation for Adaptation in Changing Environments at Minster Lovell, near Oxford. For many years, also, TWCs have been a feature of NTL's summer programme in Bethel, Maine. They have also been held on the European continent with Hautes Études Commerciales School of Management in Jouy-en-Josas (France) and the Bayswater Institute in London. The composition of the membership tends to be highly international.

The socio-ecological setting for double-task management

The accelerating rate of change in social, educational, technological, economic, and other fields—and, above all, the way these changes interact—has forced communities, organizations, and individuals to seek a greater understanding of what is going on within and around them. In learning to cope with the various environments affecting them, all organizations have had to become more open to their environments. In so doing, they become more exposed and vulnerable.

Staff specialities of many kinds have been introduced to help regulate open boundaries. There is increasing emphasis on consultation and on collaborative modes that manage both external and internal complexity under conditions of greater interdependence.

Just when the need has become greater for collaboration and interdependence, the contradictory tendency to fall back on familiar competencies and structures has asserted itself. This paradox is a more complex issue than just resistance to change. Dealing with it involves acquiring a capability for recognizing and relinquishing valued but outmoded forms of working, while at the same time using insight to face tendencies towards rivalry and envy which accompany a greater emphasis on interdependence.

In the highly charged environment of today, it is easier to acknowledge such a principle than to act on it. The exploration of options arouses pain, stress, or impatience and can result in simplistic rationalizations. This will especially be so when change involves unlearning earlier-held values and ways of thinking and acting. In the process of unlearning, those concerned must find within themselves a readiness and capability to understand and work through both conscious and unrecognized attitudes and preconceptions. These are most usefully identified and explored through the experience of examining the ways by which a system is planned, regulated, and managed. Working through experiences of this kind has become a *sine qua non* for those who have to live and work in complex and uncertain environments.

New forms of organizational design do not inevitably result in happier or easier solutions, but, rather, in a different set of prices and costs, which are often a source of disillusion if their implications are not anticipated. We need to find ways of creating catalytic experiences that provide all concerned with the opportunity to unlearn old approaches and build new ones. Organizations need to develop institutional resources, both personal and organizational, for maintaining and reviewing the new state and for ensuring continuous commitment to it.

Most organizations have been managed in a form whereby the pattern of authority was clear-cut and hierarchical. The environment exercised a much smaller influence: government intervened to a smaller degree; unions had less impact; change was recognizable but less turbulent. Schools maintained their "monastic" walls; hospitals were powers unto themselves, as were the professions and universities. Today, government intervenes increasingly. Unions, consumers, competitors, and suppliers clamour for attention. The technological explosion and other forms of social, international, and economic change impinge on all institutions. Originally, few advisers were required internally. To help interpret and cope with growing external problems—with all their internal derivatives—far more specialists are now employed. This means that management, both now and for the future, must reconcile institutional needs and environmental forces to a much greater extent than ever before.

This is a tremendous change. Not only does one spend much of one's time and effort considering external affairs, there is the need for continuously re-educating professionals, specialist advisers, and managers to ensure the viability of the enterprise.

The model of a relatively closed system is being replaced by a relatively open one (Bridger, 1980a). Subordinates manage their own environment to a greater extent. We have to learn to change from the classic family-tree type of organizational structure and authority to a new form of boundary management: the management of external uncertainty and internal interdependence. Continuing this process means that erstwhile subordinates become colleagues whose commitment is required to share the accountable leader's efforts at achieving group objectives. This development can be regarded as an operational definition of participation, which differs from an older pattern of delegating tasks by separating-off defined areas of work. Thus, the management of complexity and interdependence is more important for today and tomorrow than are the simpler prescriptions for leadership and management on which we have been brought up. The open-system model includes the special feature of a greater network component to fulfil the control and coordination function.

The key organizational areas of competence—such as control and coordination, planning, decision-making, and action—demand that institutional needs and tasks, and environmental forces and resources, be reconciled to a much greater extent than ever before. What we have called the "accountable authority" has had to develop ways of working that differ from those appropriate for the earlier model. Some of these changes will show a difference in degree, others will be different in kind. For example, giving and taking advice was a *desirable* characteristic of closed-system managing; it is *essential* in open systems. In a closed system, subordinates are more concerned about minding their own share of the "business"; in open systems, they manage their own environment to a much greater extent—throughout the organization—while relinquishing (as do their superiors) relevant control of planning, decisions, and actions for levels below them. Thus, the range of organizational forms has widened considerably from an almost exclusive concentration of the classic family-tree type of organizational structure to various combinations of the first and second models.

TABLE 5.1.   Changes in Roles and Functions

Changes from relatively closed system	Changes towards relatively open system
Control and coordination retained in the superior managerial role.	Control and coordination retained in superior role for policy, but shared with relevant staff for operational goals.
Prescriptive tasks for subordinates with some delegated authority.	Decision-making and discretion devolved to relevant staff when responsible for the action involved (i.e., executive and consultative mode).
Managing mostly within the confines of the system.	Managing at the boundary (i.e. reconciling external and internal resources and forces).
Allocation of jobs to persons and "knowing one's place".	More interdependence in working groups, but more anxiety about one's identity and independence.
Managing to eliminate conflict.	Managing the conflict by exploring its nature together.
Accountability and responsibility located together.	Accountability and responsibility may be separate.
Single accountability.	Multiple accountability.
Hierarchical assessment and appraisal (often uncommunicated).	Self-review and assessment plus mutual appraisal of performance and potential.
Career and personal development dependent on authority.	Mobility of careers and boundary-crossing for development; greater responsibility for own development.
Power rests with those occupying certain roles and having high status in hierarchy.	Power rests with those having control over uncertainty.
Finite data and resources utilized towards building a plan.	Non-finite data and resources leading towards a planning process; maintaining a choice of direction in deciding among options.
Periodic review and tendency to extrapolate (projection forward).	Control and planning requiring continuous review; prospection as well as projection forward.
Risk related to an information gap.	Risk related to information overload.
Long term/short term based on operational plans (periodic).	Long term/short term based on continuous adaptive planning process.
Concentrating on "getting on with the job" and "trouble-shooting" activities.	"Suspending business" at relevant times to explore work systems and ways of working.
Difficulty with "equality" and "freedom".	Difficulty with "fraternity".

A set of critical changes involved in moving from a relatively closed to a relatively open system is set out in Table 5.1. These changes are of such magnitude that they constitute a paradigm shift. The internal courses and external workshops described in this chapter have been designed to assist organizations in making this shift. They will do so only so far as large numbers of individuals within them make it in themselves.

Training in a form that models the new needs can accelerate the change process. In my view, training of the appropriate kind is an essential requirement for making the transition. For such a purpose, it needs first of all to be jointly worked out by all concerned. It then has to be capable of rapid diffusion and ultimately to be carried out without consultants. There is not all the time in the world to get on with this task: it has, in fact, become urgent.

CHAPTER SIX

Companionship with humans

Harold Bridger

"In his grief over the loss of a dog, a little boy stands for the first time, peering into the rueful morrow of manhood."

James Thurber

This chapter is derived from an unpublished pilot study carried out to identify the social and psychological forces underlying the keeping of pets. The study itself consisted not only of a selective exploration of related literature but also of a series of interviews, group discussions, and "teach-ins" with a wide variety of people.

The current intensified interest in ethnology, and the increased attention being paid to understanding the animal "world" and our own modes of living, is happening at a time when society itself is undergoing radical changes. Accelerating technological and economic change, accompanied by increased "openness" of national, community, institutional, and family boundaries to their environments, has made us question our control of events and the directions

---

This chapter is based on a paper presented at a conference at the Royal Society of Health, May 1970.

of the so-called progress of our interpersonal and inter-group relationships. The "openness" of boundaries, whether of the individuals in the groups to which they belong, or of the larger organizations in their professional, industrial, political, and other worlds has not been accompanied by equal growth in trust and a sense of identity. Dangerously late in man's history, we are beginning to regard the study of mankind itself and those families and groups within which each individual lives—as well as their antecedents—as needing systematic and continuous investment. Particular reference must be made here to the important work of John Bowlby with the publication of the first volume of *Attachment and Loss* (1969), which develops theories reconciling research in animal behaviour with current biological and psychoanalytic thought and human behaviour. Generally, deepening involvement in different aspects of this total field can be perceived through the general interest of the public in a wide variety of books and films.

The pet in society

Although there is a vast and rich animal "literature", whether in the fields of adventure, discovery, and science or in the realms of fairy stories, jokes, cartoons, films, and novels, relatively little has been written on the subject of the wider and deeper functions that companionship with humans can serve—whether for the individual or for families and society generally. It is as if there were an area best left alone, taken for granted, and not talked about—a delicate, embarrassing subject, even taboo. We can joke about people growing to look like their horse or dog, or selecting one to resemble themselves as closely as possible. The examination of the general principle that people might choose pets to "meet" characteristics of themselves in some special external form and to "reflect" certain aspects of the individual and family has had little or no attention. Furthermore, either nationally or internationally, we can joke about the way the British think more of their pets than they do of people or of their children in particular; we can take a defensive kind of pride in the way in which public emotion is expressed over cruelty to animals, vivisection, and the case of Little Lemon (of Russian Sputnik fame). The excitement of such public emotion or individual reaction is usually packed into such useful portmanteau words as "idiosyncrasy", "eccentricity", or even "cultural characteristics"; the whole area has the quality of being "meteorological" or "psychological"—talked about and used like the weather or the mind, respectively unpredictable (in Britain) or impossible to understand.

In the unpublished study mentioned above, the very cheerfulness and friendliness of the groups and the readiness to find a bottomless fund of interchange, mutual interest, and a common language gave an indication of the quality of pet owners, who acknowledged that this was their general experience in meeting other people with pets. Common ground could be established immediately, but it could also be seen as providing a screen beyond which one could only ascribe the inferences drawn from the "semi-anonymous" communications derived from the pet-discussion. These inferential communications were implicit in two senses:

1. the theme of the story or information about the pet and the picture it was intended to convey about the "teller" and/or the teller's family;

2. the "music behind the words" which suggested another level of significance for the "teller", whether or not recognized by the teller or by listeners.

A simple example, frequently expressed by adults as a question, was: "They're like children, aren't they?" In the first sense, there is the communication that the "teller" is like a parent to her or his pet(s); in the second, that she or he might like assurance or confirmation from other people that they too could share this closeness of feeling for their pets—and even when one is adult. At the same time, a parent's lot is not always a happy, loving one, and pets, like children, could be more than a nuisance at times.

In the process of administering a questionnaire in a more recent educational research survey, Jancis Smithells reported that the question, "What other members of the family join you when watching TV?", drew a consistent enquiry from the 12-year-old respondents: "Does our dog [cat, etc.] count?" It was also noted that the pronoun was almost always "our" rather than "my".

In trying to understand that children might not treat keeping pets simply as a hobby, and to appreciate the "music behind the words" of the question asking if the pet could be considered a member of the family, we need to recognize that satisfying reciprocal relationships provide:

1. "extensions" of ourselves, our influence, and our networks *externally*;
2. opportunity for testing out our ideas, our feelings, and, in general, our sense of reality;
3. incorporating our learning and experience from (1) and (2) and developing what we might call our "internal self" (we usually term this "personal growth", but this process also applies to animals in their relationships).

These processes therefore do not leave us as we were before the relationship matured. In addition to any building of social relationships externally to create the "extended" family, institution, or community, there is the complementary internal personal development of the individual. These two complementary dimensions also exist for the family itself. The animal—pet or horse—can be the means by which a family could be more "open" to its neighbours and their children, thus permitting the couple or the family to widen its network in the direction of those likely to have common values or, sometimes, in meeting those with whom a bond is sought. But equally, within the family the animal provides opportunities for projection and displacement of feelings as well as for direct expression of concern and care, of anxiety and fear, and for testing out capacities for power, authority, and influence within the family context. The animal often makes even a secure family setting a "safer" place to test out love and hate, preferences and rivalries, independence and cooperation, destructive and creative feelings, and so on.

The animal and the individual

To appreciate the important and often vital role that an animal can play in its relationship with a child, adult, family, or institution, it is necessary to indicate relevant aspects of the developmental process in the person from birth onwards.

In his original and fundamental studies of the earliest explicit form by which the infant demonstrates its acceptance of "disillusion-

ment" in recognizing something as "not-me", Winnicott (1951) out-
lines the distinctive phases within the "sequence of events which
starts with the new-born infant's fist-in-mouth activities" and which
passes through "to an attachment to a teddy, a doll or soft toy, or to a
hard toy". His interest in the first "not-me possession" concerns the
"area of experiencing" itself, the earliest time when the infant initiates
exploration beyond the thumb and the breast—to meet what lies
between "the subjective and that which is objectively perceived".

The process that begins here Winnicott sees as the human being
preparing to challenge illusion and the "illusory experience"—the
first "experiment in independence", as he calls it later.

It is not possible in this chapter to describe adequately Winnicott's
work in this field, but the qualities of the relationships that are involved are clearly early forms of later ones with toys, pets, and people: "Certainly it is often very helpful when a child can make use of
some object in the home; something that can be given a name, and
that often becomes almost part of the family. Out of the infant's
interest in this comes his eventual preoccupation with dolls, other
toys, and animals" (Winnicott, 1951).

Winnicott's work enables us to see how it is that there is partly a
sequence in which the individual can make gradually increasing use
of objects and partly a growth of the degree to which any object can be
used. The transitional object, as he calls the "first not-me possession",
would provide us with a basis for considering the roles and functions
of the animal in relation to the individual in the family.

The animal is not simply another object in the environment of the
individual member of the family, nor is the pet only a means for
beginning to learn at first hand about the animal world. The animal
also exists as a being in its own right, with which to enjoy life in
various ways and to experiment with in trying out behaviour and
attitudes. Beyond these aspects, however, there is a later and more
mature, complex structured area of experiencing provided by the pet
in its relationships with the individual. As distinct from the first area
of experiencing, this later one has a life of its own and provides more
uncertainty. In this new phase, the individual member of the family
can learn to confront anxieties and match the illusory experience with
reality, with greater security than might otherwise be possible. The
opportunity to find the situation that provides an inbuilt sensitive
balance and control while we learn to cope and acquire identity,
power, and authority is not often available. The animal is by no means

perfect for this purpose, but it may be one of the best we have. At least we know that the majority of people who own one or who have had one always seem to show much gratitude and affection to this "anonymous" counsellor.

The animal's contribution to human and social development in the family

Winnicott's concept of the "transitional object" and the theories associated with it have implications not only for the individual but for the family itself.

The position of the pet in the family can be regarded in two main ways. As most pet owners would describe the situation, the pet is a member of the family, with characteristics some of which are all its own and others held in common with one or more of the rest of the family. The pet can, for example, be the Alsatian guard dog contributing to the security and well-being of the family, appropriately

1.   dependent on the family for care, food, and sufficient exercise, and

2.   the member on whom the family is dependent for protection.

The pet, however, is an adopted member even when born within the family, since it has another mother and father. Furthermore, it is a possession, whether of the collective family or of one of the family members. The pet, therefore, must be capable of being perceived as a member of the family and have roles and functions that can realistically be regarded as contributing to the tasks, activities, harmony, and upbringing (e.g. educational and maturational aspects) of family life. At the same time, it must be capable of being perceived as a "not-family" possession by which it can be differentiated from other members of the family (even from actual adopted children, who can associate themselves with the adopted pet in one sense but must not allow themselves to be too closely identified with it).

Given the normal problems of families, with their crises, growth, achievements, and difficulties, one can see how a selection from the wide range of choice in pets (and combinations of them) could provide a "social catalyst" for the family group. The family would need to be "good enough" to be effective with a pet. The pet too would need to be "good enough" for the family purpose and to maintain its own controls. The advent and inclusion of a pet might, however, create conditions that permit parents and children to confront old unsolved problems in a new situation in which there is a special "member" with a gift for listening rather than talking. There will be opportunities for learning in a slightly "off-centre", different set of conditions, for perceiving influences and reactions from other angles, and for testing consciously and unconsciously different loving/ hating relations. Similarly, different balances of attention and neglect can be explored, and responsible control (in the regulating sense) can be developed.

For these purposes, the choice of pet ranges from tropical fish, which can be seen but not played with, to the highly active kitten or puppy. From the points of view of children of different ages, of parents, and of the family as a whole, the characteristics of the pet will be most important. What might be most suitable for a certain individual's needs might not be desirable for the family as a whole.

The pet should, irrespective of the unique needs of the family and the individuals comprising it, possess characteristics that will ensure the following:

1. *Survival* as a sound, sturdy example of its kind—that is, unlikely to succumb easily to illness or mishap for which the family would blame itself or for which it could be open to blame. This is all the more important because the pet has to be of such a kind that stories told about it could show the type of family the storyteller came from. These are implicit communications. The explicit material or manifest content is about the pet—the latent content of the story "said" the kind of complimentary things about the teller and her or his family that could not have been mentioned without the pet story as its overt and sanctioned purpose. It would appear that the physical health and feeding of the pet are of great importance, but not more so than the pet's stamina and stability to withstand intra-family pressure.

2. *Dependence*: to have the quality of needing "adoption" and requiring special care; to have a "lost" quality if without the family; to have the childish quality. Yet without losing these characteristics, the pet should be independent enough not to be suffocating or

over-demanding; it should know its way home and be able to behave on the basis of having grown up in the family.

3. *Pairing relationship:* to be able to make, or have ascribed to it, the capacity for such a relationship. The capacity involves being able to initiate and respond to affection. High value is put on the pet that can comprehend the groping for relationship in the aggressive baby. On the other hand, if instead of a healthy husband–wife relationship within the family there is competitive use of a child or animal to form a "preferred" pair, it will also be harmful to the development of both. Naturally, the "pairing relationship" within the family setting has an infinite variety of forms, and the extent to which it is used constructively and creatively—or destructively—for the "pair" and the family must depend on its character. For example, a child or pet may show its trust in another family member who is "under a cloud" of some kind, whereas the rest of the family is too hasty in condemnation. Many stories are built on the theme of the misunderstood pet who maintains the family objective against the anxiety and force of the family itself. An animal may be used, however, by a parent or child to obtain continuous satisfaction not forthcoming from other members of the family.

In contrast, however, to the active relationships and experience initiated by the human members of the family, the animal can, by its behaviour and use of its attributes and limitations, either further the family purposes or frustrate them. It will, however, be necessary to distinguish between those occasions when this originates in the pet and when it is "behaving" as a result of family projections into it.

From teddy bear to animal companion—
a process of growth

The special significance of the teddy bear or piece of cloth to which the young child becomes attached—and misses very much if taken away—carries all the signs of the emotional investment in the relationship made by the child. The loving and hostile acts on others and self have left much of teddy threadbare, often mutilated and patched.

There are not a few people who preserve their "transitional object" as a talisman far into adult life, if not throughout life. For most, the object is relinquished as toys, animals, hobbies, and human-relationship-widening activities take over the job and provide developing satisfactions and challenges for personal growth. Nevertheless, we all retain residues in one form or another of the phases we have travelled through. Whether as mementoes, mannerisms, or values and standards, there is often great relief and joy in finding that someone else felt the same way. Frequently, in such an experience a reluctant sense of shame turns into a capacity to own oneself.

Toys, too, are inanimate and, though often invested with thwarted or retaliatory feelings, can only provide learning, pleasure, comfort, or a sense of achievement according to the capabilities available to the child at that time. But toys, on the other hand, do provide an opportunity for the growing and maturing child that the "transitional object" cannot have. They can also act as a special medium by which parents, brothers, sisters, and others can join in playing with the child. As the value of this special medium shows its worth in the learning and satisfactions it brings, so the "transitional object" is gradually relegated to its private symbolic place in the individual's possessions. The world of experience it has provided as the first not-me possession has played its part, although derivations and residues will continue in the experience with toys, games, and animals. This aspect of a special medium that toys provide for bringing experience and for regulating and testing out attitudes of other people—that is, quite apart from what the toys themselves offer—can be regarded as a "temporary system" set up to enable the deep or vast gap between adult and child to be made manageable for meeting in appropriate joint activity.

There is, of course, an infinite number of situations occurring or being created that serve such purposes for children at this time and later—at home, at school, and elsewhere. But these may be utilized for "material" learning only, and the opportunity to create a climate of trust and confidence may have been lost. Teachers and parents today are far more aware of the importance of the part played by relationships built in the course of play, learning, and work and are not so exclusively concerned with the material lesson, skill, or intellectual information to be inculcated in the child.

It is in this connection that animals—whether as pets in the home, in extended social activities and sports such as horse-riding, or in agricultural life, etc.—have so much to *teach* humans, besides giving companionship. In their own right, animals provide many opportunities that the inanimate toy cannot provide. It is understandably difficult to get young children to "look after" their toys: even dolls may get careless treatment when not actually fulfilling their role in a game. But the seeds of a sense of responsibility for "another" can be sown in the caring and tending of a pet. Nor must we forget the reciprocal relationship that animals can provide—some, of course, much more than others. The animal with "a life of its own" requires added dimensions to be developed in a child if the child is going to adapt to relationship with it. In addition, the "temporary system" that the animal provides for the child to make relations with the world around her or him—places as well as people—is a much more complex one. It is a "temporary system" where values, standards, and morality begin to arise out of those earlier first attempts at exercising responsibility.

The animal as a "temporary system" for the development of character

The attitudes and behaviour of family members and other adults in their treatment and relationships with animals are always communicating themselves to the children in the situation. Children are wonderfully sensitive to the "music behind the words and actions" of adults. They can sense the "steel" or cruelty behind the honeyed expression, and they can sense the humanity and kindness behind the strict command. So can animals. The "temporary system" that companionship with animals creates with the child for testing out feelings, ideas, fantasies, and adventurous explorations has its counterpart in many facets of adult life.

While the series of congresses organized by the Royal Society of Health can be regarded as a "permanent system", each congress is itself a "temporary system" designed to try out and to risk our ideas with each other, a "market-place" for discovering both what others have to offer and who is interested in our experience. It also provides private satisfactions as well as public opportunities, as all good temporary systems should.

Sometimes the temporary system chosen can appear to be a frivolous waste of time or a cynical distraction from the actual essential task in hand. Many examples can be found in family life, in the international and national political scenes, and in other settings where apparently "silly" irrational arguments develop in situations of real or imagined threat, and where mutual trust is at low ebb. The months of pseudo-discussion about the shape of the conference table for the Viet-Cong–U.S. talks in Paris is an excellent example. In a positive sense, however, the shape of the table indicated the type and degree of relationship between the two sides and showed the maximum basis on which exploration of each other's intentions and values could be made. On this hypothesis, the relevant and fruitful companionship of animals on an individual or family basis can be indicative of health. While companionship with an animal cannot of its own accord confirm this, the relationship that permits trust and influence to be built in ways that bring out potentialities and talents of all concerned will be its own demonstrable proof.

A further simple but telling example of the "temporary system" aspect in animal companionship occurs when the animal becomes the introductory medium and immediate object of joint interest in "boy-meets-girl" situations. Quite apart, however, from the tactics of the occasion on the part of boy or girl, the animal can make its own contribution in the early tentative exploratory phase. Whether it is a dog in the classic park encounter, a horse at a riding-school, or pets at home, the animal's implicit communications about the humans become explicit in their conversation. In his books, Konrad Lorenz (1961, 1964) gives fascinating as well as expert advice, both direct and inferential, on the choosing of animals to match the needs, personalities, and interests of owners. It may indeed be possible that assumptions made about the British, with their particular attitude to exercising authority and responsibility, and their form of indirect communication and learning, may not be unconnected with their art of companionship with animals. Certainly, derived values and standards in the regard and duties owed to dependants and friends who share in one's education and development and not simply as an extension of oneself, or as an ornament or pastime, would give credence to this possibility.

CHAPTER SEVEN

Transitional interventions

Lisl Klein

This chapter is concerned with turning transitional thinking into practice, and it describes three experiences of transitional systems or roles. The first was devised by members of a client system, without any overt contribution from the external consultant who was working in the organization at the time. In the second, the consultant spontaneously began to take on the role of a product and, in doing so, loosened the log-jam of a design discussion that had become stuck. The third, by contrast, was a highly structured and formal experimental design. They are presented here in reverse chronological order: the first is the most recent and happened during my work from the Bayswater Institute as a consultant in the National Health Service. The second happened during my earlier nineteen years in the Tavistock Institute. And the third took place before that, while I was social sciences adviser in Esso Petroleum Company.

The notion of "transition" in human life was first put forward by the psychoanalyst D. W. Winnicott (1971), whose work is discussed in detail elsewhere in this volume. He pointed to the function that toys and forms of playing have for small children in facilitating experimentation with new and unknown aspects of the world and the working-through of anxieties and conflicts. The fundamental learning from this observation can be extrapolated to other aspects and phases of life, with very rich and creative consequences. Throughout the last decades, there have been massive and repeated discussions about the problems of technology or system implementation, how to cope with "resistance to change", and so on. The concept of "transition" (as distinct from the "management of change") helps to understand that it is very often simply not possible to go directly from A to B; at least as much thought and creativity needs to go into designing the vehicle for getting from A to B, and ensuring that the vehicle has the requisite characteristics, as goes into designing B.

In the design and implementation of technology, there are many forms of simulation, prototyping, and piloting that may be used. But for these to have the function of facilitating transition, certain conditions have to be met. They must be sufficiently flexible to permit alternatives to be demonstrated, and sufficiently realistic for the operational realities involved to be experienced or at least imagined. They must also, therefore, incorporate the human and social—or "soft systems"—aspects in a realistic way; that is, they must incorporate them in a way that is not merely the reification of wishful thinking.

In policy implementation, there is a similar need to provide a space for people to explore who and how they are in relation to the new situation. Institutions such as training courses, steering groups, or working parties will have the function of facilitating transition if they provide some "transitional space"—that is, if they create an environment where options can be explored in safety without later repercussions, where people can experiment with roles and behaviours beyond their habitual ones, and where issues can be worked through that the normal working culture may not encourage to surface.

Example 1:
The patient and the ward as aids to integration — the story of Poor Old Henry

Background

This story concerns the use of scenarios about a fictitious patient and an imaginary day in a ward to aid integrated working in a hospital. In 1990, a London hospital with 700 beds became one of three National Health Service pilot sites in the United Kingdom for installing a large integrated computerized Hospital Information Support System (HISS). Although the system selected was "off-the-shelf", there was a good deal of detailed design work left for the in-house project team to undertake. This team was drawn from different professions and departments in the hospital; as members of the team developed work in their own areas, they became increasingly aware that they were having to make assumptions about things outside their own specific knowledge. These were assumptions both about what happened in the hospital and about what would be happening in the information system. According to the nursing officer:

"We ... wrote the Operational Requirement for a lot of disparate systems—the nursing system, haematology, the labs, etc. I could understand the individual bits and what they could do, but, not being IT-literate, I had a problem fitting the bits of the system together to make the integrated HISS. Every time I asked a question I was met with 'I assume', or 'I expect'. .... So I personally became alarmed by my lack of understanding of the whole!"

The development of modules of the system forced members of the project team to make their tacit knowledge about the hospital explicit, and they became increasingly aware of the gaps. The project manager stated:

"... as we moved through the early part of 1991, where some people were doing what was called product-build (building tables and setting the system up ready to be run) and others were designing forms, some departmental managers—on the basis of what was being developed in the system—were making assumptions about what their work-load would include, and this takes us right through to menu design: what would employees have on their menus? Somebody had to do the various functions somewhere, and assumptions were being made within the team about who would do what: what nurses would do, what doctors would do, what ward clerks would do—a whole raft of people who all knit together in the real world but whose jobs became focused into the need to know exactly who would do what by the implementation of the system. A computer system is nothing more than a model of the real world. In the systems that aren't used by many people, the modelling is not that terribly important. But for a system that is a

real client system, where every individual out in the hospital is
going to play some part close to the work they do, it becomes more
significant that you understand the relationship between the real
world and the system itself. Unless the interface ... is clearly
organized, so that the people who are doing specific functions
have access and know how to do it on the system, you are in a
mess."

People in the organization had very little computing experience. It
was as new to the people setting the system up as it was to any of the
potential users waiting to start. At the same time, things were happening very fast: the system was having to be built and tested, training was being prepared, and the trainers needed to know who needed
to be trained on what. This brought to light the fact that another
whole lot of assumptions had to be made.

Two members of the project team in particular—the nursing officer and the patient administration officer—became increasingly
worried, both because they did not have a wide-enough circulation to
let people know what they themselves were doing, and because of the
gaps in their own knowledge. They approached the project manager
with the idea of an "integration day", a day on which representatives
from across the hospital would be in the same room together, so that
assumptions about each other's functions and work could be checked
out. As a vehicle for this, they proposed to try to build a case history
that would take staff through as many branches of care as possible
and use it as a focus for discussion.

The project manager liked this suggestion. As the idea was developed further, it emerged that there were really two perspectives from
which they wanted to look at issues of integration: one was that of a
patient moving through the hospital, and one that of a ward with
patients moving through it:

"We eventually came to the view that we needed to look at it from
a day in the ward, so that we could walk through a scenario which
described typical things that happened through the day in the
ward and see who felt they would make what contribution in the
interface between the real world and the information system to the
terminals and printers that would be placed on the wards. With
regard to the patient, one would see what impact various people
would have on the patient as he moved on."

To get hospital-wide attendance at such an event, support had to be obtained at senior level. The hospital's General Manager was approached, and he adopted the idea with enthusiasm. It was he who issued the invitations to the "integration day" and who ensured that key people attended.

A feature of the situation was that none of the systems had been implemented at that stage. All departments had internal departmental coordinators involved in the detailed development or build of their own part of the system. But the managers and other staff attending the integration day would at most have some familiarity with these internal departmental systems being developed.

"If you take radiology as an example, a radiology coordinator was building the system for radiology and would have involved all the department in the radiology departmental things, their internal bits, but would be making assumptions about how the interface between radiology and the rest of the hospital worked. Now, whilst this was working on a word-of-mouth or bits-of-paper basis, in other words in the old way, those assumptions could be fairly woolly. Once we were implementing a full-scale integrated information system, it was necessary to know much more clearly just what those boundaries were, how they would work, who precisely would do what, be responsible for what."

The method

Two scenarios were written, one for the day in a ward and one for the patient, who came to be known as "Poor Old Henry" because so many dire things happened to him. In the ward scenario, the aim was to capture who would typically be on the ward, what information they needed, what they did with it, as well as real-life events such as phone calls from other parts of the hospital. With regard to the patient, it had to be a typical patient but one who crossed a number of different department boundaries. The scenario was written by the diabetes consultant, so the patient was a diabetic.

In the event, integration days using scenarios of this kind to test some aspect of integration were used three times in the course of the next two years, and these are described here. Each time the trigger was a large topic that was going to have a wide impact, so that it was necessary to get everybody who would be affected together in the same room. However, the ward scenario was only used on the first integration day; it was not judged to be relevant for the other two.

The meetings were attended by internal hospital staff. Both senior and junior levels were represented—"those who thought they knew what went on, and those who actually knew what really happened". People's time in the meetings was covered informally by the hospital. Some people did not feel that they needed to stay for the whole time, but most chose to stay. Some of the more junior staff felt that they had to get back to their jobs. A decision had been taken not to invite people who were not employed by the hospital, such as social workers. This was linked to the issue of system boundaries, of who should and should not have direct access to the information system.

The work, however, was not primarily systems-oriented. It was intended to focus on people, procedures, and the integration of the hospital. This also meant getting people to understand that they could not simply write a procedure for their part of the work; they had to think in terms of the whole hospital—"Henry allowed the ripples from the pond to be followed".

The structure of the event was the same each time. One member of the project team would "walk" the audience "through" the story step by step, until a question was reached or a discussion broke out.

A member of the project board then acted as facilitator for the discussion. An important feature of the design was to let discussion go on until there was consensus and clarity about what a problem or an issue actually was, but not to let it move further on into problem-solving itself—that was too big and too complex a task to be handled within the space of the day and would very quickly lead to confusion. The role of the facilitator was to try to identify with the people present where the information they needed was to be found, where the responsibility for a particular issue lay. A few issues could be resolved on the spot; just having the relevant people together to share their knowledge and experience was in some cases enough. If a major issue that emerged was not concerned with HISS, in some instances a subset of people was convened afterwards to work on it.

The project manager and the training officer acted as scribes, recording the discussion and in particular the issues that emerged. It was felt necessary to have two people doing this, in case one of them missed something (the first integration day yielded one hundred such issues or questions).

After the event, the project manager circulated an "issues list" to all those who had attended. A distinction was made between significant discussion and assumptions on the one hand, which were printed in lower case, and issues needing to be addressed, printed in capitals. Recipients of this document were asked first to check whether they agreed that it was an accurate record of what had happened, and then to identify those issues in which they were themselves involved. The points for resolution or discussion that were circulated after the first meeting were not numbered, and it turned out to be a "nightmare" matching the replies to the issues. After that experience, issues were numbered and people identified issues by number.

The documentation following each meeting was turned around very quickly—within a week. Working on the issues was then prioritized, key issues about parts of the HISS that were being implemented next being looked at first. However, there was a chicken-and-egg element in this: afterwards, it was felt that, if some issues that were not immediately identified as urgent had been dealt with, some others would not have arisen at all. The circle was not closed in a formal way, but pencil notes on the various issues lists show that many questions were answered, sometimes very simply, or resolved. Some others, however, remained problematic.

Once the main part of the system had gone live, a regular "Issues Meeting" was institutionalized to continue working on issues that had not been resolved and on new ones that came up. Not all issues were resolved.

The first integration day

The first integration day was held to check assumptions in the building of the information system, as described earlier. The people who had instigated it were quite anxious. They knew what they wanted from the event, but were unsure what the participants would gain. The event took a whole day, with a "walk through" of the ward in the morning and of the story of Poor Old Henry in the afternoon:

"So on the ward [scenario] I was the narrator and started by saying 'It is 7.30 am . . .'" and asking 'Who is on the ward?' 'What information do they have?' 'What do they need to know?' 'Who is next onto the ward?' etc. Each of the people, representatives in the meeting, would say 'I'm on the ward, and at this time I need this piece of information etc.' Gradually the picture of the day on the ward built up. The nurse might say, 'I'm writing a report, using the nursing care plan . . .' 'Who comes next onto the ward?' 'The ward clerk' . . . 'Who next?' 'The junior doctor' . . . they all literally talked us through what they did, the processes, the interaction."

The ward scenario was chronological, dividing the day into phases. A medical ward is a very busy place: some categories of staff come on duty (nurses, junior doctors, a ward clerk; one agency nurse did not turn up) and hand over to each other when their shift ends. Other categories of staff come for specific purposes (physiotherapist, phlebotomist, pharmacist, chaplain, cardiac technician, porter). There are routine events (meals, bed-making, drug rounds) and non-routine events (a patient deteriorates unexpectedly and doctors and relatives have to be informed); there is a water leak in the bathroom; an oxygen pipe cannot be found. Staff have to have breaks, stores arrive, domestic cleaning takes place. A new patient is admitted, tests have to be ordered. Two patients are ready for discharge, but their test results have to be obtained first; transport has to be organized. Records and care plans have to be updated. A consultant does his ward round and this results in decisions that need to be implemented. And so on.

"What became apparent were things like the number of times the same pieces of information were requested for different needs— the bed state from the bed bureau, someone from A&E checking whether the beds available were male or female beds, the senior nurse phoning round trying to find out bed availability in terms of needing to move patients around the hospital . . .

"What it showed was the different disciplines that came and went from the ward, and identifying who needed information from whom, why and how. We also included a ward round and a medicine round."

One of the things the ward scenario highlighted was the number of times people in the meeting said, "The nurses will do that, it will only take them a minute". This was a function of the size of the group; they were all together, they could see the number of times the nursing staff were expected to do things. They even calculated the number of minutes that these various small tasks required, and they found that this added up to a whole morning of a nurse's time. So there was learning about the knock-on implications of one's actions.

The first story of Poor Old Henry was as follows:

THE UNFORTUNATE CASE OF MR HENRY SMITH

Henry Smith is an 82-year-old man who lives alone on the fifth floor of a tower block in Thamesmead. He has felt unwell for some time, but despite advice from his son (who visits him weekly) did not seek advice from his general practitioner until he developed a severe pain in his right foot. The following chronicles the history of events that follows:

Wednesday, 2 January: Henry attends his GP surgery. The GP, suspecting diabetes, sends him to the pathology department at the hospital for a blood-sugar test. Henry attends the department later the same morning. Later that day the results are phoned to the GP.

Wednesday, 9 January: Henry returns to his GP who confirms that he has diabetes and refers him to the Diabetic Day Care Centre urgently (by letter).

Friday, 18 January. Henry attends the Diabetic Day Care Centre. In view of his many symptoms it is decided that he should be referred to Dr Brown, and an appointment is made for him to attend Dr Brown's next clinic.

Wednesday, 23 January: Henry see Dr Brown in the outpatient department. Late-onset diabetes is confirmed, but a number of complications are also diagnosed, particularly problems with Henry's sight, not to mention his deteriorating right foot! Dr Brown arranges for him to be admitted the following Monday, takes some more blood tests, and starts him on antibiotics.

Monday, 28 January. Henry arrives at the hospital for his admission. There seems to be some difficulty in finding him a bed, but he is finally admitted to ward 2A under the care of Dr Brown. Here he is seen by both nurses and doctors and is told that, due to his numerous problems, arrangements will be made for him to see a dietician, a chiropodist, and a surgeon (Mr Green). He is also told that he will have a special examination of his leg (arteriogram) as soon as the appointment can be made and that he will need to be put on an insulin drip while he has this test.

Tuesday, 29 January. Henry has a very busy day! He spends the morning in the radiology department having his arteriogram, and in the afternoon he is seen by Mr Green. He is told that he needs some surgery "to sort out his foot and circulation problems" and that he will therefore be transferred to the care of Mr Green.

Wednesday, 30 January. Henry is transferred to ward 1G. Again, he is seen by the nurses and doctors (including an anaesthetist), and it is arranged for him to have surgery on Friday. He is also seen by the "blood lady" as he is to have a number of blood tests in preparation for his visit to theatre. He is told that he will probably need a blood transfusion and that his blood is being taken to "cross-match" it.

Friday, 1 February. Henry does not have a good day! Unfortunately he has a "nasty reaction" to one of the drugs that he is given in theatre and ends up in ITU for observation. He also wakes up minus a foot!

Saturday, 2 February. Henry seems much better today and is moved back to 1G, although this time he is in a bed right next to the nurses' station. The physiotherapist continues to visit him regularly to "beat" his chest. He is also seen again by Dr Brown, who explains that he is continuing to monitor his diabetes.

Wednesday, 6 February. Henry has been improving steadily, but today he takes a "funny turn" and is sent to the cardiac ultrasound department for an echocardiogram (which turns out to be normal).

Saturday, 9 February. No more "funny turns", so Henry is told that he can go home on Friday if all remains well. He is also told that arrangements will be made for him to visit the Limb Fitting Centre, for an occupational therapist to do a home visit, and for a social worker to see him. Later in the day he is given an appointment card for a visit to see Mr White in the Eye Clinic.

Friday, 15 February. All being well, Henry is discharged home. He is told that the local district nurse will visit him regularly to look at his wound. He is also given appointments to see both Dr Brown and Mr Green in the follow-up clinic in six weeks' time. Dr Brown has asked him to return to the hospital one week before his appointment to see him for a blood test. Fortunately, the hospital have arranged transport for all these visits.

Monday, 18 February. Henry is now recovering at home, but back at the hospital much work is going on to document Henry's stay. His case notes are sent to the medical secretaries, where one of the doctors dictates a discharge summary, and once this has been typed his notes are sent to the medical coders before finally being returned to file.

The second integration day

The method was used a second time when the pathology information-system module was about to be implemented. Ordering pathology tests and getting the results was crucial for all other departments, and it was essential to get the pathology system right, or as right as possible:

"It was really focusing on all the aspects of management that were associated with placing orders: phlebotomy, specimen collection, getting results, urgent results, cumulative reports, a whole raft of things that the organization was interested in in terms of order management for pathology, because it affected everybody. Prior to that we had order management for radiology which was not so pressurized, in the sense that fewer people use it and when they do use it they generally are not at the same level of intensity. Pathology is the thing that produces the urgent results and reports, the urgent results that somebody has to do something about."

This time, the ward was not thought to be the relevant entity, and the integration day focused only on the experiences of Poor Old Henry. A new scenario, continuing his story, was written. It still raised issues about the information system and integration in general, but included prompts and questions specifically angled at pathology. The following is a summary:

"After his last adventures, Henry had successfully gone home and lived a fairly independent life. He still visits the hospital on a regular basis for review of his diabetes in the outpatient department, where he has regular blood tests. However, for some time now Henry has not been well and is losing his independence. His GP decides to undertake some tests to identify the problem.

"He sends Henry for an X-ray, ECG, a physiotherapy assessment, blood tests and also arranges for him to attend ward 2A as a "ward attender" for a glucose tolerance test.

"Henry continues to decline and wakes up one morning with a slight left-sided weakness and appears a little confused. The home help becomes very anxious and phones immediately for an ambulance to take Henry to hospital. Several problems are diagnosed, he is admitted and spends six days in hospital. During this time, investigations are carried out and treatment is started involving several departments of the hospital. In his confused state he attempts to climb out of bed and falls, incurring a fractured femur. This involves another operation, an additional consultant, and transfers from one ward to another and back again. Discharging him involves ordering a wheelchair and getting the social work department involved, since he is now going to move into sheltered accommodation.

"Five weeks after Henry's discharge his elderly sister-in-law writes a letter of complaint to "the Matron". She is very unhappy that Henry had the fall and feels she was given little real explanation. She has not given any details on Henry other than his name. She has no telephone."

The scenario took up six pages and the integration day nearly a whole day. This time, 65 issues were identified. An example concerned people who were not on the system—such as community midwives and dentists—needing to order tests. The group identified ways of enabling orders to be put in and the implications for coding/statistical analysis of these decisions.

The method raised people's awareness of the complexity of the organization and highlighted how little many people knew about what was done, especially in the area of non-clinical support staff. By gaining an understanding of the sheer volume of work involved, they also gained insight into why there might be problems, as well as increased respect for those doing the work. For example, a high error rate in processing laboratory orders was identified, because an aspect of training had been misunderstood. Since the total number of orders was very great, the consequences were also very great. Once the problem had been understood, more focused training was given and the error rate reduced to 1% without loss of quality.

The third integration day

The third integration day was organized to help the hospital work on the implications of the then new framework of provider/purchaser contracting in the NHS. It was held towards the end of the 1992/93 round of contracting and was particularly aimed at service managers, many of whom had been recently appointed. This time, it was the Unit General Manager who asked for it to be organized, not the HISS team (the hospital had in the meantime merged with another one to form a single Provider Unit). There were over forty people in the room, both very senior and very junior people. Consultants, coders, heads of departments, service managers, the Director of Finance, were all involved in the process of making contracts. People who attended found it valuable and instructive, but wished it had happened earlier, so that the learning could have informed the contracting process that year.

Once again, only the story of Poor Old Henry was used, his adventures having many implications for the hospital's contracts. The script used on the last occasion was used again but modified slightly, to open up more implications for contracting. For example, Henry now had a son visiting him who was registered with a distant GP fundholder and who was also ill. In discussion with the service managers, some issues that had not been part of the story emerged, and these were simply added to the script.

The meeting revealed many problems of definition, such as what is a separate activity—"If I see someone in Outpatients and then do a coronary angiogram, are we then an agent of the GP practice, or is it our activity?" Or: "There will only be one consultant against the account, but it can involve up to four others 'assisting'. So where do drug costs get allocated?"

Although the amount of complexity and transfers from one consultant to another in Henry's case was unrealistic, the uncertainty about whose care he was under at any one point generated some questions in the audience about whether he was being clinically cared for. As each consultant episode was being coded separately, "Are the clinicians happy for coders to be diagnosing patients?" Moreover, the patient had a heart condition, which, in the interest generated by the subsequent technical problems, got forgotten.

One issue that surfaced at this meeting had rather wide implications: patients with certain conditions go to any hospital near which they find themselves for routine repeat treatment such as anticoagulant injections. It was thought to be much cheaper and simpler just to give the treatment than to get the extra-contractual referral (ECR) agreed by the district of residence first. (ECR is where non-emergency treatment is required for a patient with whose general practitioner or "district of residence" the hospital has no contract and agreement needs to be obtained—usually by telephone—that the treatment will be paid for.) In the course of the meeting, this seemed to become policy, in the hope that local residents away from home would get equivalent benefits where they found themselves, a matter of "swings and roundabouts". But the implication was that places where people go on holiday, for instance, would be at a disadvantage because they had more visitors than residents going away. There could also be quite substantial classes of work for which nobody billed or got paid:

> "It's not so much it was more bother to obtain an ECR, it was much more fundamental than that. The patient turned up on your doorstep asking to see the haematologist because he had this condition and he needed to have an injection. If he had come from Hartlepool we would not have a contract with Hartlepool, full stop. So in the terms of the rules, it had to be an ECR. Now for an ECR you have to ring up the Health Authority involved, tell them that you have one of their patients, what you want to do, get approval for it to be an ECR for them to pay, and the cost of the treatment might only be £3.50. Now you could actually spend £3.50 in administrative fees and telephone calls and paperwork and postage. In the meantime you have got the patient there, so what do you do? Do you keep the patient in the hospital hanging round for several hours while you get the paperwork for the ECR? The District Health Authority person in Hartlepool was not available, he will ring you back tomorrow . . . It was the nonsense of the situation which meant you treated the patient and you didn't get the contract sorted out."

Discussion

Initially, the purpose of using Henry and the ward scenario had been to help the people building modules of the information system to test their assumptions about other parts of the hospital and get a view of the whole. In addition, there was a purpose about merging the HISS project manager's knowledge of the information system with the team members' knowledge of the workings of the hospital.

However, making use of Henry turned out to have a number of other functions. It gave people across the hospital a better understanding of the problems of others, ranging from the clinical coders' difficulties in reading doctors' handwriting and the problem of what to do if a patient is unable to give his or her address, to major problems of clinical care and finance. It helped with the induction of new members of management. It highlighted the limitations within which people worked, as they became aware of the consequences for others of their own bright ideas. It helped to get responsibilities identified and ownership for problems taken up.

Example 2.
"I am a Trebor Mint"—
the consultant as product as transitional object

In the late 1970s a well-known company in the United Kingdom manufacturing sweets and confectionery was planning to build a new factory. It was a family firm, with a history of solid growth, and employed some three thousand people. In 1977 it was decided that one of its four factories, in London, could not be adequately refurbished within the existing building and site and should be replaced by an entirely new factory elsewhere. They wanted to take this opportunity to move away from traditional concepts of factory life, and they engaged a consultant to work with them on questions of work satisfaction and the design of the new jobs (Klein & Eason, 1991, chap. 7).

A project group at Board level had been formed, and when the consultant first met this group, in June 1977, a site had been acquired outside London and planning permission for the new factory obtained. At this meeting, the group was beginning to discuss the choice of architects and the general shape of the building. It was clear that the prospect of an entirely new factory was acting as a focus for a powerful vein of idealism in the company. Not only did they want the jobs in the new factory to be satisfying, they wanted the architecture to be innovative and human in scale, and to make a distinct contribution to the built environment.

Two concepts for the new factory were being debated: on the one hand, the concept of a large hangar-like structure within which there would be freedom and flexibility to arrange and rearrange things; on the other hand, the concept of a "village street", with small production units, as well as social facilities. Within a few minutes of joining the group, the consultant was confronted with the question: "What do you think—large hangar or village street?"

"I had, of course, no basis for an opinion, and I realized that we were in a dilemma. The concept I intended to work with was that of a production process as a sociotechnical system, i.e. one where the human and technical aspects are interdependent and need to be considered simultaneously, with the human aspects and needs playing a strong role. To translate this concept into practical reality, one needs to understand the manufacturing process and its technology in some detail. So within ten minutes of joining one of their meetings for the first time, I had met the major methodological difficulty in design—that of phasing. The company felt that they could not even begin to talk to architects until they had some idea of the basic shape of the building they wanted; one could not sensibly discuss the shape of the building without some idea of the production layout; and I could not contribute to discussion about the layout from the job-design point of view, without a sociotechnical analysis of the production process, which needed time. At that stage I had not even seen the manufacturing process."

At a second meeting the consultant worked with the project group to list job-design criteria, discussing priorities among them and relating them to production criteria. The consultant had the opportunity to spend a day in the old factory looking at the production process, but when she attended the third meeting of the project group, she was still far from really understanding the details of the production system. She had learned that the first of the products to be manufactured on the new site, a mint, consisted almost entirely of crushed sugar with some additives, which was then compressed into a tablet and packaged. Instinctively, she went back to basics:

"I was groping for a more detailed understanding, and said: 'Look, I still haven't understood the process properly—suppose I'm a piece of sugar. I've just been delivered. What happens to me?' Somebody said: 'Well, the first thing that happens to you is that you get blown along a tube. But there is a physical limit to how far you can be blown.' I said: 'OK, what happens next?' And somebody said, 'Next you get crushed into a powder.'

"In this way I talked my way through the process in very great detail, role-playing the product. For example, I heard myself saying: 'All right, so now I'm a granule—what happens next?' 'Next we drop mint oil on your head.' 'Might you miss?' 'Yes, we might.' 'How would that be discovered?' And so on.

"I checked back a number of times to ask whether this was just a game or whether it was useful, but they assured me that they were finding it very useful. The product was a fairly simple one, which they had been making for a long time, and their ways of thinking about it had become rather set. Now, these ways of thinking began to unfreeze, and they began to discover alternatives and to say to each other: 'It doesn't have to be like that, it could be like this, if such-and-such conditions are met'."

In particular, some things that had been customarily thought of in sequence could, it was found, be done in parallel. This meant that the logic of the production process was not necessarily a straight line, and this, in turn, meant that one could think in terms of a short, squat building. This was the eventual shape of the "product house" which emerged out of this process.

The consultant realized afterwards that her own strategy had instinctively been about leaving options open. Once the factory was staffed and experience of the work system was beginning to accumulate, there was more chance of reviewing and revising it in a short, squat building than in one where the logic of the layout led to long, straight lines.

During these design activities and partly through the work that had been done on design criteria, it had emerged that there was a very strong value—not to say ideology—in the company, concerning autonomous work groups and team working. This emphasis was strong and, in the consultant's view, somewhat romantic, in that group working was expected to solve a wide and diffuse range of problems. She found herself putting emphasis on unaccustomed ergonomic considerations and other "mundane" aspects of work to try to maintain some balance.

Because of the original experience, the idea of imaginatively playing with alternative ways of doing things became somewhat institutionalized in the company's design activities. The next phase of the
consultant's involvement was with the management team that the
company had been recruiting to develop, and later run, the new
factory. A residential seminar with them was organized, and the team
arrived with a rough model for the proposed product house. They
had invested £200 in Lego bricks and had worked very hard over a
weekend to produce a first tentative layout. This they presented, with
the question, "What do you think of it?" In a way that was similar to
the earlier experience, it seemed unreliable to translate the arrangement of the layout by a sheer act of imagination into the work experiences that might be going on around it:

> "I said, 'I'm not very good at reading drawings. I can't really think
> my way into this. What is actually happening down there? Sup-
> pose it's seven-thirty in the morning, what is going on?' One of
> them said: 'All right, I'll be a press operator.' Another said: 'We
> don't know if we're going to have press operators.' Gradually,
> they took on roles according to the tasks that needed to be done,
> and then someone said: 'OK, it's seven-thirty in the morning, the
> bell's gone and the doors are open . . .' He was interrupted—'What
> do you mean, bell? Are we going to have bells?' And there fol-
> lowed a long discussion on clocking-in. Their optimism and en-
> thusiasm about the consequences of autonomy was unbounded,
> and it was I who found myself playing devil's advocate—'Sup-
> pose a work group has a member who is persistently late? What
> will they do? How will they demonstrate it if there is no clock to
> give them the information?' The outcome of this discussion was
> that there should be space on a wall to install a time-clock if it
> turned out that the work groups themselves wanted one."

By midday the team had, in this way, worked their way through
the start-up and the first hour or so of production. In the process, a
number of things in the layout were changed, and it was interesting to
see how difficult it was to undo even as ephemeral a decision as the
arrangement of a few Lego bricks, given the hard work that had gone
into their original arrangement.

Example 3:
Refuelling at London Airport—
a structured, experimental approach

In contrast to the last example, there was very little spontaneity in the design of the final one. And yet it had the same function of allowing people to test out alternative strategies in a safe environment before becoming committed to one of them. There can be scope for transitional dynamics in places where psychodynamically oriented observers may not look for them; they may well be present even in a highly structured experimental context.

The story concerns the redesign of Esso Petroleum Company's aircraft refuelling function at London Airport (Shackel & Klein, 1976). At the time this work was done, Esso did about 40% of the refuelling at London's Heathrow Airport. The situation was that, after landing, aircraft parked at any one of about 100 stands on the long-haul and short-haul "aprons" of the airport. The turn-around time for most aircraft was about one hour, but one airline was already trying to reduce this to half an hour. In this time not only did passengers and fuel have to be loaded, but caterers, maintenance engineers, cleaners, and so on all need to park near and work on the plane. The job of the controller in the fuelling station was to make sure that fuelling trucks reached the aircraft on time, and the worst thing that could happen for him was that he should be responsible for delaying an aircraft.

For information about aircraft movements, the controller had on his desk the arrival and departure schedules of the airlines who were Esso customers; minute-to-minute information about the actual approach and arrival of the aircraft was received by two tickertape machines from the air traffic control centre; information about the specific fuelling needs of particular aircraft was supplied by electrowriter and by telephone links with the airlines; and information about the availability of drivers and trucks came from duty rosters and truck logs.

This job of controller had been becoming increasingly difficult. The rate of traffic through the airport was increasing at about 15% per year; traffic problems on the ground were increasing in proportion, and one could "lose" a truck in ground traffic for up to 40 minutes; and the company was very cost-conscious and kept to a minimum the controller's resources of trucks and drivers.

Job-design criteria concerning skill and autonomy were not a problem. In interviews with the controllers, it became clear that the importance of the job was clear to all and liked by all. They were very much identified with the success of the operation and had many ideas about its improvement. But all of them, in one way or another, complained of "stress", "fatigue", and inability to unwind. Inevitably, some informal ways of coping were being found: "When I know I'm going to get a delay, I phone my pal who's maintenance engineer for the airline. He'll pretend there's something the matter with the engine and start pulling it to bits."

Thus the first part of the project had been an interview study. The next phase, carried out by an external team of ergonomists, was the preparation of detailed analysis papers on all aspects of the system that were important to the controller or affected his task in some way. The papers included analyses of the tickertape, the documentation in the control-room, the communications with airlines, the movement of people in the control-room and other rooms, the role of the "bolster man" (a back-up support role), the shift-rotation scheme, the resources of men, the resources of trucks, and the implications for Esso of future changes at the airport. These formed a formal information base, checked and agreed by Esso staff, from which the proposed redesign was to be developed and critically evaluated.

From the information and analyses, detailed recommendations were made about the design and layout of the building, control-room, store of truck logs, and structure of the controller's desk, together with recommendations for noise control, heating and ventilation, lighting, and other storage facilities. A magnetic stateboard was designed to give the controller a schematic representation of the state of his resources (i.e. men and trucks) by means of coloured tags, attached to other tags representing aircraft, when they were sent out on a refuelling mission, and dismantled once the mission was complete.

A second set of recommendations then detailed the layout of the work area, the desk superstructure, the aircraft schedules, the stateboard and all tags, the men shift board, the men tag store, and colour schemes. Both the redesign of the various rooms and the desk, and the proposed new method of working, were discussed in detail with all the controllers and supervisors, and their suggestions and criticisms were taken into account in the final recommendations.

Once these discussions were complete, a simulated control-room, incorporating the new features, was built in a laboratory, and simulation experiments were designed. From information supplied by management, supervisors, and controllers, detailed running programmes for the simulation experiments were written by three postgraduate students, to obtain an accurate picture of the system. In effect, the programmes were word-for-word theatrical texts for continuous three-hour plays, in which the "actors" were enthusiastic to play their parts. Company personnel also played a large part in running the experiments, since this was the most realistic way of simulating some of the roles in the system. Students took the part of truck drivers.

Each experimental session lasted three hours, and the controller was able to walk into the replica of his office, sit down in the chair, and take over the job as he would in the real situation. The realism of the situation was indicated by the fact that controllers needed very little explanation of what to do, other than initial briefing with the new equipment. They found that they were able to react in very much the same way as in the real situation.

In this way, the controller and supervisors came and worked in the simulated control-room, testing and comparing in different sessions four different methods of working, under three different load conditions (the current load, the load predicted for the following year's peak period, and the anticipated load for five years ahead). Repeated questionnaires and interviews tested opinions at different stages of the experiments. The intention was that the people who would be operating the system could contribute their experience to its design, would be able to try a number of alternatives before deciding on a solution, and could have some idea of how long that solution would remain viable. In particular, they would be able to try out some ideas of the designers which were unfamiliar to them, and which they at first did not like, in safe conditions. The idea of the magnetic stateboard had caused some anxiety, because it did not provide the same permanent record as pieces of paper, since the tags representing each mission were put back into store once the mission was over. However, during the experiments the controllers discovered that they could feel safe with this method.

The solution arrived at in this way was installed and was found to be still in use and well liked four and seven years later (one indication of reduced stress for the controllers was that, where they had previously stood and hovered over the desk to do the job, especially during peak load times, they were now sitting to do the job and standing up at intervals to stretch).

Simulation and the testing of alternatives are not, of course, new concepts in design; it is unusual, however, to find such explicit and realistic attention paid to the human aspects of the situation. It is quite possible, for example, to simulate some of the "softer" aspects of social system functioning, such as the effect on a group that has interdependent roles when one member stays away or is slower than the others. In the case of the Esso refuelling controllers, it was found during the experiments that, as they gained increasing control over their own situation, having enough spare capacity through the simplification and streamlining of the work to be able to plan ahead instead of panic-reacting to events as they happened, there were consequences for industrial relations: before, rest-pauses and meal breaks for the drivers had tended to be either very short or very long; now, they were instinctively being scheduled in a much more equitable way.

Discussion

The story of Poor Old Henry has been presented in more detail than the other two cases, because it was developed by clients and because it has not been published before outside the NHS. Although the other two have been published before, it has nevertheless seemed worthwhile to recapitulate them briefly, because the set of three shows how the same ends can be achieved in ways that appear to be quite different.

All three cases, it turned out, had the necessary transitional characteristics of exploring and testing-out in a safe environment, with outcomes not known in advance. In all three there was an element of acting, of theatre. The element of play involved in the use of scenarios in the hospital, especially that concerning Henry, was a key feature in the move towards more integrated working. It undoubtedly helped that the meetings were handled in a light-hearted way and contained a good deal of wit and humour. It is a relief to be able to laugh about a patient's misfortunes, since he is only a fiction—"People became very fond of Henry". Humour also featured in the situation of a grown-up woman role-playing a confectionery product. This was not so much so in the somewhat formal situation of a simulation experiment; in the safety of the laboratory this, too, however, was relatively light-hearted compared with the real hazards of the actual job.

At the same time, it needs to be said that none of the strategies involved in these cases had been planned on this—transitional—theoretical basis. One is reminded of Molière's "Bourgeois Gentilhomme", who discovered that he had been speaking prose all his life.

CHAPTER EIGHT

The role of facilitators as mediators in transitional process: a South African case study

Colin Legum

Features of transition in political systems

Because the dramatic events in Eastern Europe in the 1980s happened to coincide with no less far-reaching changes in South Africa, there is a tendency to see similarities in these developments, but the conditions—and therefore the dynamics—of the negotiating and change processes in Eastern Europe are fundamentally different from what has occurred in South Africa. One essential difference is that whereas in Eastern Europe the struggles over changes in power relations threatened a comparatively recently established ruling class and political system, in South Africa they involved a historic transformation of a political, economic, and social system that, in its essentials, had endured for over three centuries. The political system of White supremacy is the longest surviving ideological system in the modern world. The mechanisms for safeguarding this system have, of course, changed from old-fashioned racial segregation to the newfangled system of apartheid in response to the forces of modernization, industrialization, and progressive changes in power relations between the White minority and the Black majority. But the continuum of a master–servant society remained intact until February 1990 when the ruling Afrikaner party was forced, finally, to break the historic mould, having accepted the inescapable reality that the apartheid system was no longer workable.

Yet another crucial difference between the processes of change in Eastern Europe and South Africa is that change became possible in the Soviet bloc as a result of the rapid and complete loss of the ruling party's power. This not only resulted in the collapse of the internal political system in Russia, but also encouraged the nations of the region to reassert their separate identities, their long-suppressed individualism, and their national history. In South Africa, on the other hand, although there had been a slow erosion of power, the ruling Afrikaner Nationalist Party had not completely lost power and remained a major negotiating partner in the process of transition. However, the problems facing both Eastern Europe and South Africa had one important element in common—namely, how to handle the transition from an authoritarian political system to a participatory democratic system.

In South Africa, for the first time in modern history, a still strongly entrenched and richly privileged ruling class embarked on a process of negotiation with the explicit understanding that any agreed new power relationship would not only fracture its supremacy, but would demand considerable economic sacrifices and the pain of uncertainty. By the time the decision was taken to negotiate with representative Black leaders, White society was in the grip of paranoia, fearing that a Black majority would "persecute" the White minority just as the White society had actively persecuted those it feared. By and large the White society, especially the Afrikaners, had been indoctrinated in a belief that its survival in the southern tip of Africa could be guaranteed only through a political system that ensured total political, military, and economic control by the White minority. The paranoiac environment of violence, suspicion, and fear was hardly conducive to the success of a negotiating process that President de Klerk presented to the White electorate as an exercise in "power-sharing", but without defining the basis on which power was to be shared. Was it to be the power relationship between the jockey and the race horse, as power-sharing was once defined by the former Rhodesian premier, Sir Godfrey Huggins?

In the two decades preceding President de Klerk's historic declaration of 2 February 1990, when he announced the complete reversal of the policies pursued by White ruling elites since 1652, a relatively small number of White South Africans, both Afrikaans- and English-speaking, had begun to challenge the legitimacy and morality of White supremacy. Some belonged to the liberal Progressive Federal Party (now Democratic Party); some joined protest movements such as the all-White women's Black Sash and a score or more of other campaigning pressure groups; some, motivated largely by financial interests, became active in business circles; some, like Dr van Zyl Slabbert and Alex Boraine, left parliament to establish an extra-parliamentary bridge-building group; some joined Black political movements; some began to voice their concern in the Christian churches; while others, like the poet Breyten Breytenbach, the playwright Athol Fugard, and the Dutch Reformed Church dissident, the Revd Beyers Naude, committed themselves as individuals. It is on one such individual, Professor H. W. van der Merwe, that this study focuses, both because of his rare understanding of the process of dynamic change in a society undergoing transition, and also because of his personal contribution to opening up the channels of communication between White and Black leaders. For convenience, van der Merwe is referred to in this chapter by his widely-known initials, HW. He was until 1993 the director of the Centre for Intergroup Studies (CIS) at the University of Cape Town.

The CIS, which was established in 1968 under the aegis of the University of Cape Town, is committed to the facilitation of communication between conflicting groups, both nationally and in the different communities, as a means of promoting a just peace in South Africa. The CIS has formulated a number of conceptual, ethical, and strategic principles concerning the accommodation of conflict in South Africa. These principles are summarized in a later section of this chapter. It should be noted at this stage, however, that in contrast with the widespread use of the term "conflict resolution", the CIS prefers to use the term "conflict accommodation" as a generic term to include all methods, practices, and techniques used to resolve or settle disputes. Its disagreement with the term "conflict resolution" is that it suggests the termination of a particular conflict through the elimination of its underlying causes, whereas "conflict accommodation" envisages a more comprehensive and far-reaching process than mere "conflict settlement" which is based on mutual compromise. Its approach is based on the view that the majority of conflicts in the world are settled or accommodated rather than resolved. In the complex South African situation, "resolution" could be interpreted as overambitious, unrealistic, or even irresponsible, whereas "accommodation" denotes the processes by which conflicting parties come to a settlement or to accommodating conflicting claims, aspirations, or needs, while acknowledging that the underlying structural causes of conflicts may not yet have been eradicated. Although the ideas and practices of the CIS have grown out of the South African experience, their application applies with equal cogency to serious conflict situations in other parts of the world.

The emergence of a bridge-builder in a polarized society

Peacemakers, HW has written, are always suspect on both sides. Speaking of the situation in his polarized society in Ulster, the Revd Ian Paisley has said: "Bridge-builders and traitors are alike; they both go over to the other side." It is a view that, until recently, was also widely held in South Africa and, most particularly, by Afrikaners about individuals in their own community. Unless there is a strong-enough support group, most people do not opt for the middle way for fear of falling between two stools. HW, however, succeeded in taking the middle way on his own.

HW comes from a typically traditionalist Afrikaner background. He was born in the Cape Province in 1929 and began his working life as a farmer. Drawn by strong Christian beliefs, he joined the Dutch Reformed Church Mission in Southern Rhodesia at the age of 19 as an industrial instructor and superintendent of African schools. He returned from Rhodesia still convinced that God willed the separation of White and Black in both state and church, and he refused even to shake hands with a Black man. Then, in his own words (1974), he recalls a

> new vision which suddenly dawned on me when my own elder brother referred to a Black female as a woman (*vrou*) instead of the normally derogatory maid (*meid*). I realised we were all one people of one world. A new world opened up for me. I saw myself as part of Africa: an Afrikaner became an African. My new approach

to my fellow South Africans inevitably brought tensions with my church which tenaciously clung to the traditional beliefs in apartheid or separation. I longed for an association in which I could give expression to my personal convictions.

This he found when he and his wife were resident hosts at an international student centre run by the Quakers at the University of California at Los Angeles where he had gone in 1958 to study sociology. Back in South Africa, he became involved with Quaker Service, which gave him scope to serve others and to give expression both to his political views, especially those regarding race relations, and also to his deepest religious convictions. He also learned (1975) that "concern for the welfare of any section of the population, and most of all the Black masses, cannot avoid the politics of race relations, the central issue of national politics in South Africa". However, he found it difficult to break with the Dutch Reformed Church, a step he finally took only in 1973.

Meanwhile, in 1968, he had been appointed as the first director of the CIS, which provided him with both a platform for his ideas and an opportunity to develop his thinking about the nature of conflict in South Africa. Early on he identified one major problem to be the virtually complete absence of communication between Whites and Blacks other than in a master–servant relationship. "There are", he wrote (1974), "seemingly irreconcilable differences between the government and the broadly-based Black leadership as regards their respective positions on power, equality, the pace of change and apartheid, and with each side feeling threatened with a serious erosion of its political base as if publicly seen to acknowledge the legitimacy of the other." His conclusion was that in a situation where direct communication between conflicting parties is absent, it becomes necessary for a third party to intervene to facilitate communication. This was the role he identified for himself and his Centre. In the early 1970s, he embarked on the sensitive and controversial task of trying to open up channels of communication across the dividing lines, first with the Afrikaner Studentebond, the Black SA Students Organization, and the White National Union of SA students, as well as with the Black Consciousness leader, Steve Biko. Later, during visits to England he began to develop personal relationships with officials of the African National Congress (ANC). These led to meetings with its leaders at their headquarters in Lusaka, Zambia, where he found them ready to talk with influential White South Africans. A significant breakthrough occurred in 1984 when he arranged for Piet Muller, the assistant editor of the pro-government *Beeld*, to have interviews with the ANC in Lusaka. Muller, despite a law prohibiting publication of the views of the ANC, subsequently wrote articles favourable to the idea of government talks with the ANC. In HW's view, this opening up of the lines of communication played an important part in breaking the political deadlock. Even in government circles, there was private praise for HW's "brokering" role. Soon, too, he was able to visit Nelson Mandela in prison and to establish a close relationship with him. His highly favourable impressions of Mandela, which he conveyed to government and wider circles, contributed to the decision of the minister of justice to hold private talks with Mandela, which finally led to the decision to free him.

As a Quaker, HW believes in "quiet diplomacy", but as a Quaker he also believes in non-violence, a position difficult to defend in a situation where the government's "structural violence" was countered by the liberation movement's armed struggle. After a particularly violent interaction between the government and the ANC in 1982/83 involving the latter's bomb attacks inside the country, and the army's raids on ANC cadres in neighbouring Lesotho and Mozambique, HW issued a statement (1974) expressing disapproval of violence on both sides, backed by a decision to make a personal contribution to victims on both sides. Although his statement was attacked from both sides, it nevertheless played an important role in the development of trust between himself and the ANC, as well as with the government. This, he says, enabled his role as a facilitator to develop.

The negotiating process in a society in transition

At different periods of their social, political, and economic development, most societies find themselves caught up not just in a situation demanding change, but in a transitional situation where fundamental change, controlled and self-conscious, is needed to restore an internal equilibrium by creating new power relations involving structural changes in their society. But very few modern societies have been confronted, as in the case of South Africa, with a breakdown of their entire political system. Where a transfer of power from one party to another can take place within an established and accepted political system, this presupposes the existence both of institutionalized rival political groupings and of at least a measure of freedom to pressure groups representing different interests. Such a system allows for evolutionary change. Where this does not exist, however, the society is faced with a real danger of revolutionary change. The only alternative to this is fundamental change in power relations and in the structures of the state—that is, adaptive change achieved through negotiated agreements.

Even in situations where adaptive change becomes possible, as now in the case of South Africa, a process of accommodation usually begins before there is acceptance of the need for a negotiating process. Such a process of accommodation, which calls for adjustments in the demands, behaviour, and expectations of both sides engaged in the conflict situation, should be seen as an essential preliminary stage in the negotiating process. It is a time when both sides engage in coercive actions to increase their own bargaining power and to diminish that of their opponents. It is also a testing-out period to decide whether and how far the other side can be trusted and to establish the minimal conditions likely to lead to agreement.

This preliminary stage is usually characterized by violence on both sides ("structural violence" by the state, "reactive violence" by its challengers), by accusations of ill-will generally expressed in extreme language ("terrorism", "treachery", "gross abuse of human rights", etc.), and by mutual expressions of a determination not to surrender to each other's demands. At the same time, subtle changes begin to occur, mostly not expressed in public, when the parties in the conflict begin to perceive that their own maximalist demands are unrealizable, and when damage limitation comes to be seen as being in the interests of both sides, but especially by the holders of power. Only when this point is reached does mediation become possible. Attempts at mediation before the right time are doomed to failure. Nevertheless, even in this stony period, there is a role for mediators to play in preparing the ground for meaningful negotiations. Such a role, in its early stages, excludes any attempt at intervention, even by "honest brokers". It can be defined as the role of the "facilitator" who is engaged in opening up channels of communication between the defenders of power and their challengers. This was the role defined and assumed by HW during the 27 years that preceded the final acceptance of the need for meaningful negotiations.

The pre-negotiation stage described above is typical of serious conflict situations, ranging all the way from the anti-colonial struggles in the Third World to Vietnam, Zimbabwe, Namibia, post-independence Mozambique, and Angola. Apart from violence, a major characteristic of this phase is paranoid behaviour, which is an effective barrier against meaningful communications between the parties engaged in the conflict. But within the camps of both sides, one finds the voices of sanity and realism which seek to establish a dialogue across non-communication barriers. These are the bridge-builders.

South Africa has had to face up to the imperative need for fundamental change at a late stage in its process of industrialization. The White minority community increasingly came to experience the loss of its former total political, economic, and military power, while the Black majority came increasingly to believe that White supremacy was no longer unassailable. This shift of internal power relations also began to affect the traditional views held by South Africa's friends and major trading partners in the West who began to respond, some more willingly than others, by exerting pressures on the government to abandon apartheid in favour of negotiating with its Black challengers. A climate of insecurity built up, and the country's buoyant economy went into decline. In place of the old certainties, there was a new questioning of traditional policies and attitudes and the beginning of a search for a different kind of society and a new political system: the hallmarks of a society ripe for transition.

The character of the transition period in South Africa was of population groups identifying with different national symbols such as the national anthem, the flag, and historic heroes. The polarization and tensions between the opposing trends towards greater authoritarianism and non-racial democracy reached a point of crisis where all the major parties in the conflict shrank back from all-out violence in favour of a negotiating process. This period saw the articulation of pain by both the White and the Black communities. This articulation of pain by both sides is a necessary stage in the process of turning away from the past. According to Professor L. D. Dekker (1988) in a paper distributed by the CIS, this stage called for an examination of the concepts of retribution (the past), reciprocity vs. retaliation (the present), and reparation (the future). The question is whether third-

party intervention can break the "blame syndrome" into which retribution locks the relationship and facilitate development towards
reparation when a common purpose for future relations can be identified. Dekker answers the question affirmatively "because crucial
components of the South African social system are already operating
in a transition which provides for considerable *space and time* for
action by change groups". He suggests that, as in the industrial relations system, retribution can be transformed into reparation if the
space and time potentials are utilized to the full.

Towards clarification of the role of a mediator

In situations where face-to-face negotiations between principal opponents are difficult or impossible, or where the ongoing process of
negotiation becomes deadlocked, the need for mediation by a third
party arises. The mediator is committed to an intervening role in
which she or he either offers possible solutions and ways of overcoming deadlocks in a negotiating process, or acts only to facilitate communication between the opposing sides. It is crucially important to
distinguish not only between different types of third-party intervention but also between the different roles that can be performed by a
mediator.

Three types of third-party intervention

Arbitration.   Arbitration is sometimes confused with mediation,
but there are important differences. It is, rather, a form of adjudica-
tion in which the third party decides the issues dividing the disputants, whereas in mediation the intermediary helps the disputants to
reach voluntary agreements. The arbitrator is required to reach a
decision binding on both sides; the mediator has no such authority.
The mediator, however, may engage in either of the other two types
of intervention described below.

Conciliation.   The conciliator usually plays an active role in facilitating exchange, by suggesting possible solutions and by assisting the
parties to reach a voluntary agreement. She or he can help unlock the

negotiating process by offering interpretations of what is happening in the group, clarifying points at issue, pointing up areas of agreement, and drawing attention to negative behaviour.

Facilitation. The facilitator's role is strictly confined to promoting communication between the parties in conflict. Facilitators do not suggest solutions or make proposals to help the parties reach agreement; their role is primarily technical: the improvement of communication as a means of promoting understanding and of conveying to each side what the other actually intends.

The mediator as either facilitator or conciliator

According to HW, facilitating communication is an end in itself in much the same way as one can pursue knowledge for the sake of knowledge. While the conciliator is relatively more concerned with the use made of new insights gained from reliable communication, the facilitator is primarily concerned with ensuring that the relevant parties gain reliable information regardless of what use they make of it. Facilitators are less likely than conciliators to be seen as meddlers, busybodies or preachers seeking to reconcile differences.

In situations of extreme polarization and intense suspicion, the facilitator is more likely to be acceptable to conflicting parties than is the conciliator. The neutral and almost technical services of the facilitator would appear to be more functional than the services of the conciliator morally committed to peacemaking. While having no political, economic, or military clout, facilitators working either as a team or as individuals have the freedom to be flexible, to disregard protocol, and to press the need for constructive initiatives or magnanimous gestures in order to fulfil the primary task of getting antagonists to accept the possibility that negotiations might be productive. Their role in the first place is to break the ice and to create a climate conducive to negotiations. Once the stage of negotiations has been reached, the facilitator can be helpful in clarifying misunderstandings or reducing suspicions about the antagonists' intentions and behaviour by informally clarifying and conveying information in situations where deadlock threatens the negotiating process.

In sum, the facilitator is a communication process specialist who is not overtly involved in problems under discussion and has no stake or prescriptive preferment in the outcome of negotiations, but who helps the group to come to an understanding.

In his writings, however, HW (1989a) also gives a wider description of the role of facilitator than just that of providing "neutral and almost technical services". For example, he stresses that impartiality does not mean indifference towards serious moral issues. On the contrary, impartial concern may reflect a particular view of morality. The facilitator, he says, should help parties to identify and confront the issues in an analytic and rational way. She or he must also try to help to provide favourable conditions in which to confront the issues. Parties to a conflict often try to make it easier for themselves by simplifying issues and focusing on their own viewpoints because this mobilizes their constituencies and gains support. But to strip a conflict of its complexity is to falsify it. One function of the facilitator, therefore, is to help participants to acknowledge that they are enmeshed together in a complex and multidimensional problem. Helping conflicting parties to "acknowledge" the complexities of the situation in which they are "enmeshed" with others is clearly important to the opening up of channels of communication.

Effective mediation and its context

The principles of "effective mediation" defined by Walter A. Maggiolo (1971) are incorporated in the CIS's approach. These are: (1) the mediator must understand and appreciate the problems confronting the parties; (2) the mediator must impart to the parties the fact that she or he knows and appreciates their problems; (3) the mediator creates doubts in their minds as to the validity of the position they have assumed with respect to their problems; (4) the mediator suggests alternative approaches that may facilitate agreement. In HW's role of a facilitator opening up communications between the government and the ANC, this last principle was inappropriate, but facilitators might use it in their work as neutral mediators in community conflict situations in which they are involved.

Factors that have an impact on mediator behaviour include: (1) the relationship of the parties before the dispute; (2) the anticipated relationship of the parties after the dispute is resolved; (3) the prior experience of each of the parties with the negotiation and mediation process; (4) the information gap between the parties over the issue in dispute; (5) the balance of power between the parties; (6) whether the parties are individuals, community organizations, coalitions, government entities, or other established institutions; (7) whether the issues affect only the disputants or a broader segment of society.

Third-party intervention as either neutral or partisan: the controversy

Mediators engage in roles that can be either neutral or partisan. Each role can have a valid place in conflict accommodation. Understanding the advantages and limitations of these different roles is a major contribution made by the academic work of the CIS, and particularly by HW's personal experience.

The success of a mediator depends on the degree of credibility she or he has established with both sides in a conflict. While the mediator may be impartial in the conduct of negotiations, she or he is not necessarily neutral as to the outcome. Whether a mediator can ever be truly neutral remains a subject of controversy, as has been frequently demonstrated in the role of intermediaries in civil rights conflicts, environmental issues, spouse abuse, family crises, or disputes involving apparent injustices or where there is a significant power imbalance between conflicting parties.

As a practitioner of facilitation, HW faced the difficulty of how to reconcile this role with his advocacy of change in social and economic structures that provoke conflict. This is an issue raised by Adam Curle (1988) in correspondence with HW, his fellow-Quaker:

> We both agree that the two activities I would call mediation, and work for change in social and economic structures that provoke conflict, are usually essential aspects of peacemaking. However, while I separate them ... HW considers them to be linked or perhaps unified. In my experience as an outside third party to conflict situations, it is virtually impossible to combine the roles of mediator and social agent: the impartiality necessary to the former doesn't mix with the partisan character of the latter. Moreover, having played both roles myself, though at different times, I maintain that they demand different skills and methods. For Hendrik [HW], working largely in his own society, I acknowledge that the situation is dissimilar and that for those like him (if there are any—his skill and sensitivity, courage and dedication are surely unique), it is both feasible and right to assume both

parts. But to refer to them collectively as mediation seems to me as inaccurate and confusing. There are different strands in peace-making ... and it is important that we recognize their various functions in this difficult and intricate process. Certainly, they must be woven together if just and stable peace is to be achieved, some of them perhaps in the work of a single individual or group. But I believe our collective efforts for peace will be strengthened by understanding the differing character of each strand.

Responding to Curle, HW claimed there was only a "semantic mis-understanding" between them. He explained (1988c):

I gave the impression that the mediator should sacrifice his im-partiality for the partisan character of the person who takes sides and promotes political change. Curle rightly warns against this. He also appreciates the forces that have influenced my own ap-proach. As a mediator in South Africa, I have become compara-tively more conscious of the socio-economic forces that have shaped the lives, opinions and attitudes of the political leaders of different groups. I see my task concerned with more than just removing "mental obstacles" and "subjective psychological atti-tudes". I cannot see my task as "entirely devoted to work on the mental obstacles to peace, believing that if these can be dimin-ished, so will the material ones". I believe that the socio-economic, as well as the subjective psychological ones, must be dealt with. While I agree with Adam's distinction between mediation and some kind of activism, I want to argue that attempts to remove socio-economic, structural or material obstacles to peace should not be confused with activism, that is, taking sides with one or other contending party. To give just one example: there are both psychological and structural obstacles to communication between Whites and Blacks in the apartheid system. As mediator, I see it as my task to work for the elimination of both types of obstacles. By working for the removal of apartheid as a system, I am not taking sides in the normal sense of political activity. In fact, I believe I have remained comparatively impartial between the major con-tending parties.

HW extended this argument by conceding that

mediators in real life are often also opinion-makers: by reaching out to the public they extend the negotiation process to other levels of society and facilitate the acceptance of agreements. How-ever, the blurring of the roles of private, discreet mediators and public opinion-makers causes severe tensions and can be highly controversial. . . . But, in a situation like that in South Africa, it is difficult separate the private role of the detached mediator and a public—even aggressive—educational campaign of the opinion-maker.

Both mediators and opinion-makers bring contending leaders together and they also try to influence their constituencies:

> There are sometimes convincing reasons for mediators to go public even during the process of intervention. Third parties can help in resolving disputes constructively to the extent that they are known and seen as prestigious.

HW confesses that he has experienced, and still does, "a fairly serious dilemma and considerable ambivalence between my private role as facilitator and my public role as opinion-maker"—a role that attaches to his position as director of his CIS.

Conceptions and principles underlying the mediation process in conflict accommodation

Some of the principles, work practices, and training workshops developed by the CIS are eclectic and derive from the experience of others engaged in conflict resolution or accommodation. The CIS, thanks mainly to HW's experience, has also provided new principles of its own and developed ideas about the dynamics of a negotiating process and the role skills required. But it has not, so far, articulated ideas about transitional processes; this is explored in the final section of this chapter.

Power relations between negotiating parties

Gross asymmetry of power between contending groups hampers successful negotiations; therefore, an essential component of successful negotiation is a balance of power sufficient to enable each party to exert pressures and inflict cost on the other, so that both are able to act autonomously. If one party is too weak to inflict substantial costs on its opponent, it cannot effectively affect the outcome of the process. A dominant group is more likely to consider negotiations when it perceives a state of stalemated power relations, or sees the alternative as resulting in unacceptable losses. Central to the negotiating process is a movement towards a more even power symmetry between the rival parties.

The appropriate timing of mediation

One salutary conclusion of the CIS's experience is that mediation is not possible or appropriate in all conflict situations. HW points out (1988c) that:

> major social and political changes are usually brought about by varying degrees of confrontation. Mediation must not be used to hold back the inevitable process of change. In political conflict, gross asymmetry of power inhibits the negotiation process and is detrimental to a lasting negotiated settlement. In such situations there may be a greater need for an activist who helps latent conflict to become manifest, and who promotes the process of empowerment as an important pre-condition to negotiation. If a community has generated the energy to confront authority and demand legitimate change, it would be wasteful to defuse the situation before a strong case had been made by the protesting party. It would be counter-productive for the mediator to enter this kind of situation too soon, or at the request of the establishment only, or even if asked to come in by a few faint-hearted members of the community. Under such conditions, partisan intervention on behalf of the weaker party is required together with, or even prior to, neutral intervention. . . . In situations where direct communication between conflicting parties is absent, it becomes necessary for a third party to intervene to facilitate communication.

However, in situations where violence has become merely destructive and fruitless, mediation to arrange a truce becomes a priority. This need has arisen on several occasions in South Africa in situations known as "township violence" between rival Black groups or, in Natal, between the Zulu Inkatha movement and its opponents. HW and his CIS have responded to appeals to intervene as mediators in situations where both parties have made clear their wish for a reduction of violence but without compromising their principles.

The place of coercion and violence

In situations such as in South Africa (and here one can think also of Israel, The Netherlands, and Sudan), there is no choice between negotiation and coercion; the most that can be sought for is a proper balance between them. HW argues that conflict and consensus are correlative (1988a):

> Coercion and co-operation are proper and useful modes of action in both domestic and international relations. Both are part of the dialectic of social life. It therefore seems inadvisable to distinguish too sharply between a consensus model and a conflict model of society. Conflict is a natural endemic condition of society and can serve positive functions, provided it is channelled and accommodated constructively.

HW (1989b) defines violence as "the improper use of force". The use of force to injure, harm, or constrain someone is an extreme manifestation of destructive conflict. It is a result of the failure to accommodate conflict successfully, or to regulate it:

> We define violence as the application of force, action, motive or thought in such a way ... that a person or group is injured, controlled or destroyed in a physical, psychological or spiritual sense. Violence was traditionally associated only with physical acts used by people in protest; in recent years, concepts of structural or institutional violence have been formulated. Violence committed through the legal machinery and institutions of the social system or the state is referred to as institutional or structural violence, involving the restriction of choices available to some part of a community through laws or customs which create inequalities of opportunity or treatment. While violence is usually abhorred in public rhetoric, it is almost as endemic as conflict itself. This is due to many factors, including the generally accepted view that violence *does* work, the relative aggressiveness of human nature, and the fact that, with the exception of the minute percentage of universal pacifists, war is accepted by all mankind as a legitimate instrument of last resort. All nations recognize the validity of violence in pursuit or protection of national interests. The selective use of such terms as "violence" and "force" reflect political biases.

Although HW and his CIS hold such views, and express them publicly, they did not completely alienate the government, probably because in recent years the government itself has begun to understand the dialectics of violence and counter-violence and the need to defuse the level of violence.

The credibility of a third party

Credibility of a third party can derive either from an institutional base or because of the proven credentials of an individual. In the case of the CIS, it derives from both; but, as explained above, HW admits to finding himself in a serious dilemma because of his dual role as a facilitator and his position as director of an institute that performs the role of opinion-maker. HW (1990) describes an opinion-maker as

> someone making a contribution to public thinking and political action. To the extent that he is successful and has an impact on constructive developments, he may claim and deserve credit. Such credit may, however, hamper progress if the facilitator instead of the contending parties is given the credit for progress in negotiations. Facilitators should generally stay out of the public eye.

This may be good theory, but it is not always possible in practice, for, as HW admits: (1990) "Most of us engage in both activities at one time or another depending on the occasion, the circumstances, and our own dispositions. No wonder these two roles are often confused in the public mind."

In a polarized society it is especially difficult to find an individual who is capable of gaining and retaining the confidence of both sides. Sincerity is obviously a key quality, but it is not enough. It requires, above all, the ability to empathize with the parties in a conflict, showing an understanding of the concerns and interests of all the sides, but—and this is the really difficult part—without intervenors surrendering their own moral position in a situation that calls for a moral stand. At no time did HW disguise the fact that he was motivated primarily by humanitarian concerns: an appreciation of "the fears of the Afrikaner community", as well as concern with, and sympathy for, "the deprived Black community". He wrote (1974) that "awareness of the grave injustices of the current political system brought home to me the urgent need for fundamental change in the social structure".

A number of White South Africans share these concerns and show sympathy for the oppressed in their society, but very few succeeded in gaining the confidence of African leaders without losing that of their fellow Whites to match HW's achievement. One possible explanation is that his humanitarian concern was complemented by a clear understanding of the needs of all sides in the conflict—a crucial qualification for anybody engaged in mediation.

Recognizing "needs" in conflict accommodation

The "theory of needs", which has been evolved by practitioners involved in conflict accommodation in many different situations, postulates that it is more important to stress the "needs" of parties in conflict than their "values" and "interests". Needs cannot be curbed, socialized, or negotiated. Scholars like John Burton (1979) emphasize that individuals have certain basic "needs" not only in a physical sense (e.g. food and shelter), but also as a social unit (e.g. recognition and security). According to Burton: "Needs describe those conditions or opportunities that are essential to the individual if he is to be a functioning and cooperative member of society, conditions that are essential to his development and which, through him, are essential to the organisation and survival of society."

This theory has led to acceptance of the idea that, in order to be effective, negotiations require some accommodation of the "needs" of the weaker party where a power imbalance exists. Conflicts over social needs are not of a zero-sum nature since the increase in the security of one party does not automatically lead to an equal decrease in security for other parties.

Having identified *issues, interests,* and *needs,* the mediator needs to help establish agreed norms for rational interaction, such as effective communication, mutual respect, acceptance of the use of persuasion rather than coercion, and the desirability of reaching a mutually satisfying agreement.

Achieving effective communication

Since opening up communication between parties in conflict is central to the facilitator's role, it is essential that she or he should understand the requirements of "effective communication". Communication involves transmitting messages. The meaning of "the message" must be shared between the parties; there needs to be agreement on the content of "the message". But, as pointed out by Louise Nieuwmeijer (1985) in a workshop organized by the CIS,

> This is naturally an ideal state of affairs since no person can be another person, experience his experience, knowledge and attitudes—the only way to completely comprehend the meaning of the communicator's message. But meaning can be shared . . . to a workable extent if people "meet" each other, that is, systematically work towards a shared meaning through a process of give and take.

The essential requirements for anyone engaged as a mediator in a negotiating process are a capacity for empathy and an ability to be a "good listener". According to Khalil Gibran (quoted in Nieuwmeijer, 1985): "The reality of the other person is not what he reveals to you, but what he cannot reveal to you. Therefore, if you would understand him, listen not to what he says, but rather to what he does not say." In the phrase used by the Tavistock Institute of Human Relations, one should "listen to the music behind the words". Moreover, there is in every group, as Dr Tom Main was the first to elucidate, "a hidden agenda". The golden rule of listening has been defined by Chief Justice Alan B. Gold of Quebec (1981): "What a mediator should do when she or he first comes into the picture is—Stop, Look, Listen. Stop is 'do nothing until you have learned' . . . Look is to 'identify the parties and the problems.' Listen, which is probably the most important of them all, is simply what it says: 'listen to what the parties tell you'." Professor James A. Wall (1981) reviewed 50 publications, dating back to 1952, to determine how mediators function, and he extracted 104 techniques and tactics employed by them. Not one included the word "listen".

The institutionalization and legitimation of conflict accommodation

Successful industrial relations show that the institutionalizing of conflict within structures that accept the legitimacy of both parties is essential for successful negotiation. Institutionalization of negotiations is a significant principle in dealing with other conflict situations as well, such as political conflicts.

For negotiations to succeed and to secure the effective implementation of what has been agreed, it is essential that those involved in the negotiations are seen as legitimate representatives. Legitimacy requires authority deriving from its voluntary acceptance by a commanding majority of those on whose behalf negotiators engage in talks to reach agreement. Successful negotiation can occur only if it involves legitimate representatives. Failure to understand this was a major obstacle to peacemaking in Israel until the government recognized the PLO as an acceptable negotiating partner. This was also the case in Northern Ireland until the IRA suspended its campaign of violence and made itself an acceptable negotiating partner.

Legitimacy and power are integrally related concepts. A state cannot claim to have effective power if it is not accepted as being truly representative and legitimate. In the words of Hannah Arendt (1970): "Power springs up whenever people get together and act in concert, but it derives its legitimacy from the initial getting together rather than from any action that may then follow. Legitimacy, when challenged, bases itself on an appeal to the past, while justification relates to an end that lies in the future."

The complementary goals of peace and justice

While these two goals are usually accepted by all parties and mediators, their unique relationship is not always fully appreciated. It requires an understanding that peace and justice are ideal states that can never be fully achieved; they are complementary only in the sense that the one cannot be pursued without regard to the other. The roles of conciliators seeking to achieve peace and of the proponents of justice (prophets) coexist in a state of tension, often within the same person who carries these roles within him/herself.

The mediator seeking to obtain peace at all costs is likely to underplay justice. One thinks here of the role of the British prime minister, Neville Chamberlain, at the time of Munich. By succeeding in arranging some kind of truce or apparent peace, the source of conflict, inequality, and injustice remains unchanged. On the other hand, the promotion of justice at all costs can undermine the chances of reaching an agreement that could provide the basis for a stable future society.

Determining the pace of change

Short- and long-term considerations should determine negotiating strategies. It is possible to reconcile gradual and radical change. Demands for radical change involving a rational plan of action are more likely to assure the achievement of a desired goal than is a "cataclysmic outburst".

Disagreement about the pace and rate of change is important and genuine. In the South African situation, the majority of the White community, which accepted the inevitability that fundamental structural change involves the loss of privileges, attempted whatever was in their power to determine the pace of change. It argued for incremental change, while those who wished to hasten the transition period favoured quick change. Although differences over means do constitute severe causes of conflict, they can be more amenable to rational debate than differences over goals. Where both parties favour orderly change, as happened in South Africa, the achievement of acceptable compromise is not impossible.

The importance of saving face

The mediator needs to take account of the fact that in any conflict situation, and particularly in adversarial politics, parties go out of their way to embarrass their opponents whenever they change policy or admit past errors. Leaders want, at all costs, to avoid any appearance of backing down under pressure. For this reason, negotiators have to help to make any agreement reached seem as prestigious and attractive as possible to all constituencies.

Unless this is done, negotiators risk losing their constituencies. Elementary as this approach may seem, it played a key role in the initial stages of the negotiating process between the South African government and the ANC. Once mediators—that is, active mediators—have helped to formulate solutions in the private negotiation process, they must help to develop circumstances favourable to the implementation of the proposed solutions.

Aiming for a win–win agreement

Most negotiations create expectations of a win–lose result. This is fatal to a successful outcome. What is crucially important is to change the agenda to envisage a win–win situation in which both parties stand to gain, rather than to encourage the idea of winners and losers. By demonstrating how both sides can hope to gain from a settlement, it is possible to defuse anxieties about the nature of the outcome.

Validation of HW's principles and underlying assumptions

The ultimate test of the validity of the principles of mediation summarized above is, of course, the effectiveness of the results of their application in achieving conflict accommodation. The purpose of the present section is to emphasize that the outcome of the application of HW's ideas and principles during the long process of facilitating communication and negotiation fully justifies those principles. This process in fact culminated in the holding of a Convention for a Democratic South Africa (CODESA). At this convention, national agreement was obtained in 1993 concerning the fundamental changes required in the country's society at social, political, and economic levels.

The holding of this convention, as a forum where face-to-face negotiations between the principal parties could begin, was essentially the result of HW's efforts to establish the conditions that would allow it to take place. Once agreement had been reached about the intention to hold such a forum, HW saw his role as facilitator completed, and he took no further part in the subsequent CODESA negotiations. Despite numerous difficulties and hold-ups, these negotiations progressed because CODESA provided the *time and space* for the adversaries to reach a better understanding of each other's *needs and fears,* and to accept compromises that neither side had contemplated at the outset of the negotiations. A major compromise that saved the talks was the acceptance of the need for a transitional period of five years of power-sharing in a national government.

In accounting for the success of these negotiations, the preceding work of HW in establishing and practising the principles of facilitation was without any doubt a—if not *the*—major factor. It is therefore worthwhile to consider what were HW's basic beliefs or assumptions that underlay all his work. In the opinion of the author, four of these stand out.

1. *The key role of an independent facilitator.*   HW identified the need for and the role of facilitation in opening up the lines of communication between adversaries who were not talking to each other and who were mutually mistrustful. He saw his role as establishing his credibility with both sides to enable him to convey messages across the barrier of suspicion between the ANC, based at their exile headquarters in Lusaka, Zambia, and the government in Pretoria, as well as with influential elements in the White society. His success in establishing his credibility with the ANC was acknowledged in a letter sent to him by the organization thanking him for his personal contribution and that of his CIS as "bridge-builders and mediators [which] cannot but be welcomed". He had more difficulty in winning acceptance in Pretoria, although it kept an open door for him to report to ministers. However, he did succeed (along with another mediating group, the Institute for the Development of an Alternative South Africa, whose role differed from his own by adopting an openly anti-government position) in arranging meetings between the ANC and pro-government media editors, academics, and prominent businessmen. Their reports back to Pretoria established a second line of communication, which gradually helped to change the government's attitude towards the ANC.

2. *The importance of a patient testing-out period.*   HW envisaged a period during which adversaries engaged in a bitter and suspicious relationship could establish each other's genuine commitment to reaching an agreement, as well as establishing the limits to which each side could be pushed without risking the possibility of negotiations. This period lasted for almost a year after Nelson Mandela's release from prison. This often fraught testing-out period established the *bona fide* intentions of both sides to engage in meaningful negotiations.

3. *Accepting that violence can be part of a negotiating process.*   This was perhaps the most difficult idea for both parties to accept. In this period, HW saw his role as facilitator to try to explain to both sides

the reasons for their mutually destructive behaviour. A key issue at this stage tested another of HW's ideas: the difficulty in getting parties of unequal power to meet around a conference table. The government, as the holders of power and especially with the greater military strength, was concerned to show that it was not entering the negotiations as a defeated party, and it sought to demonstrate its superiority by seeking to dictate the agenda for the negotiations. The ANC, on the other hand, though ready to suspend its armed struggle but not yet to abandon it, sought to prove that it possessed enough strength to make the country ungovernable through the use of violence, which had been transferred from "the battlefield" to new bases inside the country.

It was not until both sides became convinced of the limits of their own power that they were ready to begin talking. Although the parties were still of unequal strength, they had been made aware of the damage that each side was capable of inflicting on the other. This situation can be compared to what often happens in industrial disputes where workers use their power to strike to compel their much stronger employers to accept the need for negotiations in order to limit the damage that a prolonged strike could inflict on their business.

The testing-out period and the overlapping period of increased violence saw the government hard-pressed to deal with mass movements engaged in industrial stay-aways and in making the Black urban townships increasingly ungovernable. It was forced to resort to increasingly repressive measures.

4. *The imperative necessity for a fully representative negotiating body.* HW argued that, unless the parties engaged in negotiations were representatives of all the major constituencies involved in the conflict, any agreement reached by major, but not fully representative, parties would have difficulty in making agreement stick. By the time the agenda for CODESA was agreed, 28 parties had agreed to participate. Only two important groups boycotted the talks—the right-wing Afrikaners and the leftist Pan-Africanist Congress (PAC). Although both these absentees continued to be troublesome during the almost two years it took for agreement to be reached at CODESA, they were not strong enough to sabotage its work or, after agreement was reached, to discredit it.

In addition to the above assumptions, two final points need to be stressed in accounting for the ultimate success of the CODESA negotiations. The first was the fact that the principal adversaries shared a common objective: neither side wished to see the collapse of the country's economy as a result of escalating violence, and both were equally committed to the need for restructuring a discredited and outmoded political system. The second point was that the hour produced two remarkable leaders—Nelson Mandela and F. W. de Klerk—who developed a symbiotic relationship that ensured that the majority of the Black and White communities would support an agreement reached between them.

HW never wavered in his belief that it was not only necessary but possible to reconcile the interests of the White and Black communities, and that his own Afrikaner people would be receptive to the idea of a non-racial political system once the barriers of communication between the two communities were broken down. His personal role as a bridge builder was motivated by this far-seeing faith and was fashioned both by his understanding of the complexities of South Africa's racial politics and by the principles and ideas he had developed to enable him to fulfil such a role.

Transitional process as the basis of mediation

The ideas and approaches that evolved over the years in the work of HW and the CIS have been the outcome of direct experience of the difficult problems of conflict accommodation in a situation where mistrust, confrontation, and the potential for violence have always been just beneath the surface.

We have seen that the hallmarks of HW's ways of handling the problems have been patience and tolerance, a readiness for creative thinking to find new ways of framing the problems, and a willingness to learn from the experience of others as well as his own. In this context, it is surprising to notice that, on the one hand, the CIS seems to have had no contact with social scientists engaged with the theory and practice of transitional process; yet, on the other hand, most if not all of its thinking is highly consistent with the current theory of transitional process, which forms the basis of the present book. It will be instructive, therefore, to examine how close are the relations between the ideas and approaches of HW and the CIS to those that underlie transitional theory. In the following subsections a series of basic features of the transitional theory and approach are first summarized and then followed by a comment showing how HW's thinking and approach relates to them.

Structural change

Transition process theory in the present context is concerned with bringing about structural change in social systems. This means qualitative, not just quantitative, change in the relations between the parts of a system. It is also likely to involve both the relinquishment of certain parts of the system that have led to its declining effectiveness, and also the introduction of new parts. The driving force for such changes is the growing recognition of the failures of the existing system, whether these be ineffectiveness, its damaging consequences, or its injustice.

HW wrote (1974) that "awareness of the grave injustices of the current political system brought home to me the urgent need for fundamental change in the social structure".

Open-system thinking

Transition process theory recognizes that any social system, be it a family, a community, an industrial firm, or a nation, is made up of parts or sub-systems that are interdependent on each other. Furthermore, the system as a whole is interdependent with other systems that form its environment. Any change either within the system or in its environment will therefore be accommodated by the system only if its parts are capable of interacting with each other. If any part of the system is closed to the other parts, or if the system as a whole is closed to its environment, adaptation to change will be seriously impeded and the system itself will ultimately fail. Open-system thinking is a *sine qua non* for adaptive change in a social system.

The central problem initially identified by HW and his CIS was the virtually complete absence of meaningful and direct communication between the White and Black communities in South Africa: each sub-system of the nation was closed to the other. Their conclusion was that in situations where direct communication between conflicting parties is absent, it becomes necessary for a third party to intervene to facilitate communication. In other words, in a situation where closed-system thinking and mutual conflict exist between two sub-systems, the development of open-system thinking is dependent upon third-party intervention.

Developmental potential

The viable development of any social system can happen only if potential resources exist within the system and are effectively harnessed. The most critical for development are the human resources and, in particular, individuals who appreciate the possibilities for development and change, and who have the drive to realize them. Such individuals need to be identified, encouraged, and allowed to thrive.

In South Africa, "within the camps of both sides, one finds the voices of sanity and realism which seek to establish dialogue across non-communication barriers. These are the bridge-builders. HW was one of a relatively small number of bridge-builders." The developmental potential exemplified by HW was expressed in his mediating role as a facilitator. A particular feature of this role, furthermore, was that HW engaged himself in trying to identify and to foster the developmental potential of other individuals, both Whites and Blacks, by encouraging them and eventually enabling them to communicate with each other. By so doing, he also demonstrated that the form of third-party intervention most likely to foster developmental potential in others is not arbitration or conciliation: it is mediation and facilitation.

Facing and tolerating realities

Because deliberate structural change in a social system always involves relinquishing outdated ideas, values, and methods, it inevitably involves the experience of pain or mental anguish. It is also usual to find that the creativity needed to shift a *status quo* engenders destructiveness in some parts of the system. It is natural for people to try to avoid these kinds of experience rather than to face them. Such avoidance commonly results in attempts "to arrive without the experience of getting there", in finding solutions to problems that are only "as-if solutions" or "quick fixes". The quick fix is, of course, a recipe failure.

HW was well aware (1987) that "parties to a conflict make it easier for themselves by simplifying the issues. . . . But to strip a conflict of its complexity is to falsify it. One function of the mediator or facilitator is to help participants to acknowledge that they are enmeshed together in a complex and multi-dimensional problem." He also knew that "the articulation of pain on both sides (the White and Black communities) is a necessary stage in the process of turning away from the past".

Transitional space

Transitional change in a social system requires not only the relinquishing of established ideas and ways that are no longer viable; it also requires innovative thinking that leads to the discovery of new possibilities. Transitional space is that space in the minds and circumstances of change agents within which they can safely feel free of restrictions on their creative thinking. Like the play of a small child as it explores and tries out new possibilities in its expanding world, change agents need to feel free to let their perceptions, thoughts, and imaginings depart from the established cast of thinking towards new horizons. Only then can they discover both new relations and alignments between old and familiar things, and also new meanings and new action possibilities that lead to the genuine resolution of problems.

HW (1989a) recognized that part of the role of the mediator or facilitator is to "help to provide favourable circumstances in which the parties can confront the issues". As a result of the work of HW and others "there was a new questioning of traditional policies and attitudes, and the beginning of a search for a different kind of society and a new political system".

Transitional learning

The restructuring of a social system can only happen if there is first a restructuring in the minds of its key participants. Innovative thinking gives rise to new ideas, new objectives, and new strategies—that is, to new cognitive structures. Such structures, forming in the minds of people, have however to be tried out in the real world. Transitional learning is the process whereby the new ideas are tried out. They have to be honed or modified so that they become workable in reality, and the whole developmental process has to be steered around the inevitable obstacles in the direction that is needed. Each of the parts of the whole system has to be involved in this learning. Each must acknowledge ownership of the problems and collaborate with the others in active learning from the experience of tackling them. The process of "working-through" of the new insights must percolate throughout the system.

A number of examples of this have been mentioned in this chapter. "Subtle changes begin to occur, mostly expressed in public, when the parties in conflict begin to perceive that their own maximalist demands are unrealisable, and when damage limitation comes to be seen as being in the interests of both sides." HW recognized that mediators in real life are often also opinion-makers: "by reaching out to the public they extend the negotiation process to other levels of society and facilitate the acceptance of agreements."

The transformational situation

While sufficient transitional space and time are necessary conditions for restructuring to take place both in the minds of people and in the social system in which they live, they are not sufficient. Also required are transformational situations. In these, a particular combination of circumstances exists, or is created, that enables participating individuals to see things in new ways and to experience opportunities that would not otherwise exist. The participants are offered the opportunity, in a secure setting, for interaction with each other in ways not normally possible, for crossing boundaries that are usually tabooed, and for looking at problems more deeply or in new ways that had not previously seemed feasible.

The role of the mediator/facilitator as practised by HW is, centrally, of course, to bring about such situations. Mediators "have the freedom to be flexible, to disregard protocol, to suggest unconventional remedies or procedures, to widen or restrict the agenda, and to press for constructive initiatives or magnanimous gestures".

Conclusion

It should be clear from the above that the work of HW and his CIS is an excellent example of the transitional approach in action, as applied in the social system of a nation that has been trying to rid itself of an intolerable division into two closed sub-systems. Two additional points are worth making. First, the work raises important questions for transitional theory, not yet discussed anywhere else, about the place of power, conflict, confrontation, and violence in transition process. Second, one crucial aspect of the transition process seems to have been omitted in the work as reported—namely, the double task: the need to take time off to review what is occurring at regular stages of development. HW's role has been essentially that of a loner who appears not to have used the resources of his CIS to undertake the task of review. This may be because of the particular role of a loner, because of the great need for confidentiality, because of the lack of the CIS's resource of trained people, or simply because he was not familiar with the theory of the "double task".

REFERENCES AND BIBLIOGRAPHY

Abernathy, W. J., & Wayne, K. (1974). Limits of the learning curve. *Harvard Business Review, 52.*

Ackerman, L. S. (1982). Transition management: an in-depth look at managing complex change. *Organization Dynamics* (Summer).

Adler, N. (1983). Organizational development in a multicultural environment. *Journal of Applied Behavioral Science, 19* (3) (June).

Amado, G. (1979). Comment réussir une réunion de travail. *Revue Française de Gestion* (January–February): 20–30.

Amado, G. (1980). Psychoanalysis and organisation: a cross-cultural perspective. *Sigmund Freud House Bulletin, 4* (2): 17–20.

Amado, G. (1985). "Genesis and Efficiency of Transitional Processes." Working paper, Institute for Transitional Dynamics, Luzern.

Amado, G. (1988). Cohésion organisationnelle et illusion collective. *Revue Française de Gestion, 69:* 37–43.

Amado, G. (1993). *La résonance psychosociale.* Unpublished doctoral dissertation, University of Paris VII, Paris.

Amado, G. (1999). Groupes opérationnels et processus inconscients. *Revue Française de Psychanalyse, 3:* 909–919.

Amado, G., Faucheux, C., & Laurent, A. (Eds.) (1991). Ethno-management: a Latin provocation. *International Studies of Management and Organisation, 21* (3).

Amado, G., & Guittet, A. (1991). *Dynamique des communication dans les groupes*. Paris: Armand Colin.

Anderson P., Arrow K., & Pines, D., (1988). *The Evolutionary Paths of Global Economy Workshop*, Redwood City, CA: Addison-Wesley.

Anzieu, D. (1984). *The Group and the Unconscious*. London: Karnac Books.

Arendt, H. (1970). *On Violence*. London: Penguin.

Argyris, C. (1980). *The Inner Contradictions of Rigorous Research*. New York: Academic Press.

Argyris, C. (1983). Action science and intervention. *Journal of Applied Behavioral Science, 19* (2): 115–140.

Argyris, C. (1990). *Overcoming Organizational Defenses: Facilitating Organizational Learning*. Needham Heights, MA: Allyn and Bacon.

Argyris, C. (1993). *Knowledge for Action: A Guide to Overcoming Barriers to Organizational Change*. San Francisco, CA: Jossey Bass.

Argyris, C., & Schön, D. (1978). *Organizational Learning: A Theory of Action Perspective*. Reading, MA: Addison-Wesley.

Ashby, W. R. (1960). *Design for a Brain*. London: Chapman & Hall.

Aubert, N., & de Gaulejac, V. (1981). *Le coût de l'excellence*. Paris: Editions du Seuil.

Baba, M. L. (1995). The cultural ecology of the corporation: explaining diversity in work group responses to organizational transformation. *Journal of Applied Behavioral Science, 31* (2) (June).

Bartunek, J. M., & Moch, M. K. (1987). First-order, second-order, and third-order change and organization development interventions: a cognitive approach. *Journal of Applied Behavioral Science, 23* (4).

Barus-Michel, J., Giust-Desprairies, F., & Ridel, L. (1996). *Crises, approche psychosociale clinique*. Paris: Desclée de Brouwer.

Basaglia, F. (1967). *L'instituzione negata*. Milan: Einaudi.

Bass, B. M. (1985). *Leadership and Performance beyond Expectations*. New York: Free Press.

Bass, B. M., & Avolio, B. J. (1990). The implications of transactional and transformational leadership for the individual, team and organizational development. *Research in Organizational Change and Development, 4*: 231–272.

Bate, P. (1990). Using the culture concept in an organization development setting. *Journal of Applied Behavioral Science, 26* (1).

Beckhard, R., & Harris, R. (1977). *Organizational Transitions: Managing Complex Change*. Reading, MA: Addison Wesley.

Beckhard, R., & Pritchard, W. (1992). *Changing the Essence: The Art of Creating and Leading Fundamental Change in Organizations*. San Francisco, CA: Jossey-Bass.

Beer, M. (1980). *Organization Change and Development: A New Systems View*. Santa Monica, CA: Goodyear.

Beer, M., & Walton, A. E. (1987). Organization change and development. *Annual Review of Psychology, 38.*

Bejarano, A. (1972). Résistance et transfert dans les groupes. In: D. Anzieu et al. (Eds.), *Le travail psychanalytique dans les groupes.* Paris: Dunod.

Bennis, W. G. (1966). *Changing Organizations.* New York: McGraw-Hill.

Bennis, W. G., & Nanus, B. (1985). *Leaders: The Strategies for Taking Charge.* New York: Harper & Row.

Bernoux, P. (1985). *La sociologie des organisations.* Paris: Editions du Seuil.

Bion, W. R. (1959). *Experiences in Groups.* New York: Basic Books.

Bion, W. R. (1970). *Attention and Interpretation.* London: Tavistock Publications.

Bion, W. R., & Rickman, J. (1943). Intra-group tensions in therapy. *Lancet,* 2: 678–681.

Bitan-Weiszfeld, M., Mendel, G., & Roman, P. (1992). *Vers l'entreprise démocratique.* Paris: Editions de la Découverte.

Blake, R. R., & Mouton, J. S. (1988). Comparing strategies for incremental and transformational change. In: R. H. Kilmann, T. J. Covin, & Associates, *Corporate Transformation: Revitalizing Organizations for a Competitive World.* San Francisco, CA: Jossey-Bass.

Boston Consulting Group (1968). *Perspectives on Experience.* Boston, MA: Boston Consulting Group Inc.

Bowlby, J. (1949). The study and reduction of group tensions in the family. *Human Relations,* 2: 123–128.

Bowlby, J. (1969). *Attachment and Loss, Vol. 1: Attachment.* London: Hogarth Press.

Bradshaw-Campbell, P. (1989). The implications of multiple perspectives on power for organization development. *Journal of Applied Behavioral Science, 25* (1).

Bridger, H. (1946). The Northfield experiment. *Bulletin of the Menninger Clinic, 1* (10).

Bridger, H. (1980a). The kinds of organisational development required for working at the level of the whole organization considered as an open system. In: K. Trebesch (Ed.), *Organizational Development in Europe, Vol. 1A: Concepts.* Berne: Paul Haupt Verlag.

Bridger, H. (1980b). The relevant training and development of people for OD roles. In: K. Trebesch (Ed.), *Organizational Development in Europe, Vol. 1A: Concepts.* Berne: Paul Haupt Verlag.

Bridger, H. (1981). *Consultative Work with Communities and Organisations.* The Malcolm Millar Lecture. Aberdeen: University Press.

Bridger, H. (1987a). Courses and working conferences as transitional learning institutions. In: W. Brendan Reddy & C. C. Henderson (Eds.), *Training, Theory and Practice.* Washington, DC: NTL Institute/University Associates.

Bridger, H. (1987b). "To Explore the Unconscious Dynamics of Transition as it Affects the Interdependance of Individual, Group and Organizational Aims in Paradigm Change." Unpublished paper presented at the ISPSO symposium on Integrating Unconscious Life in Organizations: Psychoanalytic Issues in Organizational Research and Consultation. Montreal (October).

Bridger, H. (1990). The discovery of the therapeutic community: the Northfield experiments. In: E. Trist & H. Murray, *The Social Engagement of Social Science: A Tavistock Anthology, Vol. 1*. Philadelphia, PA: University of Pennsylvania Press.

Bridger, H., Gray, S., & Trist, E. (1998). L'Institut Tavistock: origines et premières années, *Revue Internationale de Psychosociologie, 10* (11).

Bridges, W. (1986). Managing organizational transitions. *Organizational Dynamics* (Summer): 24–33.

Brown, J. S., & Duguid, P. (1991). Organizational learning and communities of practice: toward a unified view of working, learning and innovation. *Organizational Science, 2* (1): 40–57.

Bryman, A. (1996). Leadership in organizations. In: S. R. Clegg, C. Hardy, & W. R. Nord (Eds.), *Handbook of Organization Studies*. London: Sage Publications.

Burke, W. W. (1980). Organization development and bureaucracy in the 1980s, *Journal of Applied Behavioral Science, 16* (3).

Burke, W. W. (1994). *Organization Development: A Process of Learning and Changing*. Reading, MA: Addison Wesley.

Burns, G. M. (1978), *Leadership*. New York: Harper & Row.

Burton, J. W. (1979). *Deviance, Terrorism and War: The Process of Solving Unsolved Social and Political Problems*. Oxford: Martin Robertson.

Cangelosi, V. E., & Dill, W. R. (1965). Organizational learning: observations toward a theory. *Administrative Science Quarterly, 10*: 175–203.

Chein, I., Cook, S., & Harding, J. (1948). The field of action research. *American Psychologist, 3* (February): 43–50.

Cherns, A. B. (1976). The principles of sociotechnical systems design. *Human Relations, 29* (8): 783–792.

Colloque de Cerisy (1994). *L'analyse stratégique—sa genèse, ses applications et ses problèmes actuels: autour de Michel Crozier*, edited by Francis Pavé. Paris: Editions du Seuil.

Conger, J. A. (1989) *The Charismatic Leader: Behind the Mystique of Exceptional Leadership*. San Francisco, CA: Jossey-Bass.

Conger, J. A., & Kanungo, R. N. (1988). *Charismatic Leadership: The Elusive Factor in Organisational Effectiveness*. San Francisco, CA: Jossey-Bass.

Crozier, M. (1963). *Le phénomène bureaucratique*. Paris: Editions du Seuil.

Crozier, M. (1974). *Où va l'administration française?* Paris: Editions d'Organisation.

Crozier, M. (1980). *Le mal américain.* Paris: Fayard.

Crozier, M., & Friedberg, E. (1977). *L'acteur et le système.* Paris: Editions du Seuil.

Curle, A. (1986). *In the Middle: Non-official Mediation in Violent Situations.* New York: St. Martin's Press.

Curle, A. (1987). Mediation—and some of the obstacles. *The Friend, 145.*

Curle, A. (1988). "Mediation and Conflict Resolution." Unpublished correspondence with H. W. van der Merwe, Centre for Intergroup Studies, Cape Town.

Curle, A. (1989). Foreword. In: H. W. van der Merwe, *Pursuing Justice and Peace in South Africa.* London: Routledge.

Cyert, R., & March, J. (1963). *A Behavorial Theory of the Firm,* Englewood Cliffs, NJ: Prentice-Hall.

Deal, T. E., & Kennedy, A. A. (1982). *Corporate Cultures: The Rites and Rituals of Corporate Life.* Reading, MA: Addison-Wesley.

Dejours, C. (1993). *Travail, usure mentale.* Paris: Bayard Editions.

Dejours, C. (Ed.) (1996). Psychodynamique du travail. *Revue Internationale de Psychosociologie, 3* (5): 3–160.

Dekker, L. D. (1988). *Retribution and Reparation: Overcoming Retaliation.* Cape Town: Centre for Intergroup Studies.

Diamond, M. A. (1986). Resistance to change: a psychoanalytic critique of Argyris and Schön's contributions to organisation theory and intervention. *Journal of Management Studies, 23* (5) (September).

d'Iribarne, A. (1989). *La logique de l'honneur.* Paris: Editions du Seuil.

Dubost, J. (1987). *L'intervention psychosociologique.* Paris: PUF.

Dubost, J., & Levy, A. (1980). L'analyse sociale. In: *L'intervention institutionnelle* (pp. 49–105). Paris: Poujot.

Duncan, R. B., & Weiss, A. (1978). Organizational learning: implications for organization design. In: B. Staw (Ed.), *Research in Organizational Behavior.* Greenwich, CT: JAI Press.

Dunphy, D. C., & Stace, D. A. (1988). Transformational and coercive strategies for planned organizational change: beyond the OD model. *Organization Studies, 9* (3).

Dutton, J., & Duncan, R. B. (1981). "The Process and Threats to Sensemaking and Their Relationship to Organizational Learning". Working Paper, Kellogg Graduate School of Management, Northwestern University.

Eden, C., & Huxham, C. (1996). Action research for management research. *British Journal of Management, 7* (1): 75–86.

Eden, C., & Huxham, C. (1997). Action research for the study of organizations. In: S. R. Clegg, C. Hardy, & W. R. Nord, (Eds.), *Handbook of Organization Studies*. London: Sage Publications.

Eden, D. (1986). OD and self-fulfilling prophecy: boosting productivity by raising expectations. *Journal of Applied Behavioral Science, 22* (1).

Edmondson, A., & Moingeon, B. (1995). Organizational learning as a source of competitive advantage: when to learn how and when to learn why. *Cahiers de Recherche HEC* (No. 552).

Elden, M. (1979). Three generations of work democracy experiments in Norway. In: C. Cooper & E. Mumford (Eds.), *The Quality of Work in Eastern and Western Europe*. London: Associated Business Press.

Elden, M., & Levin, M. (1991). Cogenerative learning: bringing participation into action research. In: W. F. Whyte (Ed.), *Participatory Action Research* (pp 127–142). London: Sage.

Elliot, J. (1978). What is action research in schools? *Journal of Curriculum Studies, 10*: 355–357.

Emery, F. E., & Thorsrud, E. (1969). *Democracy at Work*. Leiden: Martinus Nijhoff.

Emery, F. E., & Trist, E. L. (1960). Socio-technical systems. In: C. W. Churchman & M. Verlhust (Eds.), *Management Sciences, Models and Techniques, Vol. 2*. Oxford : Pergamon Press.

Emery, F. E., & Trist, E. L. (1965). The causal texture of organizational environments. *Human Relations, 18*: 21–31.

Emery, F. E., & Trist, E. L. (1973). *Towards a Social Ecology*. London: Tavistock.

Emery, M., & Emery, F. (1978). Searching: for new directions, in new ways . . . for new times. In: J. W. Sutherland (Ed.), *Management Handbook for Public Administrators*. New York: Van Nostrand Reinhold.

Enriquez, E. (1972). Problématique du changement. *Connexions, 4*: 5–45.

Enriquez, E. (1983). *De la horde à l'état*. Paris: Gallimard.

Enriquez, E. (1991). *Les figures du maître*. Paris: Arcantère.

Enriquez, E. (1992). *L'organisation en analyse*. Paris: PUF.

Enriquez, E. (1997). *Les jeux du pouvoir et du désir dans l'entreprise*. Paris: Desclée de Brouwer.

Faucheux, C., Amado, G., & Laurent, A. (1982). Organizational development and change. *Annual Review of Psychology* (Palo Alto), *33*: 343–370.

Feldman, S. P. (1986). Management in context: an essay on the relevance of culture to the understanding of organizational change. *Journal of Management Studies, 23* (6).

Fiol, C. M., & Lyles, M. A. (1985). Organizational learning. *Academy of Management Review, 10* (4).

Flamholtz, E. (1995). Managing organizational transitions: implications for corporate and human resource management. *European Management Journal, 13* (1).

Fox, W. M. (1995). Sociotechnical system principles and guidelines: past and present. *Journal of Applied Behavioral Science*, 13 (1) (March).

Frame, R. M., Nielsen, W. R., & Pate, L. E. (1989). Creating excellence out of crisis: organizational transformation at the Chicago Tribune. *Journal of Applied Behavioral Science*, 25 (2): 109–122.

Freedman, D. (1993). A "nouvelle science", "nouveau management". *Harvard—L'Expansion* (Spring): 6–13.

French, W. L., & Bell, C. H., Jr (1990). *Organization Development: Behavioural Science Interventions for Organization Improvement* (4th edition). Englewood Cliffs, NJ: Prentice-Hall.

French, W. L., & Bell, C. H., Jr (1999). *Organization Development: Behavioural Science Interventions for Organization Improvement* (6th edition). Englewood Cliffs, NJ: Prentice-Hall.

French, W. L., Bell, C. H., & Zawacki, R. A. (Eds.) (1994). *Organization Development and Transformation: Managing Effective Change*. Homewood, IL : Irwin.

Geertz, C. (1973). *The Interpretation of Cultures*. New York: Basic Books.

Geldenhus, O., & Kawa, W. (1985). *Third Party Intervention: Mediation, Facilitation and Negotiation*. Cape Town: Centre for Intergroup Studies.

Gerwin, D., & Kolodny, H. (1992). *Management of Advanced Manufacturing Technology: Strategy, Organization, and Innovation*. New York: John Wiley & Sons.

Gilmore, T. (1988). *Making a Leadership Change*. San Francisco, CA: Jossey-Bass.

Gilmore, T., Shea, G. P., & Useem, M. (1997). Side effects of corporate cultural transformations. *Journal of Applied Behavioural Science*, 33 (2, June): 174–189.

Glassman, A. M., & Cummings, T. G. (1991). *Cases in Organizational Development*. Homewood, IL: Irwin.

Gleick, J. (1988). *Chaos: The Making of a New Science*. London: Heinemann.

Gold, A. (1981). *Conflict in Today's Economic Climate: Society of Professionals*. Toronto: La Dispute.

Goldstein, J. (1994). *The Unshackled Organization: Facing the Challenge of Unpredictability through Spontaneous Reorganization*. Portland, OR: Productivity Press.

Goodman, P. S. & Kurke, L. B. (1982). Studies of change in organizations: a status report. In: P. Goodman and Associates (Eds.), *Change in Organizations*. San Francisco, CA: Jossey Bass.

Gouillart, F., & Kelly, J. (1995). *Transforming the organization*. New York : McGraw-Hill.

Gray, S. G. (1970). The Tavistock Institute of Human Relations. In: H. V. Dicks (Ed.), *50 Years of Tavistock Clinic*. London: Routledge & Kegan Paul.

Grolnick, S. (1990). *The Work and Play of Winnicott*. Northvale, NJ: Jason Aronson.

Hall, E. T., & Hall, M. R. (1990). *Understanding Cultural Differences*. Yarmouth, ME: Intercultural Press.

Hammer, M., & Champy, J. (1993). *Reengineering the Corporation: A Manifesto for Business Revolution*. New York: Harper Business.

Harrison, R. G. (1984). Reasserting the radical potential of OD: notes towards the establishment of a new basis for OD practice. *Personnel Review, 13* (2).

Hecksher, C. (1994). Defining the post-bureaucratic type. In: C. Hecksher & A. Donnellon (Eds.), *The Post-bureaucratic Organisation: New perspectives on organisational change*. London: Sage Publications.

Herbert, E. L., & Trist, E. L. (1953). The institution of an absent leader by a students' discussion group. *Human Relations, 6*: 215–48.

Herzberg, F. (1966). *Work and the Nature of Man*. Cleveland, OH: World Press.

Higgin, G., & Bridger, H. (1964). The psycho-dynamics of an inter-group experience. *Human Relations, 17*: 391–446.

Hofstede, G. (1980). *Culture's Consequences*. Beverly Hills, CA: Sage.

Holland, N. R. (1985). *The I*. New Haven, CT: Yale University Press.

Hosking, D. M. (1988). Organising, leadership, and skilful process. *Journal of Management Studies, 25*.

Hosking, D. M. (1991). Chief executives, organising processes, and skill. *European Journal of Applied Psychology, 41*.

House, R. J. (1977). A 1976 theory of charismatic leadership. In: J. G. Hunt & L. L. Larson (Eds.), *Leadership: The Cutting Edge*. Carbondale, IL: Southern Illinois University Press.

House, R. J., & Shamir, B. (1993). Toward the integration of transformational, charismatic, and visionary theories. In: M. M. Chemers & R. Ayman (Eds.), *Leadership Theory and Research: Perspectives and Directions*. New York: Academic Press.

Huber, G. P. (1991). Organizational learning: the contributing processes and the literatures. *Organization Science, 2* (1) (February).

Huse, E. F., & Cummings, T. G. (1985). *Organization Development and Change*. St. Paul, MN: West Publishing.

Janis, I. (1982). *Group Think*. Boston, MA: Houghton Mifflin.

Jaques, E. (1951). *The Changing Culture of a Factory*. London: Tavistock Publications. Reissued New York: Garland, 1987.

Jaques, E. (1995). Why the psychoanalytical approach to understanding organizations is dysfunctional. *Human Relations, 8* (4): 343–349.

Kaës, R. (1977). Processus et fonction de l'idéologie dans les groupes. *Perspectives Psychiatriques, 33*: 27–48.

Kaës, R. (1979). Introduction à l'analyse transitionnelle. In: R. Kaës, A.

Missenard, R. Kaës, D. Anzieu, & J. Guillaumin (Eds.), *Crise, rupture et dépassement*. Paris: Dunod.

Kaës, R., Anzieu D., & Guillaumin, J. (1979) *Crise, rupture et dépassement*. Paris: Dunod.

Kaës, R., Missenard, A., Kaës, R., Anzieu, D., & Guillaumin, J. (1979). *Crise, rupture et dépassement*. Paris: Dunod.

Katz, D., & Kahn, R. L. (1966). *The Social Psychology of Organizations*. New York: John Wiley.

Katzenbach, J. R., & Smith, D. K. (1993). *The Wisdom of Teams: Creating the High Performance Organisation*. Boston, MA: Harvard Business School.

Kemmis, S. (1981). Research approaches and methods: action research. In D. Anderson & C. Blakers (Eds.), *Transition from School: An Exploration of Research and Policy*. Canberra: Australian National University Press.

Kets de Vries, M. (1996). Leaders who make a difference. *European Management Journal, 14* (5) (October).

Kiel, L. D. (1994). *Managing Chaos and Complexity in Government: A New Paradigm for Managing Change, Innovation, and Organisational Renewal*. San Francisco, CA: Jossey-Bass.

Kilmann, R. H. (1989). *Managing Beyond the Quick Fix*. San Francisco, CA: Jossey-Bass.

Kilmann, R. H., Covin, T. J., & Associates (1988). *Corporate Transformation: Revitalizing Organizations for a Competitive World*. San Francisco, CA: Jossey-Bass.

Kindler, H. S. (1979). Two planning strategies: incremental change and transformational change. *Group and Organization Studies, 4*.

King, P., & Steiner, R. (1992). *The Freud-Klein Controversies, 1941–1945*. London: Routledge & The Institute of Psycho-Analysis.

Klein, L., & Eason, K. (1991). *Putting Social Science to Work*. Cambridge: Cambridge University Press.

Klein, M. (1948). *Contributions to Psycho-Analysis 1921–1945*. London: Hogarth Press.

Kolodny, H., Liu, M., Stymne, B., & Denis, H. (1996). New technology and the emerging organisational paradigm. *Human Relations, 49* (12).

Kotter, J. P. (1990). *A Force for Change: How Leadership Differs From Management*. New York: Free Press.

Kotter, J. P. (1995). Leading change: why transformation efforts fail. *Harvard Business Review* (March–April).

Kouzes, J. M., & Posner, B. Z. (1993). *Credibility: How Leaders Gain and Lose It, Why People Demand It*. San Francisco, CA: Jossey-Bass.

Laing, R. D. (1970). *Le moi divisé*. Paris: Stock.

Lapassade, G. (1967). *Groupes, organisations et institutions*. Paris: Gauthier-Villars.

Lapassade, G. (1972). L'analyste institutionelle et l'intervention. *Connexions*, 4: 65–106.

Laughlin, R. C. (1991). Environmental disturbances and organizational transitions and transformations: some alternative models. *Organization Studies*, 12 (2).

Laurent, A. (1983). The cultural diversity of western conceptions of management. *International Studies of Management and Organisation*, 13 (1–2) (Fall).

Laurent, A. (1990). A cultural view of organizational change. In P. Evans, Y. Doz, & A. Laurent (Eds.), *Human Resource Management in International Firms*. New York: St. Martin's Press.

Levy, A. (1986). Second-order planned change: definition and conceptualization. *Organizational Dynamics*, 15 (1) (Summer).

Levy, A. (1997). *Sciences cliniques et organisations sociales*. Paris: PUF.

Levy, A., & Merry, U. (1986). *Organizational Transformation: Approaches, Strategies, Theories*. New York: Praeger.

Lewin, K. (1935). *A Dynamic Theory of Personality*. New York: Macmillan.

Lewin, K. (1944). Dynamics of group action. *Educational Leadership*, 1: 195–200.

Lewin, K. (1945). Reserve program of group dynamics—the Research Center for Group Dynamics at MIT. *Sociometry*, 8 (2): 126–136.

Lewin, K. (1946). Action research and minority problems. *Journal of Social Issues*, 2: 34–36.

Lewin, K. (1947). Frontiers in group dynamics. *Human Relations*, 1: 5–11, 143–153.

Lewin, K. (1951). *Field Theory and Social Science*. New York: Harper.

Lewin, K. (1964). *Psychologie dynamique* (2nd edition). Paris: PUF.

Lewin, K., Lippitt, R., & White, R. K. (1939). Patterns of aggressive behavior in experimentally created social climates. *Journal of Social Psychology*, 10: 271–299.

Lippitt, R., Watson, J., & Westley, B. (1958). *Dynamics of Planned Change*. New York: Harcourt Brace & World.

Lorenz, K. Z. (1961). *King Salomon's Ring*. London: Methuen.

Lorenz, K. Z. (1964). *Man Meets Dog*. Harmondsworth: Penguin.

Lourau, R. (1970). *L'analyste institutionelle*. Paris: Ed. de Minuit.

Lovelady, L. (1984). The process of organisation development: a reformulated model of the change process. Part 1. *Personnel Review*, 13 (2).

Low, K. B., & Bridger, H. (1979). Small group work in relation to management development. In: B. Babington-Smith & B.A. Farrell (Eds.), *Training in Small Groups*. Oxford: Pergamon Press.

Maggiolo, W. A. (1971). *Techniques of Mediation in Labor Disputes*. New York: Oceana Publications.

Mailhiot, G. B. (1968). *Dynamique et genèse des groupes*. Paris: Epi.

Manz, C. C. & Sims, H. P. (1991). Super leadership: beyond the myth of heroic leadership. *Organizational Dynamics, 19*: 18–35.

March, J., & Olsen, J. (1976). *Ambiguity and Choice in Organizations.* Bergen: Universitetsforlaget.

Martin, J. (1992). *Cultures in Organizations: Three Perspectives.* New York: Oxford University Press.

Mason, R., & Mitroff, I. (1981). *Challenging Strategic Planning Assumptions.* New York: John Wiley.

McClean, A. (1981). Organisation development: a case of the emperor's new clothes? *Personnel Review, 10* (1).

McGregor, D. (1960). *The Human Side of Enterprise.* New York: McGraw-Hill.

Mendel, G. (1972). De la régression du politique au psychique. In: *Socio-psychanalyse, Vol. 1* (pp. 11–63). Paris: Payot.

Mendel, G. (1998). *L'acte est une aventure.* Editions de la Découverte.

Mendel, G. (1999). *Le vouloir de création.* Paris: Editions de l'Aube.

Mendel, G., & Beillerot, J. (Eds.), 1980, *L'intervention Institutionnelle.* Payot, Paris.

Menzies Lyth, I. E. P. (1988). *Containing Anxiety in Institutions: Selected Essays.* London: Free Association Books.

Menzies Lyth, I. E. P. (1989). *The Dynamics of the Social: Selected Essays.* London: Free Association Books.

Meyerson, D., & Martin, J. (1987). Cultural change: an integration of three different views. *Journal of Management Studies, 24.*

Mitroff, I., & Emshoff, J. R. (1979). On strategic assumption-making: a dialectial approach to policy and planning. *Academy of Management Review, 4* (1): 1–12.

Moingeon, B., & Edmondson, A. (1995). Organizational learning as a source of competitive advantage: when to learn how and when to learn why. *Les Cahiers de Recherche, HEC, CR 552/1995.*

Morgan, G. (1980). Paradigms, metaphors and puzzle solving in organization theory. *Administrative Science Quarterly, 25*: 605–622.

Morgan, G. (1984). Opportunities arising from paradigm diversity. *Administration and Society, 16*: 306–327.

Morgan, G. (1986). *Images of Organization.* London: Sage.

Morgan, G. (1988). *Riding the Waves of Change.* San Francisco, CA: Jossey-Bass.

Moss Kanter, R. (1983). *The Change Masters: Innovation and Entrepreneurship in the American Corporation.* New York: Simon & Schuster.

Moss Kanter, R., Stein, B. A., & Jick, T. D. (1992). *The Challenge of Organizational Change: How Companies Experience It and Leaders Guide It.* New York: Free Press.

Muzyka, D., De Koning, A., & Churchill, N. (1995). On transformation and adaptation: building the entrepreneurial corporation. *European Management Journal*, 13 (4): 346–361.

Nadler, D. A. (1982). Managing transitions to uncertain future states. *Organization Dynamics* (Summer).

Nadler, D. A., & Tushman, M. L. (1990). Beyond the charismatic leader: leadership and organisational change. *California Management Review* (Winter).

Nevis, E., Lancourt, J., & Vassallo, H. (1996). *Intentional Revolutions: A Seven-Point Strategy for Transforming Organizations.* San Francisco, CA: Jossey-Bass.

Nicolis, G., & Prigogine, I. (1989). *Exploring Complexity: An Introduction.* New York: W. H. Freeman.

Nieuwmeijer, L. (1985). *Communication Strategy as a Conflict Management Tool in Negotiation in Third Party Intervention.* Cape Town: Centre for Intergroup Studies.

Nonaka, I. (1988). Creating organizational order out of chaos: self renewal in Japanese firms. *California Management Review* (Spring): 57–73.

Pagès, M., Bonetti, M., de Gaulejac, V., & Descendre, D. (1979). *L'emprise de l'organisation.* Paris: PUF.

Paul, C. F., & Gross, A. C. (1981). Increasing productivity and morale in a municipality: effects of organization development. *Journal of Applied Behavioral Science*, 17 (1).

Pava, C. (1986). Redesigning sociotechnical systems design: concepts and methods for the 1990s. *Journal of Applied Behavioral Science*, 22 (3).

Perlaki, I. (1994). Organizational development in Eastern Europe: learning to build culture-specific OD theories. *Journal of Applied Behavioral Science*, 30 (3).

Perlmutter, H. (1965). *Towards a Theory and Practice of Social Architecture.* Tavistock Pamphlet No. 12. London: Tavistock Publications.

Perlmutter, H., & Trist, E. (1986). Paradigms for societal transition. *Human Relations*, 1: 1–27.

Peters, E. E. (1991). *Chaos and Order in the Capital Markets: A New View of Cycles, Prices, and Market Volatility.* New York: Wiley.

Peters, M., & Robinson, V. (1984). The origins and status of action research. *Journal of Applied Behavioral Science*, 20 (2).

Peters, T. J., & Waterman, R. H. (1982). *In Search of Excellence.* New York: Harper & Row.

Pettigrew, A. M. (1987). Context and action in the transformation of the firm. *Journal of Management Studies*, 24 (6) (November).

Poole, P. P., Gioia, D. A., & Gray, B. (1989). Influence modes, schema change, and organizational transformation. *Journal of Applied Behavioral Science*, 25 (3).

Porras, J. I., & Silvers, R. C. (1991). Organization development and transformation. *Annual Review of Psychology, 42.*

Porras, J. I., & Wilkins, A. (1980). Organization development in a large system: an empirical assessment. *Journal of Applied Behavioral Science, 16* (4).

Prigogine, I., & Stengers, I. (1984). *Order out of Chaos: Man's New Dialogue with Nature.* New York: Bantam Books.

Raimbault, M., & Saussois, J. M. (1983). *Organiser le changement.* Paris: Editions d'Organisation, Collection Formation.

Reason, P., & Bradbury, H. (Eds.) (2000). *Handbook of Action Research.* London: Sage.

Revans, R. (1973). *Developing Effective Managers: A New Approach to Business Education.* New York: Praeger.

Rice, A. K. (1965). *Learning for Leadership: Interpersonal and Intergroup Relations.* London: Tavistock Publications.

Riviere, J. (Ed.) (1952). *Developments in Psychoanalysis.* London: Hogarth Press.

Rueff-Escoubès, C. (1997). *La démocratie dans l'école.* Paris: Editions Syros.

Sashkin, M. (1988). The visionary leader. In J. A. Conger & R. N. Kanungo (Eds.), *Charismatic Leadership: The Illusive Factor in Organizational Effectiveness.* San Francisco, CA: Jossey-Bass.

Sashkin, M., & Burke, W. W. (1987). Organization development in the 1980s. *Journal of Management, 13* (2).

Schein, E. H. (1985). *Organisational Culture and Leadership.* San Francisco, CA: Jossey-Bass.

Schein, E. H. (1987). *The Clinical Perspective in Field Work.* Newbury Park, CA: Sage.

Schein, E. H., & Bennis, W. G. (1965). *Personal and Organizational Change Through Group Methods.* New York: John Wiley.

Schön, D. (1971). *Beyond the Stable State.* New York: Basic Books.

Schön, D. A. (1983). *The Reflective Practitioner.* New York: Basic Books.

Selznick, P. (1957). *Leadership in Administration.* Evanston, IL: Row Peterson.

Senge, P. M. (1990). *The Fifth Discipline: The Art and Practice of the Learning Organization.* London: Century Business.

Shackel, B., & Klein, L. (1976). ESSO London Airport refuelling control centre redesign—an ergonomics case study. *Applied Ergonomics 7* (1): 37–45.

Sheldon, A. (1980). Organizational paradigms: a theory of organizational change. *Organizational Dynamics* (Winter).

Shrivastava, P. (1983). A typology of organizational learning systems. *Journal of Management Studies, 20* (1).

Simon, H. (1957). *Administrative Behaviour: A Study of Decision Making Processes in Administrative Organisation*. London: Macmillan.

Sims, H. P., & Lorenzi, P. (1992). *The New Leadership Paradigm*. Newbury Park, CA: Sage.

Smircich, L. (1983). Concepts of culture and organisational analysis. *Administrative Science Quarterly, 28* (3).

Spector, B. (1995). The sequential path to transformation management. *European Management Journal, 13* (4).

Stacey, R. (1991). *The Chaos Frontier: Creative Strategic Control for Business*. Oxford: Butterworth-Heinemann.

Stacey, R. (1992). *Managing the Unknowable: Strategic Boundaries between Order and Chaos in Organisations*. San Francisco, CA: Jossey-Bass.

Stacey, R. D. (1995). The science of complexity: an alternative perspective for strategic change processes. *Strategic Management Journal, 16*.

Stacey, R. D. (1996). *Complexity and Creativity in Organisations*. San Francisco, CA: Berrett-Koehler.

Susman, G. I. (1981). Planned change: prospects for the 1980s. *Management Science, 27* (2) (February).

Tainio, R., & Santalainen, T. (1984). Some evidence for the cultural relativity of organizational development programs. *Journal of Applied Behavioral Science, 20* (2).

Tannenbaum, R., & Hanna, R. W. (1985). Holding, letting go and moving on. In: R. Tannenbaum, N. Mangulies, & F. Massarik (Eds.), *Human Systems Development*. San Francisco, CA: Jossey-Bass.

Thom, R. (1975). *Structural Stability and Morphogenesis*, translated by D.H. Fowler. Reading, MA: W.A. Benjamin.

Thorsrud, E. (1970). A strategy for research and social change industry: a report on the industrial democracy project in Norway. *Social Science Information* (October): 65–90.

Tichy, N. M., & Devanna, M. A. (1986). *The Transformational Leader*. New York: Wiley.

Tosquelles, F. (1966). Pédagogie et psychothérapie institutionnelle. *Revue de Psychothérapie Institutionnelle, 2* (3): 43–66.

Touraine, A. (1981). The voice and the eye: on the relationship between actors and analysts. *Political Psychology, 2* (1): 3–14.

Trist, E. (1983). Referent organizations and the development of inter-organizational domains. *Human Relations, 36*: 269–284.

Trist, E. (1987). "Keynote address." Einar Thorsrud Memorial Conference on Industrial Democracy, Oslo.

Trist, E. (1990). Culture as a psycho-social process. In: E. Trist & H. Murray, *The Social Engagement of Social Science: A Tavistock Anthology, Vol. 1: The Socio-Psychological Perspective*. Philadelphia, PA: University of Pennsylvania Press.

Trist, E., & Bamforth, K. (1951). Some social and psychological consequences of the long wall method of coal getting. *Human Relations, 4*.

Trist, E., & Murray, H. (Eds.) (1990). *The Social Engagement of Social Science. ATavistock Anthology, Vol. 1: The Socio-Psychological Perspective.* Philadelphia, PA: University of Pennsylvania Press.

Trist, E., & Sofer, C. (1959). *Exploration in Group Relations.* Leicester: Leicester University Press.

Trompenaars, F. (1993). *Riding the Waves of Culture.* London: Economist Books.

Vaill, B. P. (1982). The purposing of high-performing systems. *Organizational Dynamics* (Autumn): 23–39.

Van der Heijden, K. (1996). *Scenarios: The Art of Strategic Conversation.* Chichester: Wiley.

van der Merwe, H. W. (1974). *Looking at the Afrikaner Today.* Cape Town: Tafelberg.

van der Merwe, H. W. (1975). *Afrikaner as African.* Lampito: Quaker Esperanto Society.

van der Merwe, H. W. (1983). Mediation and empowerment. In A. P. Hare (Ed.), *The Struggle for Democracy in South Africa: Conflict and Conflict Resolution.* Cape Town: Centre for Intergroup Studies.

van der Merwe, H. W. (1985). "Consensus Politics or Bloodshed." Topic paper, S.A. Institute of Race Relations, Cape Town.

van der Merwe, H. W. (1987). *Negotiation and Mediation in South Africa in Perspective.* Johannesburg: S.A. International

van der Merwe, H. W. (1988a). Groundwork for political negotiations in South Africa. *Communicare* (Washington), *7* (2).

van der Merwe, H. W. (1988b). *Mediation in Practice: Towards Building Bridges in South Africa.* Cape Town: Centre for Intergroup Studies.

van der Merwe, H. W. (1988c). South African initiatives: contrasting options in the mediation process. In C. B. Mitchell & K. Webb (Eds.), *New Approaches in International Mediation.* Westport, CT: Greenwood Press.

van der Merwe, H. W. (1989a). Political mediation in South Africa: some problems and challenges. *Organization Development Journal* (Washington).

van der Merwe, H. W. (1989b). *Pursuing Justice and Peace in South Africa.* London: Routledge.

van der Merwe, H. W. (1990). *The Human Factor in Resolving Conflict.* Cape Town: Centre for Intergroup Studies.

van der Merwe, H. W. (1991). *The Creation and Communication of New Structures and Values for South Africans in the Negotiation Process.* Cape Town: Clubview.

van der Merwe, H. W., & Hund, J. (1986). *Legal Ideology and Politics in*

South Africa: A Social Science Approach. Cape Town: Centre for Intergroup Studies.

van der Merwe, H. W., Maree, J., Zaaiman, A., Philip, C., & Muller, A. D. (1991). Principles of communication between adversaries in South Africa. In: J. W. Burton & F. Dukes (Eds.), *Conflict: Readings in Management.* New York: St. Martin's Press.

van der Merwe, H. W., & Meyer, G. (1986). *Conflict Accommodation: Toward Conceptual Clarification.* Cape Town: Centre for Intergroup Studies.

van der Merwe, H. W., & Odendaal, A. (1990). *Constructive Conflict Intervention in South Africa: Some Lessons.* Cape Town: Centre for Intergroup Studies.

Vansina, L. S. (1998). The individual in organizations: rediscovered or lost forever? *European Journal for Work and Organizational Psychology, 7* (3): 265–282.

Vickers, G. (1965). *The Art of Judgment.* New York: Basic Books.

Vickers, G. (1978). Some implications of systems thinking. *The Nevis Quarterly* (October).

Vroom, V. H., & Yetton, P. W. (1973). *Leadership and Decision-Making.* Pittsburgh, PA : University of Pittsburgh Press.

Waldorp, M. M. (1992). *Complexity: The Emerging Science at the Edge of Chaos.* New York: Simon & Schuster.

Wall, J. A. (1981). Mediation: an analysis. *Journal of Conflict Resolution, 25:* 157–180.

Walter, G. A. (1984). Organizational development and individual rights. *Journal of Applied Behavioral Science, 20* (4).

Weick, K. E. (1990). Technology as univoque: Sensemaking in new technologies. In: P. S. Goodman, L. S. Sproull, et al. (Eds.), *Technology and Organization.* San Francisco, CA: Jossey Bass.

Weisbord, M. R. (1987). *Productive Work Places: Organizing and Managing for Dignity, Meaning and Community.* San Francisco, CA: Jossey-Bass.

Weiszfeld, M., Roman, P., & Mendel, G. (1993). *Vers L'entreprise démocratique.* Paris: Editions de la Découverte.

Werr, A. (1995). Approaches, methods and tools of change—a literature survey and bibliography. *Economic and Industrial Democracy, 16:* 607–651.

Wertheimer, M. (1945). *Productive Thinking* (revised edition). New York: Harper, 1959.

Westley, F. R., & Mintzberg, H. (1989). Visionary leadership and strategic management. *Strategic Management Journal, 10:* 17–32.

Wheatley, M. J. (1992). *Leadership and the New Science: Learning about Organisation from an Orderly Universe.* San Francisco, CA: Berrett-Koehler.

Wilkins, A. L., & Dyer, W. G. (1988). Toward culturally sensitive theories of culture change. *Academy of Management Review, 13* (4).

Wilmott, H. (1993). Strength is ignorance; slavery is freedom: managing culture in modern organizations. *Journal of Management Studies, 30*: 515–552.

Winnicott, D. W. (1951). Transitional objects and transitional phenomena. In: *Collected Papers: Through Paediatrics to Psycho-Analysis.* London: Tavistock Publications, 1958.

Winnicott, D. W. (1963). From dependence towards independence in the development of the individual. In: *The Maturational Processes and the Facilitating Environment.* New York: International Universities Press, 1965.

Winnicott, D. W. (1971). *Playing and Reality.* London: Tavistock Publications.

Yelle, L. E. (1979). The learning curve: historical review and comprehensive survey. *Decision Sciences, 10* (2): 302–308.

Yukl, G. A. (1981). *Leadership in Organizations.* Englewood Cliffs, NJ: Prentice-Hall.

Zaleznik, A. (1977). Managers and leaders: are they different? *Harvard Business Review, 55*: 67–78.

Zimmerman, B. J. (1992). The inherent drive towards chaos. In: P. Lorange, B. Chakravarty, A. Van de Ven, & J. Roos (Eds.), *Implementing Strategic Processes: Change, learning and cooperation.* London: Blackwell.

Zobrist, A. (1987). "Reflections on Maintenance and Review." Working paper, Institute for Transitional Dynamics, Lucerne.

INDEX